Vocabulary Workshop

Level C

Jerome Shostak

Senior Series Consultant

Alex Cameron, Ph.D.
Department of English
University of Dayton
Dayton, Ohio

Series Consultants

Sylvia A. Rendón, Ph.D.
Coord., Secondary Language Arts
and Reading
Cypress-Fairbanks I.S.D.
Houston, Texas

Mel Farberman
Supervisor of Instruction
Brooklyn High Schools
New York City Board of Education
Brooklyn, New York

John Heath, Ph.D.
Department of Classics
Santa Clara University
Santa Clara, California

Sadlier-Oxford
A Division of William H. Sadlier, Inc.

Reviewers

The publisher wishes to thank for their comments and suggestions the following teachers and administrators, who read portions of the series prior to publication.

Anne S. Crane
Clinician English Education
Georgia State University
Atlanta, GA

Susan W. Keogh
Curriculum Coordinator
Lake Highland Preparatory
Orlando, FL

Mary Louise Ellena-Wygonik
English Teacher
Hampton High School
Allison Park, PA

Lisa Anne Pomi
Language Arts Chairperson
Woodside High School
Woodside, CA

Arlene A. Oraby
Dept. Chair (Ret.), English 6–12
Briarcliff Public Schools
Briarcliff Manor, NY

Susan Cotter McDonough
English Department Chair
Wakefield High School
Wakefield, MA

Sr. M. Francis Regis Trojano
Sisters of St. Joseph (CSJ)
Educational Consultant
Boston, MA

Keith Yost
Director of Humanities
Tomball Ind. School District
Tomball, TX

Patricia M. Stack
English Teacher
South Park School District
South Park, PA

Joy Vander Vliet
English Teacher
Council Rock High School
Newtown, PA

Karen Christine Solheim
English Teacher
Jefferson High School
Jefferson, GA

Photo Credits

Archive/Sporting News: 34. *Corbis*/Lee Snider: 27; Susan Middleton & David Liitschwager: 41; Bettmann: 64, 71, 104; Charles O'Rear: 156. *Image Bank*: Ghislain & Marie David de Lossy: 83; Petrified Collection: 90; Dandy Zipper: 149. *Index Stock*/Eric Sanford: 57; Fotopic: 137; Stephen Frink: 170; Rudi Von Briel: 182. *The Johnstown Flood Museum*: 130. *Greg Lord*: 123. *Stone*/Davies & Starr: 163. *Time Pix*/Bernard Hoffman: 116. *Brooks Walker*: 97.

PREFACE

For over five decades, VOCABULARY WORKSHOP has proven a highly successful tool for guiding systematic vocabulary growth. It has also been a valuable help to students preparing for the vocabulary-related parts of standardized tests. In this, the latest edition of the series, many new features have been added to make VOCABULARY WORKSHOP even more effective in increasing vocabulary and improving vocabulary skills.

The **Definitions** sections in the fifteen Units, for example, have been expanded to include synonyms and antonyms and for each taught word an illustrative sentence for each part of speech.

In the **Synonyms** and **Antonyms** sections, exercise items are now presented in the form of phrases, the better to familiarize you with the range of contexts and distinctions of usage for the Unit words.

New to this edition is **Vocabulary in Context**, an exercise that appears at the end of each Unit and in the Reviews. In this exercise, you will read an expository passage containing a selection of Unit words. In addition to furnishing you with further examples of how and in what contexts Unit words are used, this exercise will also provide you with practice with vocabulary questions in standardized-test formats.

In the five Reviews, you will find two important new features, in addition to Analogies, Two-Word Completions, and other exercises designed to help you prepare for standardized tests. One of these new features, **Building with Classical Roots**, will acquaint you with Latin and Greek roots from which many English words stem and will provide you with a strategy that may help you find the meaning of an unknown or unfamiliar word.

Another new feature, **Writer's Challenge**, is designed to do just that—challenge you to improve your writing skills by applying what you have learned about meanings and proper usage of selected Unit words.

Finally, another new feature has been introduced in the four Cumulative Reviews. **Enriching Your Vocabulary** is meant to broaden and enhance your knowledge and understanding of the relationships, history, and origins of the words that make up our rich and dynamic language.

In this Level of VOCABULARY WORKSHOP, you will study three hundred key words, and you will be introduced to hundreds of other words in the form of synonyms, antonyms, and other relatives. Mastery of these words will make you a better reader, a better writer and speaker, and better prepared for the vocabulary parts of standardized tests.

CONTENTS

PRONUNCIATION KEY

The pronunciation is indicated for every basic word introduced in this book. The symbols used for this purpose, as listed below, are similar to those appearing in most standard dictionaries of recent vintage. The author has consulted a large number of dictionaries for this purpose but has relied primarily on *Webster's Third New International Dictionary* and *The Random House Dictionary of the English Language (Unabridged)*.

There are, of course, many English words for which two (or more) pronunciations are commonly accepted. In virtually all cases where such words occur in this book, the author has sought to make things easier for the student by giving just one pronunciation. The only significant exception occurs when the pronunciation changes in accordance with a shift in the part of speech. Thus we would indicate that *project* in the verb form is pronounced prə jekt', and in the noun form, präj' ekt.

It is believed that these relatively simple pronunciation guides will be readily usable by the student. It should be emphasized, however, that the *best* way to learn the pronunciation of a word is to listen to and imitate an educated speaker.

Vowels	ā	lake	e	stress	ü	loot, new
	a	mat	ī	knife	u̇	foot, pull
	â	care	i	sit	ə	rug, broken
	ä	bark, bottle	ō	flow	ər	bird, better
	au̇	doubt	ô	all, cord		
	ē	beat, wordy	oi	oil		

Consonants	ch	child, lecture	s	cellar	wh	what
	g	give	sh	shun	y	yearn
	j	gentle, bridge	th	thank	z	is
	ŋ	sing	th	those	zh	measure

All other consonants are sounded as in the alphabet.

Stress	The accent mark *follows* the syllable receiving the major stress: en rich'

Abbreviations	*adj.*	adjective	*n.*	noun	*prep.*	preposition
	adv.	adverb	*part.*	participle	*v.*	verb
	int.	interjection	*pl.*	plural		

THE VOCABULARY OF VOCABULARY

There are some interesting and useful words that are employed to describe and identify words. The exercises that follow will help you to check and strengthen your knowledge of this "vocabulary of vocabulary."

Denotation and Connotation

The **denotation** of a word is its specific dictionary meaning. Here are a few examples:

Word	Denotation
humane	kind and merciful
braggart	boastful person
search	look for

The **connotation** of a word is its **tone**—that is, the emotions or associations it normally arouses in people using, hearing, or reading it. Depending on what these feelings are, the connotation of a word may be *favorable* (*positive*) or *unfavorable* (*negative, pejorative*). A word that does not normally arouse strong feelings of any kind has a *neutral* connotation. Here are some examples of words with different connotations:

Word	Connotation
humane	favorable
braggart	unfavorable
search	neutral

Exercises *In the space provided, label the connotation of each of the following words* ***F*** *for "favorable,"* ***U*** *for "unfavorable," or* ***N*** *for "neutral."*

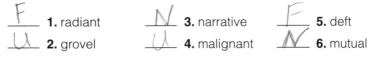

_F_ **1.** radiant   _N_ **3.** narrative   _F_ **5.** deft

_U_ **2.** grovel   _U_ **4.** malignant   _N_ **6.** mutual

Literal and Figurative Usage

When a word is used in a **literal** sense, it is being employed in its strict (or primary) dictionary meaning in a situation (or context) that "makes sense" from a purely logical or realistic point of view. For example:

On our hike we picked berries, *mushrooms*, and other wild plants.

In this sentence, *mushrooms* is employed literally. The mushrooms are real fungi.

Sometimes words are used in a symbolic or nonliteral way in situations that do not "make sense" from a purely logical or realistic point of view. We call this nonliteral application of a word a **figurative** or **metaphorical** usage. For example:

Sometimes a minor border incident *mushrooms* into a major international crisis.

In this sentence, *mushrooms* is not being used in a literal sense. That is, the mushrooms are not real. Rather, the word is intended to convey graphically that the problem is growing rapidly.

Exercises In the space provided, write **L** for "literal" or **F** for "figurative" next to each of the following sentences to show how the italicized expression is being used.

L **1.** Fireworks displays on the Fourth of July usually include *skyrockets*, Roman candles, and other spectacular illuminations.

F **2.** During a period of sharp inflation, prices of consumer goods *skyrocket* at an alarming rate.

F **3.** Every spring, companies all over the country are *deluged* with mail from college students looking for summer employment.

Synonyms

A **synonym** is a word that has *the same* or *almost the same* meaning as another word. Here are some examples:

cheerful—glad
attempt—try
salary—pay

select—choose
mercy—kindness
careful—cautious

Exercises In each of the following groups, circle the word that is most nearly the **synonym** of the word in **boldface** type.

1. praise	**2. halt**	**3. pleasant**	**4. thief**
a. flattery	a. cry	a. tall	a. lieutenant
b. ability	b. begin	b. mighty	b. follower
c. excitement	c. hold	c. agreeable	c. burglar
d. sight	d. stop	d. noisy	d. chief

Antonyms

An **antonym** is a word that means *the opposite* of or *almost the opposite* of another word. Here are some examples:

generous—stingy
give—take
cheerful—sad

love—hate
swift—slow
conceal—reveal

Exercises In each of the following groups, circle the word that is most nearly the **antonym** of the word in **boldface** type.

1. graceful	**2. certain**	**3. linger**	**4. glorious**
a. good	a. real	a. hasten	a. patriotic
b. awkward	b. guilty	b. fish	b. shameful
c. gracious	c. dark	c. eat	c. dangerous
d. polite	d. questionable	d. study	d. hard

VOCABULARY STRATEGY: USING CONTEXT

How do you go about finding the meaning of an unknown or unfamiliar word that you come across in your reading? You might look the word up in a dictionary, of course, provided one is at hand. But there are two other useful strategies that you might employ to find the meaning of a word that you do not know at all or that is used in a way that you do not recognize. One strategy is to analyze the **structure** or parts of the word. (See pages 11 and 12 for more on this strategy.) The other strategy is to try to figure out the meaning of the word by reference to context.

When we speak of the **context** of a word, we mean the words that are near to or modify that word. By studying the context, we may find **clues** that lead us to its meaning. We might find a clue in the immediate sentence or phrase in which the word appears (and sometimes in adjoining sentences or phrases, too); or we might find a clue in the topic or subject matter of the passage in which the word appears; or we might even find a clue in the physical features of a page itself. (Photographs, illustrations, charts, graphs, captions, and headings are some examples of such features.)

One way to use context as a strategy is to ask yourself what you know already about the topic or subject matter in question. By applying what you have learned before about deserts, for example, you would probably be able to figure out that the word *arid* in the phrase "the arid climate of the desert" means "dry."

The **Vocabulary in Context** exercises that appear in the Units and Reviews and the **Choosing the Right Meaning** exercises that appear in the Reviews and Cumulative Reviews both provide practice in using subject matter or topic to determine the meaning of given words.

When you do the various word-omission exercises in this book, look for ***context clues*** built into the sentence or passage to guide you to the correct answer. Three types of context clues appear in the exercises in this book.

A ***restatement clue*** consists of a *synonym* for, or a *definition* of, the missing word. For example:

> When I told my landlord that I was planning to _____
> my apartment, he didn't seem too unhappy to see me depart.
> a. clean   (b. vacate)   c. furnish   d. redecorate

In this sentence, *depart* is a synonym of the missing word, *vacate*, and acts as a restatement clue for it.

A ***contrast clue*** consists of an *antonym* for, or a phrase that means the *opposite* of, the missing word. For example:

> Though some of my classmates are decidedly skinny, others are
> definitely (**thin,** (**overweight**)).

In this sentence, *skinny* is an antonym of the missing word, *overweight*. *Skinny* thus functions as a contrast clue for *overweight*.

An **inference clue** implies but does not directly state the meaning of the missing word or words. For example:

"Only a <u>trial</u> in a bona fide court of law can <u>determine</u> the _____ of the <u>charges</u> leveled at <u>my client</u>," the _____ said.

a. effect . . . prosecutor
b. relevance . . . judge
c. validity . . . defense attorney
d. appropriateness . . . juror

In this sentence, there are several inference clues: (a) the word *trial* suggests the word *validity* because the purpose of a trial is to decide whether charges are true or false; the word *determine* suggests the same thing; (b) the words *charges* and *my client* suggest a *defense attorney* because accusations are brought against a defendant rather than a plaintiff.

Exercises   Use context clues to choose the word or words that complete each of the following sentences or sets of sentences.

1. Though I was brought up in a completely (**rural, urban**) environment, life in the big city suits me to a tee.

2. People with _____ ideas are always thinking up new and different things to do or say or make.

a. vague
b. simple
c. old-fashioned
d. original

3. Because a medieval castle was primarily a fortress, scholars point out that it was built more for _____ than for _____.

a. decoration . . . usefulness
b. defense . . . comfort
c. aggression . . . protection
d. pageantry . . . style

VOCABULARY STRATEGY: WORD STRUCTURE

One important way to build your vocabulary is to learn the meaning of word parts that make up many English words. These word parts consist of **prefixes, suffixes,** and **roots,** or **bases.** A useful strategy for determining the meaning of an unknown word is to "take apart" the word and think about the parts. For example, when you look at the word parts in the word *invisible,* you find the prefix *in-* ("not") + the root *-vis-* ("see") + the suffix *-ible* ("capable of"). From knowing the meanings of the parts of this word, you can figure out that *invisible* means "not capable of being seen."

Following is a list of common prefixes. Knowing the meaning of a prefix can help you determine the meaning of a word in which the prefix appears.

Prefix	Meaning	Sample Words
bi-	two	biannual, bicycle
com-, con-	together, with	compatriot, contact
de-, dis-	lower, opposite	devalue, disloyal
fore-, pre-	before, ahead of time	forewarn, preplan
il-, im-, in-, ir, non-, un-	not	illegal, impossible, inactive, irregular, nonsense, unable
in-, im-	in, into	inhale, import
mid-	middle	midday, midterm, midway
mis-	wrongly, badly	mistake, misbehave
re-	again, back	redo, repay
sub-	under, less than	submarine, subzero
super-	above, greater than	superimpose, superstar
tri-	three	triangle

Following is a list of common suffixes. Knowing the meaning and grammatical function of a suffix can help you determine the meaning of a word.

Noun Suffix	Meaning	Sample Nouns
-acy, -ance, -ence, -hood, -ity, -ment, -ness, -ship	state, quality, or condition of, act or process of	adequacy, attendance, persistence, neighborhood, activity, judgment, brightness, friendship
-ant, -eer, -ent, -er, -ian, -ier, -ist, -or	one who does or makes something	contestant, auctioneer, resident, banker, comedian, financier, dentist, doctor
-ation, -ition, -ion	act or result of	organization, imposition, election

Verb Suffix	Meaning	Sample Verbs
-ate	to become, produce, or treat	validate, salivate, chlorinate
-en	to make, cause to be	shorten, lengthen, weaken
-fy, -ify, -ize	to cause, make	liquefy, glorify, legalize

Adjective Suffix	Meaning	Sample Adjectives
-able, -ible	able, capable of	believable, incredible
-al, -ic	relating to, characteristic of	natural, romantic
-ful, -ive, -ous	full of, given to, marked by	beautiful, protective, poisonous
-ish, -like	like, resembling	foolish, childlike
-less	lacking, without	careless

A **base** or **root** is the main part of a word to which prefixes and suffixes may be added. Many roots come to English from Latin, such as *-socio-,* meaning "society," or from Greek, such as *-logy-,* meaning "the study of." Knowing Greek and Latin roots can help you determine the meaning of a word such as *sociology,* which means "the study of society."

In the **Building with Classical Roots** sections of this book you will learn more about some of these Latin and Greek roots and about English words that derive from them. The lists that follow may help you figure out the meaning of new or unfamiliar words that you encounter in your reading.

Greek Root	Meaning	Sample Word
-astr-, -aster-, -astro-	star	astral, asteroid, astronaut
-auto-	self	autograph
-bio-	life	biography
-chron-, chrono-	time	chronic, chronological
-cosm-, -cosmo-	universe, order	microcosm, cosmopolitan
-cryph-, -crypt-	hidden, secret	apocryphal, cryptographer
-dem-, -demo-	people	epidemic, democracy
-dia-	through, across, between	diameter
-dog-, -dox-	opinion, teaching	dogmatic, orthodox
-gen-	race, kind, origin, birth	generation
-gnos-	know	diagnostic
-graph-, -graphy-, -gram-	write	graphite, autobiography, telegram
-log-, -logue-	speech, word, reasoning	logic, dialogue
-lys-	break down	analysis
-metr-, -meter-	measure	metric, kilometer
-micro-	small	microchip
-morph-	form, shape	amorphous
-naut-	sailor	cosmonaut
-phon-, -phone-, -phono-	sound, voice	phonics, telephone, phonograph
-pol-, -polis-	city, state	police, metropolis
-scop-, -scope-	watch, look at	microscopic, telescope
-tele-	far off, distant	television
-the-	put or place	parentheses

Latin Root	Meaning	Sample Word
-cap-, -capt-, -cept-, -cip-	take	capitulate, captive, concept, recipient
-cede-, -ceed-, -ceas-, -cess-	happen, yield, go	precede, proceed, decease, cessation
-cred-	believe	incredible
-dic-, -dict-	speak, say, tell	indicate, diction
-duc-, -duct-, -duit-	lead, conduct, draw	educate, conduct, conduit
-fac-, -fact-, -fect-, -fic-, -fy-	make	faculty, artifact, defect, beneficial, clarify
-ject-	throw	eject
-mis-, -miss-, -mit-, -mitt-	send	promise, missile, transmit, intermittent
-note-, -not-	know, recognize	denote, notion
-pel-, -puls-	drive	expel, compulsive
-pend-, -pens-	hang, weight, set aside	pendulum, pension
-pon-, -pos-	put, place	component, position
-port-	carry	portable
-rupt-	break	bankrupt
-scrib-, -scribe-, -script-	write	scribble, describe, inscription
-spec-, -spic-	look, see	spectator, conspicuous
-tac-, -tag-, -tang-, -teg-	touch	contact, contagious, tangible, integral
-tain-, -ten-, -tin-	hold, keep	contain, tenure, retinue
-temp-	time	tempo, temporary
-ven-, -vent-	come	intervene, convention
-vers-, -vert-	turn	reverse, invert
-voc-, -vok-	call	vocal, invoke

WORKING WITH ANALOGIES

Today practically every standardized examination involving vocabulary, especially the SAT-I, employs the **analogy** as a testing device. For that reason, it is an excellent idea to learn how to read, understand, and solve such verbal puzzles.

What Is an Analogy?

An analogy is a kind of equation using words rather than numbers or mathematical symbols and quantities. Normally, an analogy contains two pairs of words linked by a word or symbol that stands for an equal sign (=). A complete analogy compares the two pairs of words and makes a statement about them. It asserts that the logical relationship between the members of the first pair of words is *the same as* the logical relationship between the members of the second pair of words. This is the only statement a valid analogy ever makes.

Here is an example of a complete analogy. It is presented in two different formats.

Format 1   **Format 2**
maple is to tree as rose is to flower   maple : tree :: rose : flower

Reading and Interpreting Analogies

As our sample indicates, analogies are customarily presented in formats that need some deciphering in order to be read and understood correctly. There are a number of these formats, but you need concern yourself with only the two shown.

Format 1: Let's begin with the format that uses all words:

> maple is to tree as rose is to flower

Because this is the simplest format to read and understand, it is the one used in the student texts of VOCABULARY WORKSHOP. It is to be read exactly as printed. Allowing for the fact that the word pairs change from analogy to analogy, this is how to read every analogy, no matter what the format is.

Now you know how to read an analogy. Still, it is not clear exactly what the somewhat cryptic statement "maple is to tree as rose is to flower" means. To discover this, you must understand what the two linking expressions *as* and *is to* signify.

- The word *as* links the two word pairs in the complete analogy. It stands for an equal sign (=) and means "is the same as."

- The expression *is to* links the two members of each word pair, so it appears twice in a complete analogy. In our sample, *is to* links *maple* and *tree* (the two words in the first pair) and also *rose* and *flower* (the two words in the second word pair). Accordingly, the expression *is to* means "has the same logical relationship to" the two words it links.

Putting all this information together, we can say that our sample analogy means:

> The logical relationship between a *maple* and a *tree* is *the same as* (=) the logical relationship between a *rose* and a *flower*.

Now you know what our sample analogy means. This is what every analogy means, allowing for the fact that the word pairs will vary from one analogy to another.

Format 2: Our second format uses symbols, rather than words, to link its four members.

> maple : tree :: rose : flower

This is the format used on the SAT-I and in the *TEST PREP Blackline Masters* that accompany each Level of Vocabulary Workshop. In this format, a single colon (:) replaces the expression *is to*, and a double colon (::) replaces the word *as*. Otherwise, format 2 is the same as format 1; that is, it is read in exactly the same way ("maple is to tree as rose is to flower"), and it means exactly the same thing ("the logical relationship between a *maple* and a *tree* is the same as the logical relationship between a *rose* and a *flower*").

Completing Analogies

So far we've looked at complete analogies. However, standardized examinations do not provide the test taker with a complete analogy. Instead, the test taker is given the first, or key, pair of words and then asked to *complete* the analogy by selecting the second pair from a given group of four or five choices, usually lettered *a* through *d* or *e*.

Here's how our sample analogy would look on such a test:

1. maple is to tree as
a. acorn is to oak
b. hen is to rooster
c. rose is to flower
d. shrub is to lilac

or

1. maple : tree ::
a. acorn : oak
b. hen : rooster
c. rose : flower
d. shrub : lilac

It is up to the test taker to complete the analogy correctly.

Here's how to do that in just four easy steps!

Step 1: *Look at the two words in the key (given) pair, and determine the logical relationship between them.*

In our sample analogy, *maple* and *tree* form the key (given) pair of words. They indicate the key (given) relationship. Think about these two words for a moment. What is the relationship of a maple to a tree? Well, a maple is a particular kind, or type, of tree.

Step 2: *Make up a short sentence stating the relationship that you have discovered for the first pair of words.*

For our model analogy, we can use this sentence: "A maple is a particular kind (type) of tree."

Step 3: *Extend the sentence you have written to cover the rest of the analogy, even though you haven't completed it yet.*

The easiest way to do this is to repeat the key relationship after the words *just as*, leaving blanks for the two words you don't yet have. The sentence will now read something like this:

A maple is a kind (type) of tree, just as a ? is a kind of ? .

Step 4: *Look at each of the lettered pairs of words from which you are to choose your answer. Determine which lettered pair illustrates the same relationship as the key pair.*

The easiest and most effective way to carry out step 4 is to substitute each pair of words into the blanks in the sentence you made up to see which sentence makes sense. Only one will.

Doing this for our sample analogy, we get:

a. A maple is a kind of tree, just as an acorn is a kind of oak.
b. A maple is a kind of tree, just as a hen is a kind of rooster.
c. A maple is a kind of tree, just as a rose is a kind of flower.
d. A maple is a kind of tree, just as a shrub is a kind of lilac.

Look at these sentences. Only *one* of them makes any sense. Choice *a* is clearly wrong because an acorn is *not* a kind of oak. Choice *b* is also wrong because a hen is *not* a kind of rooster. Similarly, choice *d* is incorrect because a shrub is *not* a kind of lilac, though a *lilac* is a kind of shrub. In other words, the two words are in the wrong order. That leaves us with choice *c*, which says that a rose is a kind of flower. Well, that makes sense; a rose is indeed a kind of flower. So, choice *c* must be the pair of words that completes the analogy correctly.

Determining the Key Relationship

Clearly, determining the nature of the key relationship is the most important and the most difficult part of completing an analogy. Since there are literally thousands of key relationships possible, you cannot simply memorize a list of them. The table on page 16, however, outlines some of the most common key relationships. Study the table carefully.

Table of Key Relationships

Complete Analogy	Key Relationship
big is to **large** as **little** is to **small**	**Big** means the same thing as **large**, just as **little** means the same thing as **small**.
tall is to **short** as **thin** is to **fat**	**Tall** means the opposite of **short**, just as **thin** means the opposite of **fat**.
brave is to **favorable** as **cowardly** is to **unfavorable**	The tone of **brave** is **favorable**, just as the tone of **cowardly** is **unfavorable**.
busybody is to **nosy** as **klutz** is to **clumsy**	A **busybody** is by definition someone who is **nosy**, just as a **klutz** is by definition someone who is **clumsy**.
cowardly is to **courage** as **awkward** is to **grace**	Someone who is **cowardly** lacks **courage**, just as someone who is **awkward** lacks **grace**.
visible is to **see** as **audible** is to **hear**	If something is **visible**, you can by definition **see** it, just as if something is **audible**, you can by definition **hear** it.
invisible is to **see** as **inaudible** is to **hear**	If something is **invisible**, you cannot **see** it, just as if something is **inaudible**, you cannot **hear** it.
frigid is to **cold** as **blistering** is to **hot**	**Frigid** is the extreme of **cold**, just as **blistering** is the extreme of **hot**.
chef is to **cooking** as **tailor** is to **clothing**	A **chef** is concerned with **cooking**, just as a **tailor** is concerned with **clothing**.
liar is to **truthful** as **bigot** is to **fair-minded**	A **liar** is by definition not likely to be **truthful**, just as a **bigot** is by definition not likely to be **fair-minded**.
starvation is to **emaciation** as **overindulgence** is to **corpulence**	**Starvation** will lead to **thinness**, just as **overindulgence** will lead to **fatness**.
practice is to **proficient** as **study** is to **knowledgeable**	**Practice** will make a person **proficient**, just as **study** will make a person **knowledgeable**.
eyes are to **see** as **ears** are to **hear**	You use your **eyes** to **see** with, just as you use your **ears** to **hear** with.
sloppy is to **appearance** as **rude** is to **manner**	The word **sloppy** can refer to one's **appearance**, just as the word **rude** can refer to one's **manner**.
learned is to **knowledge** as **wealthy** is to **money**	Someone who is **learned** has a great deal of **knowledge**, just as someone who is **wealthy** has a great deal of **money**.

Exercises   *In each of the following, circle the item that best completes the analogy. Then explain the key relationship involved.*

1. neat is to **tidy** as
a. normal is to unusual
b. gigantic is to colossal
c. deep is to dry
d. tall is to short

2. hammer is to **tool** as
a. soprano is to opera
b. tree is to forest
c. typewriter is to machine
d. horse is to vehicle

3. veterinarian is to **animals** as
a. druggist is to vagrants
b. lawyer is to fees
c. theologian is to angels
d. warden is to prisoners

4. kindle is to **extinguish** as
a. live is to dwell
b. study is to examine
c. listen is to learn
d. start is to stop

VOCABULARY AND WRITING

When you study vocabulary, you make yourself not only a better reader but also a better writer. The greater the number of words at your disposal, the better you will be able to express your thoughts. Good writers are always adding new words to their personal vocabularies, the pool of words that they understand *and* know how to use properly. They use these words both when they write and when they revise.

There are several factors to consider when choosing words and setting the tone of your writing. First, your choice of words should suit your purpose and your audience. If you are writing an essay for your social studies teacher, you will probably want to choose words that are formal in tone and precise in meaning. If you are writing a letter to a friend, however, you will probably choose words that are more informal in tone and freer in meaning. Your **audience** is the person or people who will be reading what you write, and your **purpose** is the reason why you are writing. Your purpose, for example, might be to explain; or it might be to describe, inform, or entertain.

Almost any kind of writing—whether a school essay, a story, or a letter to a friend—can be improved by careful attention to vocabulary. Sometimes you will find, for example, that one word can be used to replace a phrase of five or six words. This is not to say that a shorter sentence is always better. However, readers usually prefer and appreciate **economy** of expression. They grow impatient with sentences that plod along with vague, unnecessary words rather than race along with fewer, carefully chosen ones. Writing can also be improved by attention to **diction** (word choice). Many writers use words that might make sense in terms of *general* meaning but that are not precise enough to convey *nuances* of meaning. In the **Writer's Challenge** sections of this book, you will have an opportunity to make word choices that will more clearly and precisely convey the meaning you intend.

Exercises   *Read the following sentences, paying special attention to the words and phrases underlined. From the words in the box, find better choices for the underlined words and phrases.*

1. Because we had a long journey ahead of us, we could not remain or stay any longer.

talk	tarry	listen	play

2. The pioneers had to bear many weights on their journey across the continent.

storms	delays	skirmishes	burdens

3. Our assignment is to write a brief statement giving a general view of the novel's plot.

synopsis	criticism	essay	preface

4. The chair was covered with a vulgar and scratchy fabric.

colorful	cheap	coarse	costly

5. I hope to receive a prosperous bonus at the end of the year.

nice	substantial	important	tangible

This test contains a sampling of the words that are to be found in the exercises in this Level of VOCABULARY WORKSHOP. It will give you an idea of the types of words to be studied and their level of difficulty. When you have completed all the units, the Final Mastery Test at the end of this book will assess what you have learned. By comparing your results on the Final Mastery Test with your results on the Diagnostic Test below, you will be able to judge your progress.

Synonyms

*In each of the following groups, circle the word or phrase that **most** **nearly** expresses the meaning of the word in **boldface** type in the given phrase.*

1. refuse to **capitulate**
   a. ask   b. listen   c. surrender   d. cooperate

2. write a **sequel**
   a. letter   b. follow-up   c. novel   d. summary

3. **perceptible** changes
   a. sudden   b. noticeable   c. painful   d. costly

4. **infiltrated** enemy lines
   a. destroyed   b. avoided   c. strengthened   d. penetrated

5. do her **stint**
   a. share   b. best   c. worst   d. least

6. a **plausible** excuse
   a. reasonable   b. lengthy   c. silly   d. confused

7. **plundered** the treasury
   a. set up   b. attacked   c. robbed   d. reformed

8. the **plaudits** of the people
   a. wishes   b. complaints   c. praises   d. fears

9. a vague **premonition** of disaster
   a. cause   b. rumor   c. echo   d. forewarning

10. have **ample** opportunity
   a. little   b. rare   c. unusual   d. sufficient

11. **solicitous** about our problems
   a. contented   b. concerned   c. confused   d. careless

12. a **dire** result
   a. favorable   b. dreadful   c. sensible   d. predictable

13. surrounded by **servile** followers
   a. cringing   b. patriotic   c. brave   d. faithful

14. an **avowed** enemy
   a. deadly   b. weak   c. declared   d. defeated

15. handle **gingerly**
   a. quickly   b. successfully   c. too late   d. cautiously

16. the **acme** of success
    a. cause   b. lack   c. cost   d. top

17. convey our regrets
    a. feel   b. send   c. cause   d. soothe

18. become a **nonentity**
    a. voter   b. leader   c. nobody   d. scholar

19. choose an appropriate **excerpt**
    a. topic   b. title   c. selection   d. leader

20. peruse the report
    a. write   b. read   c. vote on   d. approve

21. struck a **discordant** note in the proceedings
    a. welcome   b. jarring   c. strange   d. sensible

22. garnish a salad
    a. eat   b. toss   c. prepare   d. decorate

23. facetious remarks
    a. sensible   b. dull   c. interesting   d. humorous

24. deface public property
    a. damage   b. sell   c. repair   d. steal

25. devoid of pity
    a. full   b. empty   c. result   d. cause

26. filled with **anguish**
    a. distress   b. joy   c. patience   d. annoyance

27. a **detriment** to success
    a. reaction   b. aid   c. block   d. opening

28. preclude failure
    a. anticipate   b. prevent   c. cause   d. reveal

29. oblique glances
    a. angry   b. loving   c. longing   d. sideways

30. a man whose deeds have been **vilified** by history
    a. remembered   b. celebrated   c. badmouthed   d. ignored

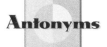

Antonyms

*In each of the following groups, circle the word that is **most nearly opposite** in meaning to the word in **boldface** type in the given phrase.*

31. appease a bully
    a. satisfy   b. avoid   c. enrage   d. protect

32. excised the meaningless sentence
    a. wrote   b. inserted   c. questioned   d. ignored

33. negligent owners
    a. overworked   b. elderly   c. responsible   d. happy-go-lucky

34. a **judicious** choice of words
    a. sensible   b. cautious   c. sensitive   d. foolish

35. new evidence that will bolster our case
a. improve   b. weaken   c. clinch   d. concern

36. outlandish behavior
a. weird   b. embarrassing   c. normal   d. rude

37. kindred spirits
a. intoxicating   b. warlike   c. happy   d. unlike

38. tried to minimize my part in the victory
a. increase   b. ignore   c. reduce   d. match

39. was rational when he committed the crime
a. guilty   b. intelligent   c. responsible   d. insane

40. inert officials
a. active   b. stupid   c. frightened   d. greedy

41. tractable mules
a. strong   b. unmanageable   c. tame   d. hungry

42. a skittish driver
a. new   b. confident   c. careless   d. timid

43. increased the enmity between the two countries
a. friendship   b. trade   c. hostility   d. tourism

44. a haughty young man
a. clever   b. wealthy   c. angry   d. humble

45. disgruntled customers
a. satisfied   b. demanding   c. numerous   d. rich

46. a very volatile situation
a. explosive   b. puzzling   c. stable   d. unusual

47. a group of ramshackle buildings
a. sturdy   b. ancient   c. battered   d. vacant

48. a cryptic message
a. verbal   b. clear   c. lengthy   d. sad

49. upbraided the children for what they had done
a. fined   b. praised   c. scolded   d. punished

50. a whimsical account of her travels
a. lengthy   b. funny   c. humorless   d. short

Definitions

Note carefully the spelling, pronunciation, part(s) of speech, and definition(s) of each of the following words. Then write the word in the blank space(s) in the illustrative sentence(s) following. Finally, study the lists of synonyms and antonyms given at the end of each entry.

1. adage
(ad' ij)

(*n.*) a proverb, wise saying

One way to begin an informal speech or an oral report is to quote an old _____.

SYNONYMS: maxim, saw, aphorism

2. bonanza
(bə nan' zə)

(*n.*) a rich mass of ore in a mine; something very valuable, profitable, or rewarding; a source of wealth or prosperity; a very large amount; sudden profit or gain

The thrilling adventure movie set in Alaska proved to be a box-office _____.

SYNONYMS: windfall

3. churlish
(chər' lish)

(*adj.*) lacking politeness or good manners; lacking sensitivity; difficult to work with or deal with; rude

The store manager instructed all the salesclerks to avoid _____ replies to customers' questions.

SYNONYMS: surly, ill-tempered
ANTONYMS: courteous, civil, well-mannered

4. citadel
(sit' ə del)

(*n.*) a fortress that overlooks and protects a city; any strong or commanding place

A medieval _____ once guarded the capital city of the Greek island of Rhodes.

SYNONYMS: fort, stronghold, bulwark, bastion

5. collaborate
(kə lab' ə rāt)

(*v.*) to work with, work together

Several students plan to _____ on a geology project for the annual science fair.

SYNONYMS: team up, join forces
ANTONYM: work alone

6. decree
(di krē')

(*n.*) an order having the force of law; (*v.*) to issue such an order; to command firmly or forcefully

"There went forth a _____ from Caesar Augustus that all the world should be taxed" (Luke 2:1).

Why does nature always seem to _____ nasty weather for our annual family picnic?

SYNONYMS: (*n.*) proclamation, edict; (*v.*) proclaim

7. discordant
(dis kôr′ dənt)

(*adj.*) disagreeable in sound, jarring; lacking in harmony, conflicting

Their little spat struck a _____ note in our otherwise happy family get-together.

SYNONYMS: grating, shrill, different, divergent
ANTONYMS: harmonious, in agreement

8. evolve
(ē välv′)

(*v.*) to develop gradually; to rise to a higher level

Authors hope that their notes, descriptions, and character sketches will _____ into a book.

SYNONYMS: unfold, emerge
ANTONYMS: wither, shrivel up, atrophy

9. excerpt
(ek′ sərpt)

(*n.*) a passage taken from a book, article, etc.; (*v.*) to take such a passage; to quote

My essay includes a long _____ from a speech by Sojourner Truth.

If you _____ some material from a reference book, be sure to enclose it in quotation marks.

SYNONYMS: (*n.*) portion, section, extract

10. grope
(grōp)

(*v.*) to feel about hesitantly with the hands; to search blindly and uncertainly

When the power failed, we had to _____ in the dark to find a working flashlight.

SYNONYMS: fumble for, cast about for

11. hover
(həv′ ər)

(*v.*) to float or hang suspended over; to move back and forth uncertainly over or around

A large group of vultures _____ in the air above the wounded animal.

SYNONYMS: linger, waver, seesaw
ANTONYM: soar

12. jostle
(jäs′ əl)

(*v.*) to make or force one's way by pushing or elbowing; to bump, shove, brush against; to compete for

I tried not to _____ other riders as I exited the crowded bus.

SYNONYM: push

13. laggard
(lag′ ərd)

(*n.*) a person who moves slowly or falls behind; (*adj.*) falling behind; slow to move, act, or respond

Tour guides often have to urge _____ to keep up with the rest of the group.

Tenants who are _____ in paying rent run the risk of being forced to move.

SYNONYMS: (*n.*) slowpoke, straggler; (*adj.*) sluggish
ANTONYMS: (*n.*) early bird; (*adj.*) swift, speedy, prompt

14. plaudits
(plô′ ditz)

(*n. pl.*) applause; enthusiastic praise or approval

The skaters who won the gold medals gratefully accepted the
_____ of their fans.

SYNONYMS: cheers, acclaim
ANTONYMS: boos, disapproval, ridicule

15. preclude
(prē klüd′)

(*v.*) to make impossible, prevent, shut out

Three wrong answers will _____
any contestant from entering the quiz show's final round.

SYNONYMS: hinder, check, stop
ANTONYMS: help, promote, facilitate

16. revert
(rē vərt′)

(*v.*) to return, go back

Control of a property usually _____
to the legal owner when a lease is up.

SYNONYMS: relapse, regress
ANTONYMS: progress, advance

17. rubble
(rəb′ əl)

(*n.*) broken stone or bricks; ruins

Bulldozers and wrecking balls soon reduced the damaged
building to a heap of smoking _____.

SYNONYMS: wreckage, debris

18. servile
(sər′ vīl)

(*adj.*) of or relating to a slave; behaving like or suitable for a
slave or a servant, menial; lacking spirit or independence,
abjectly submissive

Most serious performers prefer constructive criticism to
_____ flattery.

SYNONYMS: slavish, groveling, fawning
ANTONYMS: masterly, overbearing

19. vigil
(vij′ əl)

(*n.*) a watch, especially at night; any period of watchful attention

Thousands attended the solemn _____
at the Vietnam Veterans Memorial.

20. wrangle
(raŋ′ gəl)

(*v.*) to quarrel or argue in a noisy, angry way; to obtain by
argument; to herd; (*n.*) a noisy quarrel

My brother and sister always _____
over whose turn it is to take out the trash.

The customer got into a nasty _____
with the shopkeeper.

SYNONYMS: (*v.*) squabble, bicker
ANTONYMS: (*v.*) agree, concur

Completing the Sentence

From the words for this unit, choose the one that best completes each of the following sentences. Write the word in the space provided.

1. The swiftest members of the herd escaped the trappers' nets, but the __laggards__ were caught.

2. Your silly pride about doing everything on your own __precludes__ your getting the help you need so badly.

3. On the ground, teams of paramedics administered first aid to the victims of the accident, while police helicopters __hovered__ overhead.

4. They had such a long __wrangle__ over the use of the bicycle that their mother finally wouldn't allow either of them to use it.

5. As we discussed our coming vacation, we gradually __evolved__ a plan for a bicycle trip through New England.

6. With tireless devotion, the ailing child's parents kept an anxious __vigile__ at her bedside.

7. Let me read aloud a few __excerpts__ from the newspaper review of the new movie.

8. The cafeteria line was so crowded that I was __jostled__ past the desserts before I could take one.

9. During his eleven years of "personal rule," King Charles I of England bypassed Parliament and ruled the country by royal __decree__.

10. For two nights, he did his homework faithfully; then he __reverted__ to his usual lazy ways.

11. After the walls of their city fell to the enemy, the inhabitants withdrew to the __citadel__ and continued the struggle from there.

12. When the lights suddenly went out, I __groped__ my way into the kitchen to find a candle and matches.

13. Our teacher gave the two of us permission to __collaborate__ on our reports because we were investigating related problems.

14. The Emancipation Proclamation of 1863 was the first step in releasing African Americans from their __servile__ bonds.

15. Suddenly the __discordant__ voices of two people engaged in a quarrel burst upon my ears and jarred me out of my daydream.

16. What is the exact wording of the __adage__ about early birds and worm-catching?

17. If you will only show a little patience, that business investment may grow into a(n) __bonanza__ for you.

18. A word of praise from the coach meant more to me than all the loud but thoughtless _plaudits_ of the crowd.

19. Before the new housing project could be built, it was necessary to tear down the old houses and remove the _rubble_.

20. You hurt her feelings when you reacted to her comments in such a(n) _churlish_ way, especially since you asked for her advice.

Synonyms

*Choose the word from this unit that is **the same** or **most nearly the same** in meaning as the **boldface** word or expression in the given phrase. Write the word on the line provided.*

1. as the ad campaign slowly **unfolded** ___evolve___
2. tried to **prevent** further objections to the bill ___preclude___
3. an inspiring **maxim** to live by ___adage___
4. **pushed** the table so hard that it tipped over ___jostle___
5. **fumble** for an answer to the question ___grope___
6. represented quite a **windfall** for the company ___bonanza___
7. crushed beneath many tons of **debris** ___rubble___
8. plan to **team up** to write an original skit ___collaborate___
9. annoyed by all that **fawning** attention ___servile___
10. the Roman siege of the **stronghold** at Masada ___citadel___
11. an **extract** from the poet's best-known work ___excerpt___
12. **go back** to an earlier stage of development ___revert___
13. **lingered** around the 100-degree mark for days ___hover___
14. according to a papal **proclamation** ___decree___
15. kept a **watch** at their father's coffin ___vigil___

Antonyms

*Choose the word from this unit that is **most nearly opposite** in meaning to the **boldface** word or expression in the given phrase. Write the word on the line provided.*

16. surprised by the **harmonious** ending of the piece ___discordant___
17. usually **agreed** about the way to proceed ___wrangle___
18. not accustomed to such **courteous** service ___churlish___
19. known for being **early birds** ___laggard___
20. did not expect such **disapproval** from the audience ___plaudits___

Choosing the Right Word

*Circle the **boldface** word that more satisfactorily completes each of the following sentences.*

1. All those who (**decreed, collaborated**) with the enemy in the hope of gaining special favors will be punished severely.

2. The assembly speaker may have been boring, but that was no excuse for the students' (**laggard, churlish**) behavior toward him.

3. I have always regarded our colleges and universities as (**citadels, plaudits**) of learning and bastions against ignorance and superstition.

4. The fact that he was found guilty of a felony many years ago doesn't (**preclude, evolve**) his running for mayor.

5. When I fumbled the ball on the three-yard line, the (**plaudits, excerpts**) of the crowd suddenly turned into jeers and catcalls.

6. I refuse to accept the excuse that the pressures of a new job caused you to (**revert, grope**) to your old habit of cigarette smoking.

7. After the operation, we sat in the hospital lounge, keeping a nightlong (**bonanza, vigil**) until we heard from the doctor.

8. For weeks an anxious world (**wrangled, hovered**) between war and peace as diplomats desperately struggled to resolve the crisis.

9. Every time he quotes an old (**vigil, adage**), he looks as though he has just had a brilliant new idea.

10. She raised so many objections to attending the dance that it was obvious she was (**groping, precluding**) for an excuse not to go.

11. A president needs people who will tell him frankly what they really think, rather than just offer (**servile, discordant**) approval of everything he does.

12. There are times when we all need to be (**jostled, reverted**) away from old, familiar ideas that may no longer be as true as they once seemed.

13. The principal was quick to approve new programs for our club but (**servile, laggard**) in providing financial support for them.

14. The little club that they set up to talk over community problems (**evolved, jostled**) over the years into a national political organization.

15. The "broken-down old furniture" that the woman left to her children turned out to be a (**bonanza, rubble**) of valuable antiques.

16. The committee found it impossible to reach any agreement on the matter because the views of its members were so (**churlish, discordant**).

17. After I had broken curfew for the third time in one week, my angry parents (**decreed, precluded**) that I was grounded for the rest of the term.

18. As we searched through the (**rubble, citadel**) after the earthquake, it was heartbreaking to find such articles as a teakettle and a child's doll.

19. From the hundreds of newspaper items, the lawyer carefully (**excerpted, collaborated**) three short paragraphs that supported his case.

20. Under the Articles of Confederation, the thirteen states (**hovered, wrangled**) so much that the nation seemed to be in danger of breaking up.

Read the following passage, in which some of the words you have studied in this unit appear in **boldface** type. Then complete each statement given below the passage by circling the letter of the item that is **the same** or **almost the same** in meaning as the highlighted word.

A Dynamic and Creative Duo

(Line)

Have you ever heard a musical **excerpt** from *H.M.S. Pinafore* or *The Pirates of Penzance*? If so, you've had a taste of the work of one of England's most famous creative teams. Playwright William S. Gilbert (1836–1911) and composer Arthur S. Sullivan (1842–1900) teamed up to write fourteen popular musical plays in the late

(5)   nineteenth century.

It may seem curious that these two men came to **collaborate** on some of the most enduring and tuneful works in the history of the musical theater. They

(10)   had very different personalities. Gilbert was a difficult man who was known to be remote and arrogant. Sullivan was a gifted musician with a sociable and easygoing manner.

(15)   You may know famous American musicals such as *The King and I*, *West Side Story*, or *Rent*. The style of works such as these **evolved** over time to blend music, dance, and theater into

Scene from *The Pirates of Penzance*

(20)   a seamless whole. Previously, popular musicals (called *comic operas* or *operettas*) were less unified. They were excuses to string together an amusing assortment of songs, dance numbers, and stage spectacles.

Then along came Gilbert and Sullivan. Sullivan's sweet melodies and lush orchestrations balanced Gilbert's witty plays and lyrics. Their twenty-five-year

(25)   partnership earned them **plaudits** from audiences, critics, and fellow artists the world over.

Eventually, their working relationship began to decline. Each man was jealous of the other's success. Each was annoyed by the other's temperament. They **wrangled** over artistic and personal issues. A short time after the first performance of *The Gondoliers*,

(30)   they reached the breaking point. Their final split came after an awful fight over—of all things—the purchase of a carpet for the theater in which their works were performed.

---

1. The meaning of **excerpt** (line 1) is
  a. idea   c. passage
  b. sound   d. masterpiece

2. Collaborate (line 7) most nearly means
  a. join forces   c. intrude
  b. concentrate   d. disagree

3. Evolved (line 18) is best defined as
  a. withered   c. retreated
  b. repeated   d. developed

4. The meaning of **plaudits** (line 25) is
  a. orders   c. ridicule
  b. praise   d. profits

5. Wrangled (line 28) most nearly means
  a. lingered   c. squabbled
  b. puzzled   d. concurred

Definitions

Note carefully the spelling, pronunciation, part(s) of speech, and definition(s) of each of the following words. Then write the word in the blank space(s) in the illustrative sentence(s) following. Finally, study the lists of synonyms and antonyms given at the end of each entry.

1. antics
(an' tiks)

(*n. pl.*) ridiculous and unpredictable behavior or actions

The _____ of the chimpanzees amused the crowds at the zoo.

SYNONYMS: pranks, shenanigans

2. avowed
(ə vaùd')

(*adj., part.*) declared openly and without shame, acknowledged

The governor was an _____ supporter of the plan to aid public libraries throughout the state.

SYNONYMS: admitted, sworn
ANTONYMS: unacknowledged, undisclosed

3. banter
(ban' tər)

(*v.*) to exchange playful remarks, tease; (*n.*) talk that is playful and teasing

There is nothing my friends and I enjoy more than to

_____ good-naturedly for hours.

Casual _____ helps to pass the time during a long journey.

SYNONYMS: (*n.*) joking, raillery
ANTONYM: (*n.*) serious talk

4. bountiful
(baùnt' i fəl)

(*adj.*) giving freely, generous; plentiful, given abundantly

On Thanksgiving Day, people all over America celebrate the

_____ gifts of nature.

SYNONYMS: liberal, abundant, copious
ANTONYMS: scarce, scanty, in short supply

5. congested
(kən jest' id)

(*adj., part.*) overcrowded, filled or occupied to excess

The doctor grew very concerned when the patient's lungs became _____ with fluid.

SYNONYMS: jammed, packed, choked
ANTONYMS: uncluttered, unimpeded

6. detriment
(det' rə mənt)

(*n.*) harm or loss; injury, damage; a disadvantage; a cause of harm, injury, loss, or damage

The home team survived a six-game losing streak with almost no _____ to its standing in the league.

SYNONYMS: hindrance, liability
ANTONYMS: advantage, help, plus

7. durable
(dùr' ə bəl)

(*adj.*) sturdy, not easily worn out or destroyed; lasting for a long time; (*n. pl.*) consumer goods used repeatedly over a series of years

Denim is a very _____ kind of fabric.

Most people own household _____
such as furniture and appliances.

SYNONYMS: (*adj.*) long-lasting, enduring
ANTONYMS: (*adj.*) fragile, perishable, fleeting, ephemeral

8. enterprising
(ent' ər prī ziŋ)

(*adj.*) energetic, willing and able to start something new; showing boldness and imagination

An _____ young person may turn a
hobby into a way of earning money to pay for college.

SYNONYMS: vigorous, ambitious, aggressive, audacious
ANTONYMS: lazy, indolent, timid, diffident

9. frugal
(frü' gəl)

(*adj.*) economical, avoiding waste and luxury; scanty, poor, meager

At home, we usually prepare _____
but nourishing and delicious meals.

SYNONYMS: thrifty, skimpy
ANTONYMS: wasteful, improvident, lavish, extravagant

10. gingerly
(jin' jər lē)

(*adj., adv.*) with extreme care or caution

Difficult and demanding customers should be handled in a
_____ and courteous manner.

Pedestrians made their way _____
along the slippery, snow-covered streets.

SYNONYMS: (*adv.*) cautiously, warily, circumspectly
ANTONYMS: (*adv.*) firmly, confidently, aggressively

11. glut
(glət)

(*v.*) to provide more than is needed or wanted; to feed or fill to the point of overstuffing; (*n.*) an oversupply

Hollywood studios _____ theaters
with big-budget action movies during the summer season.

When there is a _____ of gasoline
on the market, prices at the pump may drop dramatically.

SYNONYMS: (*v.*) flood, inundate; (*n.*) surplus, plethora
ANTONYMS: (*n.*) shortage, scarcity, dearth, paucity

12. incognito
(in käg nē' tō)

(*adj., adv.*) in a disguised state, under an assumed name or identity; (*n.*) the state of being disguised; a person in disguise

Just before the battle of Agincourt, Shakespeare's King Henry V
prowls through his camp _____.

In a way, makeup artists are practitioners of the fine art of

_____.

ANTONYM: (*adj.*) undisguised

13. invalidate
(in val' ə dāt)

(v.) to make valueless, take away all force or effect

Lawyers will try to _____ the contract.

SYNONYMS: cancel, annul, disapprove, discredit
ANTONYMS: support, confirm, back up, legalize

14. legendary
(lej' ən der ē)

(adj.) described in well-known stories; existing in old stories (legends) rather than in real life

Ajax was one of the _____ Greek heroes who fought before the walls of Troy.

SYNONYMS: mythical, fabulous, famous, celebrated

15. maim
(mām)

(v.) to cripple, disable, injure, mar, disfigure, mutilate

Each year, falls _____ thousands of people, some of them for life.

16. minimize
(min' ə mīz)

(v.) to make as small as possible, make the least of; to make smaller than before

Whenever you are in a car, you should wear your seatbelt to _____ the risk of injury in an accident.

SYNONYMS: belittle, downplay, underrate
ANTONYMS: magnify, enlarge, exaggerate

17. oblique
(ō blēk')

(adj.) slanting or sloping; not straightforward or direct

The boxer's _____ blow left his opponent unscathed.

SYNONYMS: diagonal, indirect
ANTONYMS: direct, straight to the point

18. veer
(vēr)

(v.) to change direction or course suddenly, turn aside, shift, swerve

The huge storm finally _____ out to sea, leaving much destruction in its wake.

19. venerate
(ven' ə rāt)

(v.) to regard with reverence, look up to with great respect

In a number of religions, it is customary for people to _____ saints and martyrs to the faith.

SYNONYMS: worship, revere, idolize
ANTONYMS: despise, detest, ridicule, deride

20. wanton
(wänt' ən)

(adj.) reckless; heartless, unjustifiable; loose in morals; (n.) a spoiled, pampered person; one with low morals

The gas chambers at Auschwitz are a grim testimony to the _____ cruelty of the Nazis.

The main character in the popular miniseries was a charming but heartless _____ .

SYNONYMS: (adj.) rash, malicious, spiteful, unprovoked
ANTONYMS: (adj.) justified, morally strict, responsible

Completing the Sentence

From the words for this unit, choose the one that best completes each of the following sentences. Write the word in the space provided.

1. An inability to get along smoothly and effectively with other people will be a great _____ to you in any career you may choose.

2. Even the most _____ materials will in time be worn away by flowing water.

3. Although he had been severely _____ in the automobile accident, he was determined to return to his job and lead a normal life.

4. Instead of walking straight from the farmhouse to the road, we set off in a(n) _____ direction across the field.

5. I would never have expected members of the senior class to take part in such childish _____!

6. We admired the _____ immigrant who set up a small shop and developed it into a large and prosperous business.

7. We desperately needed every bit of help we could find, but what we got was a(n) _____ of advice and a scarcity of cold cash.

8. We should be willing to share our _____ food supplies with less fortunate people in other parts of the world.

9. In American law, the fact that the person accused of a crime is poor does not _____ his or her right to adequate legal representation.

10. To avoid the children in the street, the truck _____ sharply to the right and sideswiped several parked cars.

11. Isn't it strange for a(n) _____ music lover to show no interest in our school orchestra?

12. The vandals broke windows, overturned desks, and left the school a scene of _____ destruction.

13. Although she tried to cover it up with lively _____, I could see that her feelings had been deeply hurt.

14. Since I was afraid of banging my bare feet against the furniture, I walked through the darkened room very _____.

15. What a change from the _____ streets of the inner city to the wide-open spaces of the Great Plains!

16. Although his income was small, his _____ living habits enabled him to save a large sum of money over the years.

17. The film star traveled _____ in order to avoid the attentions of her adoring fans.

18. As Americans, we _____ the great ideals of human freedom expressed in the Bill of Rights.

19. While I do not wish to alarm you, I will not _____ the danger if you refuse to have the children vaccinated.

20. Davy Crockett was a real person, but so many tall stories have been told about him that he has become a(n) _____ figure.

Synonyms

Choose the word from this unit that is **the same** or **most nearly the same** in meaning as the **boldface** word or expression in the given phrase. Write the word on the line provided.

1. the child prodigy's **celebrated** talent _____

2. laughed at the **shenanigans** of the comedian _____

3. **swerved** to avoid a pothole _____

4. cared for those **injured** in the fire _____

5. a **sworn** opponent of higher taxes _____

6. stuck with a **surplus** of zucchini _____

7. **joked** with my teammates after the game _____

8. **underrated** the importance of the discovery _____

9. made **ambitious** plans for the company _____

10. **revere** the writings of Shakespeare _____

11. a need to remain **disguised** _____

12. **malicious** damage to public property _____

13. an **indirect** reference to an embarrassing event _____

14. received **copious** praise for their work _____

15. a serious **liability** to my future plans _____

Antonyms

Choose the word from this unit that is **most nearly opposite** in meaning to the **boldface** word or expression in the given phrase. Write the word on the line provided.

16. the **uncluttered** aisles of the supermarket _____

17. a garment made of a very **fragile** fabric _____

18. **confirm** the results of the election _____

19. stepped **confidently** into the mountain lake _____

20. served the guests a **lavish** meal _____

Choosing the Right Word

*Circle the **boldface** word that more satisfactorily completes each of the following sentences.*

1. As a(n) (**avowed, gingerly**) supporter of women's rights, she believes that men and women should receive the same pay if they do the same jobs.

2. We are grateful for the (**frugal, bountiful**) legacy that our great artists and composers have given us.

3. Why do you suppose someone whose face is known all over the world would want to travel (**obliquely, incognito**)?

4. I will not try to (**minimize, banter**) the difficulties we face, but I am sure that we can overcome them by working together.

5. Children may be (**maimed, avowed**) in spirit as well as in body if they do not have a secure and loving home environment.

6. The (**legendary, wanton**) deeds of Sherlock Holmes are so well known that many people think he really lived.

7. Self-confidence is a good quality; but if it is carried too far, it can be a (**detriment, glut**) to success in life.

8. Instead of just waiting for things to get better by themselves, we must be more (**incognito, enterprising**) in working for improvements.

9. Because of his repeated traffic violations, his driver's license has been (**congested, invalidated**).

10. We were shocked by their (**bountiful, wanton**) misuse of the money their parents had left them.

11. Your speech would have been better if you had stayed with your main idea instead of (**bantering, veering**) off to side issues.

12. After living for so long on a (**frugal, durable**) diet, I was amazed when I saw the variety of rich dishes served at the banquet.

13. Building a new skyscraper there will bring additional thousands of people into an area that is already (**invalidated, congested**).

14. The mad Roman emperor Caligula believed that he was a god and expected people to (**venerate, veer**) him as such.

15. I didn't want Charlotte to know that I was watching her, but occasionally I managed to steal a few (**oblique, legendary**) glances at her.

16. Although I love sports, I sometimes feel that television is becoming (**glutted, maimed**) with athletic events of all kinds.

17. Instead of approaching him in that timid and (**frugal, gingerly**) manner, tell him frankly what is on your mind.

18. When they saw that they had been caught red-handed, they resorted to all kinds of (**detriments, antics**) in a vain attempt to prove their "innocence."

19. Our friendship has proved to be (**durable, enterprising**) because it is based on mutual respect and honesty.

20. It was bad taste on your part to use that (**venerating, bantering**) tone when we were discussing such a sad event.

Read the following passage, in which some of the words you have studied in this unit appear in **boldface** type. Then complete each statement given below the passage by circling the letter of the item that is **the same** or **almost the same** in meaning as the highlighted word.

The Oldest Rookie

(Line)

In the 1930s and 1940s, the **legendary** Leroy "Satchel" Paige was one of the best pitchers in baseball. The astounding Alabama-born right-hander first gained national attention in the 1920s as one of the leading players in the Negro Leagues. Many factors

contributed to Paige's huge popularity with fans. He had a casual and humorous manner and often engaged in (5) crowd-pleasing **banter**. He had an easy-to-remember nickname, and his pitching style was unusual.

However, the primary reason for Paige's fame was his **bountiful** athletic talent. Sportswriters recognized him as one of the finest pitchers in the history of the (10) game. He had a blazing fastball, flawless control, and a **durable** arm that served him well for an amazing number of years. Joe DiMaggio said that Paige was "the best and fastest pitcher" he ever faced.

In 1947, Jackie Robinson broke baseball's color (15) barrier. The following year, Satchel Paige took the mound for the Cleveland Indians, becoming the first African American pitcher in the American League. At age forty-two, he was also baseball's oldest rookie.

Some critics tried to **minimize** the importance of (20) Paige's move to the American League. They accused Indians owner Bill Veeck of signing Paige for the publicity. Veeck replied that the right-hander was "the best available player" to help the team win the pennant.

In 1965, at the age of fifty-nine, Paige pitched for (25) Kansas City, becoming the oldest player ever to take part in a major-league game. His last public appearance was for the Atlanta Braves in 1969. In 1971, Satchel Paige took his rightful place in baseball's Hall of Fame.

Satchel Paige on the mound in 1965

Fans and players alike **venerate** the memory of this (30) great African American athlete.

---

1. The meaning of **legendary** (line 1) is
a. celebrated
b. amateur
c. cheerful
d. unknown

2. Banter (line 6) most nearly means
a. smiles
b. arguments
c. joking
d. skills

3. Bountiful (line 9) is best defined as
a. unusual
b. scarce
c. amazing
d. abundant

4. The meaning of **durable** (line 12) is
a. fragile
b. long
c. sturdy
d. muscular

5. Minimize (line 20) most nearly means
a. exaggerate
b. belittle
c. legalize
d. explain

6. Venerate (line 30) is best defined as
a. look up to
b. acknowledge
c. downplay
d. discuss

Definitions

Note carefully the spelling, pronunciation, part(s) of speech, and definition(s) of each of the following words. Then write the word in the blank space(s) in the illustrative sentence(s) following. Finally, study the lists of synonyms and antonyms given at the end of each entry.

1. allot
(ə lät′)

(v.) to assign or distribute into shares or portions

The teacher _____ books and supplies to each student on the first day of school.

SYNONYMS: apportion, parcel out, allocate

2. amass
(ə mas′)

(v.) to bring together, collect, gather, especially for oneself; to come together, assemble

A prudent investor can _____ a fortune in the stock market over the long run.

SYNONYMS: accumulate, pile up, garner
ANTONYMS: scatter, dissipate, squander, waste

3. audacious
(ô dā′ shəs)

(adj.) bold, adventurous, recklessly daring

The audience cheered the _____ feats of the trapeze artists.

SYNONYMS: enterprising, brave
ANTONYMS: timid, cowardly

4. comply
(kəm plī′)

(v.) to yield to a request or command

Employees who fail to _____ with a company's rules may lose their jobs.

SYNONYMS: submit to, consent to, acquiesce in
ANTONYMS: reject, refuse, decline

5. devoid
(di void′)

(adj.) not having or using, lacking

The old well on my grandparents' property has long been _____ of water.

SYNONYMS: wanting, bereft
ANTONYMS: full, teeming, abounding

6. elite
(ā lēt′)

(n.) the choice part of a group of people or things; (adj.) superior

Each year, the social _____ of the community sponsors several events to benefit local charities.

You can get a fine education regardless of whether or not you attend an _____ school.

SYNONYMS: (n.) cream of the crop, upper crust
ANTONYMS: (n.) rank and file, dregs of society

7. grapple
(grap′ əl)

(n.) an iron hook used to grab and hold; (v.) to come to grips with, wrestle or fight with

A ship equipped with _____ may be used to recover large pieces of wreckage from the ocean floor.

Store employees _____ with the thieves and held them until the police arrived.

SYNONYMS: (v.) tackle, confront, struggle with

8. incapacitate
(in kə pas′ ə tāt)

(v.) to deprive of strength or ability; to make legally ineligible

In the 1940s and 1950s, polio _____ many thousands of people each year all over the world.

SYNONYMS: disable, debilitate, paralyze, cripple
ANTONYMS: rehabilitate, restore

9. instigate
(in′ stə gāt)

(v.) to urge on; to stir up, provoke, start, incite

Several demonstrators in the angry crowd did their best to _____ a riot.

ANTONYMS: stop, quell, squelch, quash

10. longevity
(län jev′ ə tē)

(n.) long life, long duration, length of life

The sea turtle is known for its _____ .

ANTONYMS: brevity, transience

11. myriad
(mir′ ē əd)

(adj.) in very great numbers; (n.) a very great number

Scientists continue to make new discoveries in their studies of the _____ life-forms of the jungle.

You will find information on a _____ of subjects on the Internet.

SYNONYMS: (adj.) innumerable, countless
ANTONYMS: (adj.) few, scant, sparse

12. perspective
(pər spek′ tiv)

(n.) a point of view or general standpoint from which different things are viewed, physically or mentally; the appearance to the eye of various objects at a given time, place, or distance

The designs for the children's playhouse were drawn to scale and in the right _____ .

SYNONYMS: viewpoint, sense of proportion

13. perturb
(pər tərb′)

(v.) to trouble, make uneasy; to disturb greatly; to throw into confusion

The rude and disruptive behavior of several party guests _____ the host and hostess.

SYNONYMS: upset, agitate, anger, irritate
ANTONYMS: delight, gladden, please

14. prodigious
(prə dij′ əs)

(adj.) immense; extraordinary in bulk, size, or degree

Few intellects have rivaled the _____ mind of Albert Einstein.

SYNONYMS: gigantic, tremendous, astounding
ANTONYMS: puny, minuscule, insignificant

15. relevant
(rel' ə vənt)

(*adj.*) connected with or related to the matter at hand

I found several Web sites that provided information _____ to the topic of my research paper.

SYNONYMS: pertinent, germane, applicable
ANTONYMS: unconnected, extraneous

16. skittish
(skit' ish)

(*adj.*) extremely nervous and easily frightened; shy or timid; extremely cautious; unstable, undependable

Only an experienced and confident rider should mount a _____ horse.

SYNONYMS: jumpy, restive, capricious, fickle
ANTONYMS: bold, daring, reckless, cool, unflappable

17. tether
(teth' er)

(*n.*) a rope or chain used to fasten something to a fixed object; the outer limit of strength or resources; (*v.*) to fasten with a rope or chain

Some young people find it difficult to break the emotional and financial _____ that bind them to their parents.

Before the storm, I _____ the boat securely to the dock.

SYNONYMS: (*v.*) tie up, chain up, leash
ANTONYMS: (*v.*) untie, let loose

18. unison
(yü' nə sən)

(*n.*) a sounding together; agreement or accord

The members of our new student orchestra need to practice playing in _____ .

SYNONYMS: harmony, concord, assent

19. vie
(vī)

(*v.*) to compete; to strive for victory or superiority

Many actors _____ for the leading role in the famous director's new film.

SYNONYMS: contend, rival

20. willful
(wil' fəl)

(*adj.*) stubbornly self-willed; done on purpose, deliberate

After lengthy deliberations, the jury found the defendant guilty of _____ murder.

SYNONYMS: headstrong, obstinate, premeditated
ANTONYMS: docile, obedient, tractable

From the words for this unit, choose the one that best completes each of the following sentences. Write the word in the space provided.

1. He joined the _____ group of athletes who have run a mile in under four minutes.

2. The disease had so _____ the poor woman that she was no longer able to leave her bed.

3. If all the members of the cast work in _____, I am sure we will have a successful class show.

4. I refuse to _____ with any order issued by a person who has absolutely no knowledge of the project I'm working on.

5. I know that you are a brilliant student, but I am still amazed that you could _____ such a vast store of information so quickly.

6. Before we set out on the camping trip, our Scout leader _____ special tasks and responsibilities to each one of us.

7. The _____ child insisted on wearing sneakers to her sister's wedding.

8. We can thank modern medical science for the increased _____ of human beings in most parts of the world.

9. Trying to navigate through rush-hour traffic on a high-speed expressway can be a nightmare for a(n) _____ driver.

10. A number of cities _____ with one another to be chosen as the site of a national political convention.

11. Since the town meeting tonight has been called to deal with conservation, only discussion _____ to that subject will be allowed.

12. You will have to use a(n) _____ to recover the lobster trap from the bottom of the bay.

13. Though we have made many outstanding contributions to the conquest of space, landing men on the moon is probably our most _____ achievement.

14. The autumn night sky, with its _____ of stars, always fills me with awe and wonder.

15. Father said, "I am _____, not because you failed the exam, but because you still seem unable to understand *why* you failed it."

16. There in the middle of the garden was a goat _____ to a stake.

17. When he seemed hopelessly defeated, General George Washington crossed the Delaware River and launched a(n) _____ surprise attack on the Hessians.

18. I am completely _____ of sympathy for anyone who loses a job because of carelessness and indifference.

19. In wartime, it is not unusual for secret agents to be sent behind enemy lines in an effort to _____ a rebellion.

20. Someday, when you see this event in its proper _____, you will realize that it is not as important as it seems now.

Synonyms

*Choose the word from this unit that is **the same** or **most nearly the same** in meaning as the **boldface** word or expression in the given phrase. Write the word on the line provided.*

1. innumerable opportunities to learn something new _____

2. repeated delays that **irritated** the passengers _____

3. when considered from another **viewpoint** _____

4. allocated four tickets to each member of the cast _____

5. accumulated a huge collection of folk art _____

6. contended for first prize at the science fair _____

7. are in **agreement** on a course of action _____

8. chose only the **cream of the crop** _____

9. behaves in a **headstrong** fashion _____

10. tried to calm the **jumpy** children _____

11. had to **tackle** a difficult problem _____

12. an illness that **disables** young and old alike _____

13. seems determined to **provoke** an argument _____

14. submit to the terms of the treaty _____

15. a **tremendous** effort by the entire team _____

Antonyms

*Choose the word from this unit that is **most nearly opposite** in meaning to the **boldface** word or expression in the given phrase. Write the word on the line provided.*

16. timid when faced with a challenge _____

17. a river **teeming with** fish _____

18. untied the pair of carriage horses _____

19. evidence that is **extraneous** to the investigation _____

20. the **brevity** of the public's interest in the story _____

Choosing the Right Word

*Circle the **boldface** word that more satisfactorily completes each of the following sentences.*

1. In the next chorus, *please* try to sing in (**unison, compliance**).

2. We will never have a well-organized or effective club if all the members insist (**willfully, prodigiously**) on having their own way.

3. As I stared at the luscious chocolate swirl cake, I bravely (**incapacitated, grappled**) with temptation—but the chocolate cake won!

4. Can you imagine what a (**relevant, prodigious**) amount of research is needed for a multivolume reference book such as the *Encyclopaedia Britannica*?

5. People who come from rich and socially prominent families don't always belong to the intellectual (**myriad, elite**).

6. Great new discoveries in science can be made only by men and women with intellectual (**compliance, audacity**).

7. By the twentieth mile of a marathon, many runners have reached the end of their (**perspective, tether**).

8. The bitter strike closed shops, shut down factories, and (**incapacitated, perturbed**) an entire industry for months.

9. I wonder why the camp directors were unwilling to (**comply, vie**) with my request to keep a pet snake in my tent.

10. Unless you want to (**instigate, amass**) a quarrel, don't make insulting remarks about my friends and family.

11. How do you explain the fact that in practically every country the (**elite, longevity**) of women is greater than that of men?

12. The defense has told you about the defendant's unhappy childhood, but how is this (**relevant, willful**) to the question of innocence or guilt?

13. Perhaps in the long-term (**longevity, perspective**) of history, some events that seem very important now will prove to be minor.

14. I don't think anyone can hope to (**vie, grapple**) with Gloria in the election for "Most Popular Student."

15. Jane Addams was not only profoundly (**perturbed, instigated**) by the suffering of other people but also tried hard to help them.

16. If we have to share the same locker, please try to keep your things in the space (**allotted, amassed**) to you.

17. She delivered a simple, low-key speech, completely (**devoid, relevant**) of fancy language or emotional appeals.

18. He has had such bad experiences with motorcycles that he has become extremely (**audacious, skittish**) of them.

19. Our course in life sciences has given us some idea of the (**myriad, unison**) varieties of plants and animals inhabiting the earth.

20. She had devoted her life to (**amassing, allotting**) not material riches but the love, respect, and thanks of every member of this community.

*Read the following passage, in which some of the words you have studied in this unit appear in **boldface** type. Then complete each statement given below the passage by circling the letter of the item that is **the same** or **almost the same** in meaning as the highlighted word.*

The Other Rain Forests

(Line)

When people hear the term *rain forest*, they think of extremely dense foliage, monkeys howling, and parrots shrieking, all in a steamy, exotic, tropical setting. But there is an entirely different kind of rain forest that is completely **devoid of** the plants and animals of the tropics. It is known as a *temperate* rain forest. Temperate

(5) rain forests are found both north and south of the tropics, in places with mild (temperate) climates. Most are coastal, are near or on mountains, and are very wet and rainy.

The longest unbroken stretch of temperate rain forest is located along the west coasts of Canada

(10) and the United States, stretching from Alaska south to Oregon. This habitat is as complex and varied as its tropical counterparts. It supports **myriad** plant and animal species. Some of the oldest, largest trees in the world grow in it.

(15) Temperate rain forests have been drastically reduced in size because of the worldwide demand for wood. Environmentalists and the logging industry **vie** for influence on the policies that will determine the fate of the forests.

(20) Environmentalists have used the Endangered Species Act to prevent or limit logging. The spotted owl became a symbol of these efforts. This small bird requires large areas of old-growth forest, in which trees grow to **prodigious** heights.

Spotted owls nest in old-growth forests.

(25) Without such trees, the spotted owl has no place to nest. Loggers, however, argue that jobs and even entire communities will be lost if logging is limited.

In the coming years, it will be up to the parties directly involved and to American and Canadian voters to consider the various arguments **relevant** to this debate. Like other rain forests all over the world, North America's temperate rain forests

(30) face an uncertain future.

---

1. The meaning of **devoid of** (line 3) is
a. filled with   c. lacking in
b. hidden from   d. suitable for

2. Myriad (line 13) most nearly means
a. countless   c. colorful
b. unusual   d. sparse

3. Vie (line 18) is best defined as
a. wait   c. pay
b. settle   d. compete

4. The meaning of **prodigious** (line 24) is
a. average   c. uniform
b. puny   d. gigantic

5. Relevant (line 28) most nearly means
a. interesting   c. unconnected
b. pertinent   d. hostile

Analogies *In each of the following, circle the item that best completes the comparison.*

1. miser is to **amass** as
a. spendthrift is to squander
b. thief is to inherit
c. banker is to embezzle
d. wanton is to save

2. lungs are to **congested** as
a. streets are to deserted
b. citadels are to strong
c. vigils are to nightly
d. drains are to clogged

3. words are to **banter** as
a. pictures are to adages
b. actions are to antics
c. ideas are to bonanzas
d. deeds are to plaudits

4. agitator is to **instigate** as
a. saint is to venerate
b. laggard is to hurry
c. spark is to ignite
d. perspective is to evolve

5. myriad is to **many** as
a. devoid is to none
b. scarce is to much
c. glutted is to little
d. congested is to few

6. durable is to **longevity** as
a. relevant is to great wealth
b. unified is to great variety
c. elite is to great wisdom
d. prodigious is to great size

7. gingerly is to **care** as
a. laggard is to speed
b. diplomatic is to tact
c. skittish is to courage
d. churlish is to courtesy

8. amass is to **much** as
a. minimize is to little
b. reduce is to much
c. increase is to little
d. shrink is to much

9. veer is to **away** as
a. inflate is to down
b. revert is to back
c. wither is to up
d. decline is to forward

10. daredevil is to **audacious** as
a. spendthrift is to frugal
b. laggard is to enterprising
c. tattletale is to prodigious
d. coward is to skittish

11. avowed is to **openness** as
a. frank is to concealment
b. stealthy is to openness
c. incognito is to concealment
d. underhanded is to openness

12. tether is to **rope** as
a. hover is to bird
b. maim is to detriment
c. grapple is to hook
d. minimize is to tool

13. boor is to **churlish** as
a. traitor is to faithful
b. angle is to oblique
c. lion is to skittish
d. toady is to servile

14. audacious is to **plaudits** as
a. legendary is to heroes
b. prodigious is to strength
c. clownish is to antics
d. cowardly is to jeers

15. wrangle is to **discordant** as
a. agree is to harmonious
b. grope is to certain
c. comply is to willful
d. perturb is to pleasant

16. wanton is to **unfavorable** as
a. servile is to favorable
b. durable is to unfavorable
c. enterprising is to favorable
d. gingerly is to unfavorable

17. scarce is to **devoid** as
a. bountiful is to glutted
b. legendary is to relevant
c. unison is to discordant
d. servile is to decreed

18. frugal is to **bountiful** as
a. oblique is to slanting
b. timid is to audacious
c. churlish is to expensive
d. willful is to graceful

Word Associations

In each of the following groups, circle the word that is best defined or suggested by the given phrase.

1. to assign storage space to all the tenants
a. invalidate   b. allot   c. evolve   d. amass

2. a small group of the best students chosen for a special course
a. vigil   b. elite   c. rubble   d. bonanza

3. to keep going back to one's old habits
a. revert   b. vie   c. instigate   d. minimize

4. an order having the force of law
a. grapple   b. wrangle   c. decree   d. rubble

5. a highly profitable investment
a. wanton   b. bonanza   c. tether   d. citadel

6. a parched and arid wasteland
a. myriad   b. devoid   c. avowed   d. incognito

7. a ray of light hitting a window at an angle
a. relevant   b. oblique   c. avowed   d. wanton

8. "Try to look at it from my point of view."
a. vigil   b. citadel   c. banter   d. perspective

9. storm clouds hanging over the city
a. jostling   b. evolving   c. hovering   d. veering

10. "A penny saved is a penny earned."
a. banter   b. excerpt   c. adage   d. tether

11. a celebrated star of stage and screen
a. legendary   b. bountiful   c. frugal   d. durable

12. to cause worry and grief to parents by one's conduct
a. venerate   b. perturb   c. preclude   d. evolve

13. what remains when a city has been heavily bombed
a. adage   b. detriment   c. rubble   d. wrangle

14. with no concern for right or justice
a. wanton   b. laggard   c. servile   d. legendary

15. searched confusedly for the right word
a. jostled   b. groped   c. wrangled   d. veered

16. the sentry's lonely watch
a. antics   b. vigil   c. perspective   d. decree

17. scattered paragraphs from the Constitution
a. plaudits   b. decrees   c. excerpts   d. gluts

18. a worker who has lost a finger in an industrial accident
a. prodigious   b. gingerly   c. churlish   d. maimed

19. so many troubles that I can't begin to count them
a. legendary   b. devoid   c. oblique   d. myriad

20. to take steps to prevent something from happening
a. jostle   b. preclude   c. veer   d. hover

Vocabulary in Context

*Read the following passage, in which some of the words you have studied in Units 1–3 appear in **boldface** type. Then complete each statement given below the passage by circling the item that is **the same** or **almost the same** in meaning as the highlighted word.*

Built to Last

(Line)

Long before Europeans reached the Americas, native people erected massive **citadels**. Many of these ancient buildings still stand,
(5) delighting and fascinating both scholars and tourists. But the durability of these structures raises puzzling questions. Many Native American civilizations arose in
(10) earthquake zones or near active volcanoes. All the structures built in these areas were subject to stresses that could easily have reduced them to **rubble**. What
(15) factors account for the **longevity** of these great monuments to Native American inventiveness and skill? Why have these structures survived while so many European-style
(20) buildings have not?

Because scholars have few written documents from this period to turn to, they must **grapple with** physical and cultural evidence. They compare the
(25) clues they find with what they know about modern architecture and building practices.

Scholars now believe that Native American architects knew the secrets
(30) of building durable structures on unstable ground. Inca masons, for example, found a way to fit large blocks of stone together snugly to form walls that were both strong and
(35) flexible, able to withstand tremors and quakes. The tapered shape of the temple pyramids was also a contributing factor. Many early architects understood that the
(40) combination of **oblique** angles and straight, parallel lines give a building stability.

Comparison with European architecture provides another
(45) **perspective**. Unlike their European counterparts, Native American architects did not construct arches. The arch, widely used in European buildings to achieve height, is very
(50) vulnerable to stresses that can cause it to collapse. In contrast, most early Native American structures rose in height with the support of heavy, solid walls.
(55) These elements may explain why so many of these superb structures remain for us to appreciate today.

---

1. The meaning of **citadels** (line 3) is
a. bridges
b. strongholds
c. apartments
d. malls

2. Rubble (line 14) most nearly means
a. ashes
b. nothing
c. debris
d. slums

3. Longevity (line 15) is best defined as
a. long halls
b. design
c. popularity
d. long life

4. The meaning of **grapple with** (line 23) is
a. ignore
b. doubt
c. tackle
d. accept

5. Oblique (line 40) most nearly means
a. sloping
b. unusual
c. sharp
d. wide

6. Perspective (line 45) is best defined as
a. theory
b. argument
c. viewpoint
d. topic

Choosing the Right Meaning

Read each sentence carefully. Then circle the item that best completes the statement below the sentence.

By a famous constitutional compromise, the "official" population of the pre–
Civil War Southern states was determined by adding three-fifths of the
servile population to the total free population. (2)

1. In line 3 the word **servile** most nearly means

    a. enslaved   b. fawning   c. submissive   d. domestic

One of the indicators by which experts measure the state of the economy tracks
national sales of cars, refrigerators, and other durables. (2)

2. In line 2 the word **durables** most nearly means

    a. heavy equipment   c. grains and cereals
    b. technological gadgetry   d. substantial consumer goods

Serious fighting broke out well before the bulk of either of the opposing armies had
amassed on the battlefield. (2)

3. The best meaning for **amassed** in line 2 is

    a. brought together   b. hoarded   c. assembled   d. garnered

"It's amazing that they can work such long hours under such difficult conditions
with no apparent detriment to their health," she observed. (2)

4. The phrase **detriment to** in line 2 is used to mean

    a. change in   b. damage to   c. improvement in   d. source of harm to

Thereupon ensued the laughable spectacle of the old king's courtiers jostling
with upstarts for places in the new king's retinue. (2)

5. The word **jostling** in line 1 is best defined as

    a. bumping   b. debating   c. shoving   d. vying

Antonyms

*In each of the following groups, circle the word or expression that is most nearly the **opposite** of the word in **boldface** type.*

1. relevant	**3. durable**	**5. laggard**	**7. gingerly**
a. unrelated	a. easy	a. untimely	a. quickly
b. false	b. nice	b. early	b. boldly
c. good	c. fragile	c. punctured	c. sadly
d. pleasant	d. dangerous	d. behindhand	d. slowly
2. preclude	**4. incapacitate**	**6. minimize**	**8. comply**
a. give back	a. kindle	a. prevent	a. refuse
b. take out	b. adjust	b. smother	b. struggle
c. make shorter	c. rehabilitate	c. insist	c. receive
d. make possible	d. disfigure	d. exaggerate	d. annoy

9. audacious
a. tired
b. timid
c. hard
d. lasting

10. instigate
a. blame
b. return
c. ignore
d. stop

11. bountiful
a. cautious
b. stingy
c. large
d. tough

12. willful
a. stingy
b. selfish
c. solid
d. obedient

13. incognito
a. smartly
b. simply
c. openly
d. directly

14. oblique
a. early
b. careful
c. direct
d. simple

15. discordant
a. jarring
b. heartfelt
c. harmonious
d. playful

16. venerate
a. proclaim
b. revere
c. hunt
d. despise

Word Families

A. *On the line provided, write the word you have learned in Units 1–3 that is related to each of the following nouns.*
EXAMPLE: willfulness—**willful**

1. invalidation, invalidity, invalidator _____

2. minimum _____

3. allotment, allotter, allottee _____

4. veneration, venerator _____

5. churl, churlishness _____

6. collaboration, collaborator _____

7. instigator, instigation _____

8. evolvement, evolution _____

9. audacity, audaciousness _____

10. frugality, frugalness _____

11. incapacitation, incapacity _____

12. enterprise, enterpriser, entrepreneur _____

13. discord, discordance, discordancy _____

14. compliance, compliancy _____

B. *On the line provided, write the word you have learned in Units 1–3 that is related to each of the following verbs.*
EXAMPLE: invalidate—**invalidation**

15. applaud _____

16. serve _____

17. endure _____

18. congest _____

19. avow _____

20. unite _____

Two-Word Completions

Circle the pair of words that best complete the meaning of each of the following passages.

1. He was a man of prodigious energy and _____. In no time at all, he rose from relatively humble beginnings to the very _____ of power.
a. enterprise . . . citadels
b. compliance . . . perspectives
c. longevity . . . antics
d. audacity . . . durables

2. The clownish _____ of cartoon characters, both animal and human, have won the hearts and _____ of many generations of delighted children.
a. banter . . . bonanzas
b. antics . . . plaudits
c. adages . . . vigils
d. tethers . . . decrees

3. It isn't wise to give very young children toys that will break easily. They need playthings that are _____ because they haven't yet learned to handle fragile items _____.
a. servile . . . churlishly
b. durable . . . gingerly
c. frugal . . . willfully
d. prodigious . . . wantonly

4. "If he weren't so rude, I'd be glad to _____ with him on the project," I said. "But I don't think I can work with someone who always behaves in such a _____ manner."
a. wrangle . . . servile
b. collaborate . . . churlish
c. banter . . . relevant
d. vie . . . unison

5. If you are careless with your money, you will always be penniless. But if you are _____, you may be able to _____ a sizable personal fortune.
a. bountiful . . . evolve
b. enterprising . . . maim
c. frugal . . . amass
d. audacious . . . preclude

6. The TV marathon not only garnered _____ amounts of money for Africa's starving millions but also yielded an unexpectedly rich _____ of publicity for their plight.
a. myriad . . . rubble
b. legendary . . . allotment
c. prodigious . . . bonanza
d. bountiful . . . banter

7. "A person has to expect a little accidental bumping and pushing in a crowded bus," I observed to my companion. "It's just not possible to avoid _____ another passenger when the center aisle is _____ with people."
a. maiming . . . devoid
b. grappling . . . elite
c. minimizing . . . glutted
d. jostling . . . congested

Building with Classical Roots

vers, vert—to turn

This root appears in **revert** (page 23), which means "to return, to go back to a previous, or lower, condition." Some other words based on the same root are listed below.

controversy	inverse	reversal	verse
conversant	pervert	traverse	vertiginous

From the list of words above, choose the one that corresponds to each of the brief definitions below. Write the word in the blank space in the illustrative sentence below the definition.

1. a lengthy dispute ("*a turning against*")

A new development in medical technology may spark a heated _____.

2. a change or overthrow; a change of fortune (usually for the worse), setback

The press criticized the Supreme Court's _____ of the state court's decision.

3. to turn away from the right course; to lead astray, distort ("*thoroughly, utterly turned*")

The defendant was accused of paying bribes to try to _____ the justice system.

4. turned upside down or inside out; referring to a relationship in which one item increases as the other decreases

Division is the _____ of multiplication.

5. familiar by use or study; acquainted ("*turning with*")

Before we remodeled our house, we sought expert advice from someone _____ with the town's building code.

6. whirling or spinning; tending to make dizzy; affected by or suffering from dizziness

The _____ rides in amusement parks are popular with children of all ages.

7. a line of poetry; poetic writing ("*a turning, as of a line*")

The teacher asked each student to recite a _____ of a favorite poem.

8. to travel across; to cross and recross; to extend over

We plan to _____ the countryside by bicycle this summer.

From the list of words above, choose the one that best completes each of the following sentences. Write the word in the space provided.

1. You should get along well in your new community, since you already seem to be thoroughly _____ with local customs.

2. A(n) _____ over a close election may eventually be resolved in the courts.

3. A string of unexpected setbacks and _____ turned the happy-go-lucky young man into an embittered curmudgeon.

4. She claimed that the editors had _____ her thoughtful article on varsity football into an attack on the school team.

5. In its proposal, the traffic commission recommended an elevated superhighway to _____ the congested business district.

6. How many people can remember the title of the famous poem of which the opening _____ is "'Twas the night before Christmas, when all through the house"?

7. The train ride along the edge of the _____ mountain cliff brought on a sudden dizzy spell that left me quite woozy.

8. During the heat wave we observed that there is a(n) _____ relationship between the temperature and the amount of work people can do.

---

*Circle the **boldface** word that more satisfactorily completes each of the following sentences.*

1. The climb to the top of the lighthouse on a narrow spiral staircase may be described as truly (**conversant, vertiginous**).

2. Some people seem to thrive on (**controversy, reversal**), while others seek to achieve consensus.

3. When the supply of goods is abundant, the price falls; but when supply is scarce, the (**verse, inverse**) occurs.

4. Do you think that too much commercialism (**traverses, perverts**) the meaning of many holidays?

5. Most Americans can quote a few (**controversies, verses**) of "The Star-Spangled Banner" and "America, the Beautiful."

6. The pioneers faced many challenges and hardships as they (**perverted, traversed**) the continent.

7. Some new members of the legislature were not (**conversant, vertiginous**) with the rules of parliamentary procedure.

8. King Lear undergoes a tragic (**reversal, inverse**) of fortune when he hands over his kingdom to his two hard-hearted daughters.

Writer's Challenge

Read the following sentences, paying special attention to the words and phrases underlined. From the words in the box below, find better choices for these underlined words and phrases. Then use these choices to rewrite the sentences.

WORD BANK				
audacious	comply	laggard	minimize	servile
banter	detriment	legendary	perturb	skittish
churlish	elite	longevity	preclude	venerate
collaborative	grapple	maim	relevant	wanton

FDR and the Media

1. Today there is little the public doesn't know about the private lives of politicians, regardless of whether the information is <u>connected with or related to the matter at hand</u>.

_____

_____

2. Reporters seem positively <u>rude and lacking sensitivity</u> when compared with the more discreet and respectful journalists of the past. Consider, for example, those who covered the career and presidency of Franklin Delano Roosevelt.

_____

_____

3. As a young man, Roosevelt contracted polio, a crippling disease that <u>marred</u> him for life.

_____

_____

4. Roosevelt, who wore heavy iron leg braces and used canes and, later, a wheelchair, did what he could to <u>make as small as possible</u> the public's awareness of his condition.

_____

_____

5. He was concerned that the people might be <u>shy and timid</u> about his fitness to govern if they knew the full extent of his physical disability.

_____

_____

6. He sought the cooperation of the press, and reporters <u>yielded to the request</u>.

_____

_____

7. Roosevelt's outstanding leadership of the nation during times of economic crisis and war proved that physical disability need not be a <u>cause of harm or damage</u> to great achievement.

_____

_____

Definitions

Note carefully the spelling, pronunciation, part(s) of speech, and definition(s) of each of the following words. Then write the word in the blank space(s) in the illustrative sentence(s) following. Finally, study the lists of synonyms and antonyms given at the end of each entry.

1. annul
(ə nəl′)

(*v.*) to reduce to nothing; to make ineffective or inoperative; to declare legally invalid or void

The state legislators voted by an overwhelming majority to _____ the out-of-date law.

SYNONYMS: cancel, abolish, invalidate, nullify
ANTONYMS: validate, authorize, ratify

2. blasé
(blä zā′)

(*adj.*) indifferent, bored as a result of having enjoyed many pleasures; apathetic

Battle-hardened soldiers may tend to become a bit _____ about the dangers they face.

ANTONYMS: enthusiastic, passionate, fervent

3. bolster
(bōl′ stər)

(*v.*) to support, give a boost to; (*n.*) a long pillow or cushion; a supporting post

When you write a research paper, you should always use appropriate facts to _____ your case.

The sofa has four comfortable _____.

SYNONYMS: (*v.*) strengthen, reinforce, buttress, validate
ANTONYMS: (*v.*) undermine, weaken, impair

4. deplore
(di plôr′)

(*v.*) to feel or express regret or disapproval

Social critics _____ what they believe is a widespread decline in good manners.

SYNONYMS: lament, bemoan, bewail
ANTONYMS: approve, commend, extol

5. frivolous
(friv′ ə ləs)

(*adj.*) of little importance, not worthy of serious attention; not meant seriously

I'll ignore your _____ suggestion.

SYNONYMS: silly, foolish, inane, petty, trifling
ANTONYMS: serious, important, significant

6. muster
(məs′ tər)

(*v.*) to bring together for service or battle; to gather or summon; to amount to, comprise, include; (*n.*) a list of men for military service; a gathering, accumulation

You will need to _____ up your courage to face the bully who has been tormenting you.

The sleepy new recruits assembled on the parade ground for the early morning _____.

SYNONYMS: (v.) mobilize, marshal; (n.) roster, inventory
ANTONYMS: (v.) disband, dismiss, disperse

7. nonentity
(nän en' tə tē)

(n.) a person or thing of no importance

We may not be movie stars, but we did not deserve to be treated as _____ by the presumptuous headwaiter.

SYNONYM: nobody
ANTONYMS: celebrity, superstar

8. obsess
(äb ses')

(v.) to trouble, haunt, or fill the mind

If you allow fear of failure to _____ you, you will find it difficult or even impossible to achieve your goals in life.

SYNONYM: preoccupy

9. ornate
(ôr nāt')

(adj.) elaborately decorated; showily splendid

If you ask me, an _____ gilded frame distracts the viewer's eye from a simple drawing.

SYNONYMS: fancy, elaborate, flashy, flamboyant
ANTONYMS: simple, plain, stark, austere

10. oust
(aůst)

(v.) to remove, drive out of a position or place

Military leaders _____ the duly elected president and took over the government.

SYNONYMS: expel, eject
ANTONYMS: admit, welcome

11. peruse
(pə rüz')

(v.) to read thoroughly and carefully

It is wise to have a lawyer _____ an agreement before you sign it.

SYNONYMS: study, pore over, scrutinize

12. porous
(pôr' əs)

(adj.) full of tiny holes; able to be penetrated by air or water

Some synthetic materials are as _____ and strong as natural sponges.

SYNONYMS: leaky, permeable
ANTONYMS: airtight, waterproof, impermeable

13. promontory
(präm' ən tôr ē)

(n.) a high point of land extending into water

We chose a high _____ overlooking the sea as the perfect spot for our picnic lunch.

SYNONYMS: cliff, headland

14. prone
(prōn)

(adj.) lying face down; inclined, likely

Unfortunately, I am _____ to earaches and sinus infections.

SYNONYMS: prostrate, liable, apt
ANTONYMS: standing upright, unlikely

15. qualm
(kwäm)

(*n.*) a pang of conscience, uneasiness, misgiving, or doubt; a feeling of faintness or nausea

Don't you have serious _____ about voting for such a relatively unknown and inexperienced candidate?

SYNONYMS: regret, second thought, scruple

16. recourse
(rē' kôrs)

(*n.*) a person or thing turned to for help or advice; the act of seeking help or protection

If my letter of complaint fails to get results, I will still have _____ to a higher authority.

SYNONYMS: redress, remedy, resort

17. residue
(rez' ə dü)

(*n.*) a remainder, that which remains when a part has been used up or removed

A _____ of sticky taffy made the pan difficult to clean.

SYNONYMS: remnant, remains, leavings

18. solicitous
(sə lis' ət əs)

(*adj.*) showing concern or care; fearful or anxious about someone or something

Neighbors made _____ inquiries about the state of the elderly couple's health.

SYNONYM: concerned
ANTONYMS: unconcerned, indifferent, apathetic

19. staid
(stād)

(*adj.*) serious and dignified; quiet or subdued in character or conduct

Many companies have a dress code which requires that all employees wear _____ colors such as navy or gray.

SYNONYMS: sedate, sober, prim
ANTONYMS: gaudy, jaunty, unconventional

20. sustain
(sə stān')

(*v.*) to support, nourish, keep up; to suffer, undergo; to bear up under, withstand; to affirm the validity of

You may _____ a serious eye injury if you forget to wear your safety goggles when you work with chemicals or power tools.

SYNONYMS: foster, maintain

Completing the Sentence

From the words for this unit, choose the one that best completes each of the following sentences. Write the word in the space provided.

1. Some people seem to have no _____ about manipulating others to gain their own ends.

2. I do not criticize people for trying to get ahead, but I _____ any attempt to take unfair advantage of others.

3. A lighthouse was built on the tip of the _____, where it served as a beacon for ships many miles away.

4. "In that barren wasteland," the explorer said, "we had great difficulty finding enough food to _____ life."

5. It is now time for you to take your work seriously and to give up some of the _____ activities of your earlier years.

6. Her public statements became so embarrassing that club members tried to _____ her from the presidency.

7. When we heard about our teacher's serious illness, we visited him daily in the hospital to _____ his low morale.

8. The two sisters are very different—one lively and fun loving, the other quiet and rather _____.

9. If you feel that you have been cheated, your only _____ is to make a complaint to the department of consumer affairs in your city.

10. I will not allow a single act of carelessness to _____ the results of years of hard work.

11. When we tried to carry water from the well, we found to our dismay that the bottom of the old bucket was _____.

12. Every able-bodied citizen will be _____ into active military service to fight off the invading force.

13. People who constantly _____ about their weight or figure may develop serious eating disorders.

14. The furnishings in their house are so _____ that the place looks more like a museum than a family home.

15. There I was—an utter _____ in a group of famous and accomplished persons!

16. Certain saltlike chemicals may effectively prevent the streets from icing up in winter, but the powdery _____ they leave behind can damage footwear.

17. You should _____ the instructions with great care before you fill out your application for admission.

18. She is the kind of _____ teacher who aids and encourages her students in every way she can.

19. When my cousin returned home after his first year in college, he tried to impress us with his sophisticated and _____ manner.

20. Because the villagers have so few dealings with the outside world, they are _____ to regard strangers with deep distrust.

Synonyms

*Choose the word from this unit that is **the same** or **most nearly the same** in meaning as the **boldface** word or expression in the given phrase. Write the word on the line provided.*

1. named on the regiment's **roster** _____

2. **apt** to take unnecessary chances _____

3. resisted efforts to **expel** the captain _____

4. annoyed by the reporter's **foolish** questions _____

5. settled the dispute without **resort** to the law _____

6. may **strengthen** your ability to resist colds _____

7. chose a very **elaborate** silverware pattern _____

8. cleared away the **remains** of last night's dinner _____

9. special exercises to **maintain** muscle tone _____

10. the spectacular view from the **headland** _____

11. painful memories that **haunted** the survivors _____

12. made of a **permeable** fabric _____

13. **bemoan** conditions in the refugee camp _____

14. had **regrets** about missing my friend's party _____

15. **scrutinized** the lease before signing it _____

Antonyms

*Choose the word from this unit that is **most nearly opposite** in meaning to the **boldface** word or expression in the given phrase. Write the word on the line provided.*

16. arrived wearing a **gaudy** outfit _____

17. **enthusiastic** about the glittering guest list _____

18. an **indifferent** attitude toward those in need _____

19. expect the committee to **ratify** the settlement _____

20. a room crowded with **celebrities** _____

Choosing the Right Word

Circle the **boldface** word that more satisfactorily completes each of the following sentences.

1. When the mile run began, Ken quickly took the lead, but we knew that he could not (**sustain, obsess**) that pace for the entire race.

2. Because they failed to deliver the goods on time, we felt justified in (**annulling, perusing**) the entire contract.

3. I hope someday to build a house on that (**promontory, nonentity**) commanding a beautiful view of the bay.

4. The way the witness blushed and stuttered when questioned (**bolstered, ousted**) my suspicions that he was not telling the truth.

5. Isn't it strange that such great writers as Poe and Dickinson were considered (**nonentities, promontories**) in their own lifetimes?

6. After the claims of all the creditors have been satisfied, the (**residue, qualms**) of the estate will be shared by the children.

7. I like jokes as much as anyone, but I don't approve of making such (**frivolous, porous**) remarks when a serious matter is under discussion.

8. It is all very well to criticize and (**bolster, deplore**) the mistakes of young people, but why don't you also give them credit for their good qualities?

9. We learned that behind the old professor's (**ornate, staid**) exterior there was a keen wit and a lively sense of what life is all about.

10. I admire the way Anne delivered a long, involved speech entirely without (**muster, recourse**) to written notes.

11. Only a person who is (**obsessed, bolstered**) with a desire to create beautiful music can become a great pianist or violinist.

12. If you want to learn to play chess, I suggest that you begin by (**deploring, perusing**) a summary of the rules.

13. While my sister's memory is as retentive as a steel trap, mine seems to be as (**porous, blasé**) as a sieve.

14. The team doctor ran onto the field toward the (**prone, solicitous**) figure of the injured football player.

15. "It will take all the strength we can (**annul, muster**) to dislodge the enemy from that hill," the general observed grimly.

16. I believed at the time that I was justified in refusing to help them, but later I felt some (**qualms, recourse**) about it.

17. That wonderful woman could not have been more (**solicitous, frivolous**) about me if she had been my own mother.

18. The novelist is known for her very (**staid, ornate**) writing style, using many unusual words, figures of speech, and involved constructions.

19. After being the apple of her eye for years, I suddenly found myself (**ousted, sustained**) from her affections by an upstart rival.

20. My brother tried to appear (**obsessed, blasé**) when he was named to the honor society, but I know that he was thrilled.

Vocabulary in Context

*Read the following passage, in which some of the words you have studied in this unit appear in **boldface** type. Then complete each statement given below the passage by circling the letter of the item that is **the same** or **almost the same** in meaning as the highlighted word.*

Crazy About Bikes

(Line)

If you've ever heard the song "A Bicycle Built for Two," you may have smiled at its old-fashioned images. But in the 1890s, the safety bicycle was new, liberating, and just plain irresistible. Earlier bicycles were uncomfortable and difficult to maneuver, but safety bicycles resembled today's bikes. They had air-filled tires,
(5) wheels of equal size linked by gears and chains, a padded seat, handlebars that could be adjusted, and easy-to-use brakes.

People were **obsessed** with bicycles. In 1884, there were about twenty thousand bicycles in the United States. A decade later, there were ten million! Bicycles soon took over the leisure time of the middle class. Merchants grumbled that people
(10) were spending their money on bicycles rather than on jewelry, clothes, or shoes. Book dealers complained that people who were busy cycling around day and night would have no time for reading. Music
(15) hall owners tried to **bolster** business by offering discounts to lure cyclists inside.

The tremendous interest in bicycling shocked **staid** society.
(20) Some clergy members **deplored** the bicycle as an invitation to idleness. They also condemned the newfound freedom that young people had to cycle off beyond
(25) the watchful eyes of adults.

Tandem bikes have come a long way since the 1890s.

The bicycle proved to be more than a **frivolous** fad. It had many practical uses. Doctors rode their bikes on house calls to sick patients. Salespeople used bicycles to make their rounds. City dwellers had few **qualms** about owning bicycles, which were much easier, cheaper, and cleaner to maintain than a horse and buggy. The bicycle
(30) frenzy died down when the automobile came along, but the safety bike forever changed the way Americans got around.

---

1. The meaning of **obsessed** (line 7) is
  a. preoccupied   c. amused
  b. frightened   d. confused

2. Bolster (line 15) most nearly means
  a. undermine   c. change
  b. boost   d. reorganize

3. Staid (line 19) is best defined as
  a. wealthy   c. anxious
  b. friendly   d. dignified

4. The meaning of **deplored** (line 20) is
  a. welcomed   c. decorated
  b. repaired   d. lamented

5. Frivolous (line 26) most nearly means
  a. significant   c. trifling
  b. expensive   d. unlikely

6. Qualms (line 28) is best defined as
  a. doubts   c. dreams
  b. thoughts   d. arguments

Definitions

Note carefully the spelling, pronunciation, part(s) of speech, and definition(s) of each of the following words. Then write the word in the blank space(s) in the illustrative sentence(s) following. Finally, study the lists of synonyms and antonyms given at the end of each entry.

1. aghast
(ə gast')

(*adj.*) filled with amazement, disgust, fear, or terror

People were _____ at the senseless brutality of the crime.

SYNONYMS: shocked, horrified, stupefied
ANTONYMS: delighted, overjoyed, unmoved

2. ample
(am' pəl)

(*adj.*) more than enough, large, spacious

Thanks to the wet spring weather, birds and other animals will have an _____ supply of food for the rest of the year.

SYNONYMS: sufficient, adequate, considerable
ANTONYMS: insufficient, inadequate

3. apparition
(ap ə rish' ən)

(*n.*) a ghost or ghostly figure; an unexplained or unusual appearance

The vivid _____ seemed so real that it completely unnerved me.

SYNONYMS: phantom, specter

4. assert
(ə sərt')

(*v.*) to declare or state as truth, maintain or defend, put forward forcefully

Throughout the trial and the lengthy appeal process that followed, the defendant firmly _____ her innocence.

SYNONYMS: affirm, avow

5. cower
(kaủ' ər)

(*v.*) to crouch or shrink away from in fear or shame

The tiny kittens _____ in the corner, obviously frightened by the huge, growling dog.

SYNONYMS: cringe, flinch
ANTONYM: stand up to

6. disdain
(dis dān')

(*v.*) to look upon with scorn; to refuse scornfully; (*n.*) a feeling of contempt

I emphatically _____ their cowardly behavior.

Fair-minded people have only _____ for racism in all its forms.

SYNONYMS: (*v.*) spurn, reject
ANTONYMS: (*v.*) revere, venerate, esteem, respect

7. epitaph
(ep' ə taf)

(*n.*) a brief statement written on a tomb or gravestone

Most people never stop to consider the words that might one day appear as their own _____.

SYNONYM: tombstone inscription

8. ethical
(eth' ə kəl)

(*adj.*) having to do with morals, values, right and wrong; in accordance with standards of right conduct; requiring a prescription for purchase

New developments in medicine often lead to discussions of important _____ questions.

SYNONYMS: upright, virtuous, honorable
ANTONYMS: immoral, unscrupulous, dishonest

9. facetious
(fə sē' shəs)

(*adj.*) humorous, not meant seriously

We had to laugh at her _____ remarks.

SYNONYMS: comical, witty, tongue-in-cheek
ANTONYMS: serious, humorless

10. inaudible
(in ô' də bəl)

(*adj.*) not able to be heard

Some high-frequency sounds are _____ to even the keenest human ear.

SYNONYMS: faint, indistinct
ANTONYMS: audible, easily heard

11. indiscriminate
(in dis krim' ə nət)

(*adj.*) without restraint or control; unselective

The _____ slaughter of right whales brought that species to the brink of extinction.

SYNONYMS: haphazard, random, uncritical
ANTONYMS: selective, discriminating, judicious

12. intrigue
(*n.*, in' trēg;
v., in trēg')

(*n.*) crafty dealings, underhanded plotting; (*v.*) to form and carry out plots; to puzzle or excite the curiosity

Investigators uncovered a shocking network of lies and international _____.

The old album full of faded family pictures and postcards from exotic places _____ me.

SYNONYMS: (*n.*) scheme, plot, conspiracy
ANTONYM: (*n.*) fair play

13. jurisdiction
(jür is dik' shən)

(*n.*) an area of authority or control; the right to administer justice

Cases involving robbery and assault are usually tried under the _____ of the state courts.

SYNONYM: purview

14. plausible
(plô' zə bəl)

(*adj.*) appearing true, reasonable, or fair

Their story didn't sound _____ to me.

SYNONYMS: believable, probable
ANTONYMS: improbable, far-fetched

15. plebeian
(plə bē′ ən)

(*adj.*) common, vulgar; belonging to the lower class; (*n.*) a common person, member of the lower class

>   Despite the couple's enormous wealth, their taste in cars and houses is surprisingly _____ .

>   At one time, the _____ of ancient Rome were excluded from holding public office of any kind.

SYNONYMS: (*adj.*) lowborn, proletarian, coarse, unrefined
ANTONYMS: (*adj.*) aristocratic, refined, cultivated

16. prodigal
(präd′ ə gəl)

(*adj.*) wastefully extravagant; lavishly or generously abundant; (*n.*) one who is wasteful and self-indulgent

>   We have a tight budget, but we make an exception for _____ celebrations on family birthdays.

>   The elderly man told us that he greatly regretted the years he spent living the life of a _____ .

SYNONYMS: (*adj.*) improvident; (*n.*) spendthrift, wastrel
ANTONYMS: (*adj.*) frugal, economical, stingy, miserly

17. proximity
(präk sim′ ə tē)

(*n.*) nearness, closeness

>   People with children often choose a house because of its _____ to schools.

ANTONYMS: distance, remoteness

18. pulverize
(pəl′ və rīz)

(*v.*) to grind or pound to a powder or dust; to destroy or overcome (as though by smashing into fragments)

>   At many old mills in Vermont, granite stones were used to _____ the grain.

SYNONYMS: crush, demolish

19. sequel
(sē′ kwəl)

(*n.*) that which follows, a result; a literary work or film continuing the story of one written or made earlier

>   Readers are eagerly awaiting a _____ to the author's best-selling mystery novel.

SYNONYMS: follow-up, continuation
ANTONYMS: prelude, overture, curtain-raiser

20. volatile
(väl′ ə təl)

(*adj.*) highly changeable, fickle; tending to become violent or explosive; changing readily from the liquid to the gaseous state

>   A person who is usually calm and collected may nevertheless sometimes behave in a _____ manner.

SYNONYMS: unstable, erratic
ANTONYMS: stable, steady, static, inert, dormant

Completing the Sentence

From the words for this unit, choose the one that best completes each of the following sentences. Write the word in the space provided.

1. Observers on the ground were _____ to see the rocket explode and plunge back to earth seconds after launch.

2. Although they did not dare to attack the emperor's favorite publicly, they _____ in secret to bring about his downfall.

3. Since you were given _____ time to prepare your report, I can see no excuse for your failure to complete it.

4. The giant crushers lifted the boulders and quickly _____ them into a uniform gray powder.

5. In answer to unfair criticisms, we _____ proudly that Americans have been most generous in giving aid to the needy.

6. The way the child _____ in fear whenever an adult spoke to him gave me the impression that he had been mistreated from infancy.

7. A(n) _____ TV viewer, who watches any program, good or bad, is bound to waste a lot of time.

8. Because the public-address system was not working, the voice of the speaker was completely _____ to most of the people in the hall.

9. The planning board refused to allow the construction of a factory in close _____ to our school building.

10. Who would be so proud or so foolish as to _____ a helping hand in time of real need?

11. The writer of the mystery story set up an interesting situation, but in my opinion the ending was not _____ .

12. Regulation of radio and TV stations falls within the _____ of the federal government.

13. People of all religions strive to live up to the _____ standards summarized in the Ten Commandments.

14. Although nature has been far from _____ with its gifts to Japan, that nation has become highly productive and prosperous.

15. Did Ben Jonson write the _____ that is engraved on Shakespeare's tombstone?

16. I hope he was just being _____ when he said that my dancing reminded him of a trained bear.

17. In that elegant French restaurant, which serves all kinds of fancy foods, she ordered a(n) _____ ham and cheese on rye.

18. The "ghostly figure" you think you saw in the graveyard was no more than a(n) _____ created by your imagination.

19. The movie about invaders from outer space was so successful that the studio is preparing a(n) _____ .

20. For the moment the crowd was quiet and subdued, but we knew that it was so _____ that it might become ugly and dangerous at any time.

Synonyms

*Choose the word from this unit that is **the same** or **most nearly the same** in meaning as the **boldface** word or expression in the given phrase. Write the word on the line provided.*

1. wrote a **witty** caption for the photograph _____

2. **crushed** turquoise to use as paint pigment _____

3. within the **purview** of the United Nations _____

4. enjoyed the **follow-up** more than the original _____

5. **puzzled** by their unusual behavior _____

6. a fondness for **coarse** entertainments _____

7. known for having a highly **erratic** disposition _____

8. the clearest way to **affirm** our freedom _____

9. **cringed** in terror as the tornado roared past _____

10. can barely read the **tombstone inscription** _____

11. terrified by **phantoms** _____

12. **spurned** their offers of friendship _____

13. **honorable** standards for doing business _____

14. refused to help the **wastrel** _____

15. **horrified** at the sight of the sickly children _____

Antonyms

*Choose the word from this unit that is **most nearly opposite** in meaning to the **boldface** word or expression in the given phrase. Write the word on the line provided.*

16. a person of **judicious** spending habits _____

17. offered us a **far-fetched** alibi _____

18. made a reply that was **easily heard** _____

19. **insufficient** food for all the guests _____

20. bought the property because of its **remoteness** _____

Choosing the Right Word

*Circle the **boldface** word that more satisfactorily completes each of the following sentences.*

1. In recent decades, we were forced to make greater use of our (**ample, inaudible**) coal resources to meet our growing energy needs.

2. Finally the voters, (**volatile, aghast**) that such scandalous goings-on could have occurred in their town, demanded the mayor's immediate resignation.

3. It will take the two of us months of strict economizing to make up for that one (**prodigal, ethical**) shopping spree.

4. We Americans do not believe that people who come from poor families should be regarded as (**plebeians, apparitions**).

5. Only a foolish snob would show such (**disdain, intrigue**) for someone who doesn't belong to a country club.

6. His explanation that he is failing math because "the teacher is down on me" doesn't seem (**plausible, volatile**).

7. The purpose of this experiment is to find out whether a substance will dissolve more rapidly in water if it is thoroughly (**cowered, pulverized**).

8. I find my friend's stories about her life in her native country when she was a child most (**plebeian, intriguing**).

9. When Jim missed practice for two days, he never thought that the (**sequel, disdain**) to this would be dismissal from the team.

10. During the Cuban missile crisis, the (**apparition, proximity**) of nuclear war between the superpowers once again raised its ugly head.

11. Your thoughtless remarks hurt me deeply, even though you say that you were merely trying to be (**plausible, facetious**).

12. The (**proximity, epitaph**) of the two men's ideas on many subjects made it easy for them to work together during that critical period of our history.

13. My neighbor's furniture is supposed to be "original" and "colorful," but I think it is a(n) (**indiscriminate, facetious**) collection of junk.

14. I thought that my whispers to you were (**prodigal, inaudible**), but I learned otherwise when the teacher told me in no uncertain terms to be quiet.

15. Deciding who is or isn't eligible for school athletic teams is not within the (**proximity, jurisdiction**) of the student council.

16. Although I may not agree with what you have to say, I will always (**assert, disdain**) your right to say it.

17. It takes a practiced eye to make out the (**epitaphs, sequels**) on old, weather-beaten tombstones in a country churchyard.

18. You can show respect for your supervisors without seeming to (**assert, cower**) whenever one of them speaks to you.

19. Her moods are so (**ample, volatile**) that we never know if she will be in a good humor or down in the dumps.

20. Lawyers may be punished by disbarment if it can be shown that they have violated the (**ethics, jurisdiction**) of the legal profession.

Read the following passage, in which some of the words you have studied in this unit appear in **boldface** type. Then complete each statement given below the passage by circling the letter of the item that is **the same** or **almost the same** in meaning as the highlighted word.

American Man of Letters

(Line)

The American author Washington Irving was born to a wealthy New York City family. This circumstance allowed him to lead a **prodigal** existence for much of his life. At age sixteen, Irving began to study law. However, he soon **disdained** the

college education that many young men of his social position chose. Rather, he preferred to (5) travel and to write. Thanks to his family's fortune, he was able to devote himself to both these passions.

Washington Irving had a quick mind and a lively wit, and he was determined to apply his (10) intelligence to becoming a writer. Using the pen name Jonathan Oldstyle, he wrote humorous essays. Later, he and his brother William began to publish their own magazine, called *Salmagundi*. (The name refers to a spicy dish.) (15) This short-lived periodical featured **facetious** essays poking fun at New York society.

Irving first toured Europe between 1804 and 1806. He returned to Europe in 1815 and lived there until 1832. Two of his most famous and (20) beloved stories, "The Legend of Sleepy Hollow" and "Rip Van Winkle," were written during this period. They appeared in his short

Washington Irving (1783–1859)

story collection *The Sketch Book*, published in 1820. Irving found **ample** ideas for his writing in the European customs, legends, and folktales that charmed him. (25)

Because Irving spent so many years abroad, some critics questioned his devotion to America. The best way he knew to serve his country, he **asserted**, was with the strength of his pen. Washington Irving has been called "the first American man of letters." How remarkable that some of his most enduring tales, so distinctly American in tone, were penned abroad! (30)

1. The meaning of **prodigal** (line 2) is
a. miserly
b. unstable
c. uncritical
d. self-indulgent

2. Disdained (line 3) most nearly means
a. rejected
b. respected
c. regretted
d. repeated

3. Facetious (line 16) is best defined as
a. lengthy
b. bland
c. comical
d. serious

4. The meaning of **ample** (line 24) is
a. delightful
b. original
c. unusual
d. considerable

5. Asserted (line 27) most nearly means
a. answered
b. maintained
c. appealed
d. denied

Definitions

Note carefully the spelling, pronunciation, part(s) of speech, and definition(s) of each of the following words. Then write the word in the blank space(s) in the illustrative sentence(s) following. Finally, study the lists of synonyms and antonyms given at the end of each entry.

1. abashed
(ə basht′)

(*adj., part.*) embarrassed, ashamed, or nonplussed

I was thoroughly _____ by the foolish mistake that I made at the dinner party.

ANTONYMS: unembarrassed, unashamed

2. aloof
(ə lüf′)

(*adj.*) withdrawn, standing apart from others (usually as a matter of choice)

In almost every office or business, there are some people who keep decidedly _____ from their coworkers.

SYNONYMS: distant, cold, standoffish
ANTONYMS: involved, sociable

3. anguish
(aŋ′ gwish)

(*n.*) great mental suffering, distress, or pain; (*v.*) to be deeply tormented by pain or sorrow

Survivors of a natural disaster often suffer great mental _____ long after their terrible ordeal is over.

The child's disappearance _____ every member of the community.

SYNONYMS: (*n.*) misery, woe, torment
ANTONYMS: (*n.*) joy, delight, peace of mind

4. articulate
(*v.*, är tik′ yü lāt;
adj., är tik′ yə lit)

(*v.*) to pronounce distinctly; to express well in words; to fit together into a system; (*adj.*) able to use language effectively; expressed clearly and forcefully

A successful candidate can _____ ideas in a way that makes them acceptable to voters.

To be successful as a professional lecturer, a person must, of necessity, be _____ .

SYNONYMS: (*v.*) enunciate, expound; (*adj.*) glib, eloquent
ANTONYMS: (*adj.*) tongue-tied, mumbled, incoherent

5. bask
(bask)

(*v.*) to be in, or expose oneself to, pleasant warmth; to take pleasure in or derive enjoyment from

Because they are cold-blooded creatures, lizards and other reptiles must _____ in the sun to regulate their body temperature.

SYNONYMS: wallow, revel

6. defect
(*n.,* dē' fekt;
v., di fekt')

(*n.*) an imperfection, flaw, or blemish of some kind; (*v.*) to desert a cause or organization

There is no one who does not have at least one serious character _____ .

In 1948 the Dixiecrats _____ from the Democratic Party and held their own presidential nominating convention.

7. finesse
(fi nes')

(*n.*) delicate skill; tact and cleverness; (*v.*) to accomplish something by cleverness, good judgment, or skillful evasion

To become a champion, a tennis player needs to combine power with _____ .

Skilled politicians know how to _____ their answers to embarrassing questions from reporters.

SYNONYM: (*n.*) delicacy
ANTONYMS: (*n.*) clumsiness, awkwardness

8. flaunt
(flônt)

(*v.*) to wave or flutter showily; to display in a conceited, offensive way

Some people seem to need to _____ their wealth and good fortune in life.

SYNONYMS: show off, parade
ANTONYMS: hide, downplay

9. forthright
(fôrth' rīt)

(*adj.*) frank, direct, straightforward

I appreciate the _____ way in which you express your opinions, even when they do not agree with my own.

SYNONYMS: candid, blunt
ANTONYMS: indirect, evasive, deceitful, two-faced

10. genial
(jēn' yəl)

(*adj.*) cordial, pleasantly cheerful or warm

The _____ host and hostess made each party guest feel especially welcome.

SYNONYMS: friendly, amiable
ANTONYMS: cold, unfriendly, unsociable

11. instill
(in stil')

(*v.*) to add gradually; to introduce or cause to be taken in

How can parents best _____ in their children a love for reading?

SYNONYMS: implant, infuse, inculcate
ANTONYMS: root out, eradicate, extirpate

12. ostracize
(äs' trə sīz)

(*v.*) to exclude from a group, banish, send away

Society _____ those who commit acts of treason.

SYNONYMS: cast out, expel, blackball, snub
ANTONYMS: fraternize with, associate with

13. premonition
(prē mə nish′ ən)

(*n.*) forewarning or foreboding of a future event

I felt a vague _____ of danger
as I entered the abandoned building.

SYNONYM: presentiment

14. pseudonym
(sü′ də nim)

(*n.*) a pen name, name assumed by a writer

It is wise to use a _____ to
protect your privacy when you chat on the Internet.

SYNONYM: nom de plume

15. purge
(pərj)

(*v.*) to wash away impurities, clean up; (*n.*) the process of
getting rid of something or someone decisively

A soaking rainstorm will usually _____
the air of pollutants.

The change of government was achieved through a peaceful
election rather than a brutal _____.

SYNONYMS: (*v.*) cleanse, purify
ANTONYMS: (*v.*) pollute, contaminate, defile

16. rehabilitate
(rē hə bil′ ə tāt)

(*v.*) to make over in good form; to restore to good condition or
to a former position

Over the years government agencies have spent a good deal
of money trying to _____ run-down
inner-city neighborhoods.

SYNONYMS: reclaim, rebuild, reform

17. repercussion
(rē pər kəsh′ ən)

(*n.*) an effect or consequence of some action or event, result;
an echo or reverberation

The _____ of the 1929 stock
market crash were felt all over the world.

ANTONYMS: cause, source

18. resolute
(rez′ ə lüt)

(*adj.*) bold, determined; firm

Commencement-day speakers generally urge new graduates
to be _____ in pursuit of their dreams.

SYNONYMS: steadfast, unflinching
ANTONYMS: weak, spineless, indecisive

19. retentive
(ri tent′ iv)

(*adj.*) able to hold, keep, or recall; retaining knowledge easily

A _____ memory is a great asset
for any actor, especially one who performs on stage.

ANTONYMS: porous, forgetful

20. scapegoat
(skāp′ gōt)

(*n.*) a person or thing carrying the blame for others

In ancient times, a messenger who brought bad news was
often made the _____ for it and killed.

SYNONYMS: fall guy, whipping boy

Completing the Sentence

From the words for this unit, choose the one that best completes each of the following sentences. Write the word in the space provided.

1. Good citizens don't try to remain _____ from the problems and troubles in their communities.

2. Although every form of government has its _____, democracy has more pluses and fewer minuses than any other.

3. I criticize him not because he makes mistakes but because he constantly looks for a(n) _____ to take the blame for them.

4. The defendant was found not guilty at his trial, but his punishment came when he was _____ by all his friends.

5. We learned that beneath the old man's quiet and withdrawn manner, there was a charming and _____ personality.

6. Although Hal was the only boy at the party wearing sneakers and an old sweatshirt, he did not seem at all _____ .

7. Instead of a(n) _____ answer, all we got from her was, "In one sense, yes, but on the other hand, perhaps no."

8. It took four years of civil war to _____ this nation of the curse of slavery.

9. Since we all know that you sing and play the piano beautifully, what need is there for you to _____ your musical talents?

10. I have learned over the years that it is often possible to accomplish more by _____ than by brute force.

11. Even though I assured my dying grandfather that I would visit him soon, I had a strange _____ that I would never see him again.

12. I think you will know who William S. Porter was if I tell you that he used the _____ O. Henry.

13. The star basketball player _____ in the admiration of every small child in the neighborhood.

14. She has such a(n) _____ mind that she seems able to master complicated details without even taking notes.

15. The speaker could not be understood easily because he swallowed his words instead of _____ them clearly.

16. By the example of their own conduct, our parents _____ in us a deep respect for people of all races, nationalities, and religions.

17. In recent years, pollution of our waterways has had serious and sometimes fatal _____ on the wildlife that inhabits them.

18. The city planner said that in addition to building new housing, we should plan to _____ many old buildings.

19. Can anything equal the overwhelming _____ of a mother at the death of her child?

20. After the infamous attack on Pearl Harbor, the American people were _____ in their determination to defeat the fascist powers.

Synonyms

*Choose the word from this unit that is **the same** or **most nearly the same** in meaning as the **boldface** word or expression in the given phrase. Write the word on the line provided.*

1. fortunate to have **amiable** traveling companions _____

2. **snubbed** the newcomers _____

3. prepared to deal with any and all **consequences** _____

4. **inculcate** discipline in the new recruits _____

5. welcomed **candid** comments on the plan _____

6. refuse to be made the **fall guy** again _____

7. **cleanse** the body of toxins _____

8. **showed off** an expensive new wardrobe _____

9. a rather **standoffish** disposition _____

10. **reveled** in the company of good friends _____

11. used a **pen name** to conceal my identity _____

12. filled with **presentiments** of doom _____

13. letters that revealed the depth of their **misery** _____

14. **restores** antique cars as a hobby _____

15. **imperfections** easily covered with a little makeup _____

Antonyms

*Choose the word from this unit that is **most nearly opposite** in meaning to the **boldface** word or expression in the given phrase. Write the word on the line provided.*

16. **unembarrassed** by their remarks _____

17. has a very **forgetful** mind _____

18. **indecisive** in moments of crisis _____

19. handled the matter with surprising **clumsiness** _____

20. gave an **incoherent** statement to reporters _____

*Circle the **boldface** word that more satisfactorily completes each of the following sentences.*

1. An actor who has (**basked, instilled**) for so long in the favor of the public finds it hard to realize that he is no longer popular.

2. It will be better if we all take responsibility for the mistake instead of letting one employee be the (**pseudonym, scapegoat**).

3. My (**anguish, finesse**) at the loss of a loved one was all the greater when I realized that my carelessness had caused the accident.

4. Many female authors once used male (**repercussions, pseudonyms**) because it was considered improper for women to write novels.

5. We should now be just as (**resolute, genial**) in fighting for peace as the Americans of two hundred years ago were in fighting for independence.

6. How can we ever forgive him for (**defecting, purging**) from our great cause at the very time we needed him most?

7. Although he was trying to look unconcerned, I could see that he was much (**abashed, aloof**) by the teacher's criticism.

8. Shakespeare tries to convey Brutus's (**defects, premonitions**) of defeat at Philippi by having Caesar's ghost appear to him the night before the battle.

9. His prejudices are so strong that he wants to (**ostracize, bask**) anyone who belongs to a minority religious group.

10. The purpose of our prison system is not just to punish offenders but to (**flaunt, rehabilitate**) them.

11. Fortunately, the soil is so (**resolute, retentive**) of moisture that the weeks of dry weather did not damage our crops.

12. It would be good taste on his part not to (**flaunt, ostracize**) all the honors and awards that he has won.

13. He's a clever man who has managed to (**anguish, finesse**) his way into a very important position in this company.

14. I did not think that such an innocent conversation could have such serious (**repercussions, scapegoats**) on the outcome of an election.

15. The new governor's address was an unusually (**articulate, abashed**) and effective description of the challenges facing the state in the years ahead.

16. She has lived (**aloof, retentive**) from other people for so long that it is hard for her to take part in everyday social affairs.

17. She is not the most (**forthright, genial**) person in the world, but in her own way she is at least trying to be friendly.

18. No matter how much time or effort it takes, I will (**purge, instill**) these unfair charges of disloyalty from my reputation!

19. It is possible to be honest and (**forthright, articulate**) in stating your views and opinions without being cruel or tactless.

20. Is it our duty to try to (**rehabilitate, instill**) a faith in democracy in the people of other lands?

Vocabulary in Context

*Read the following passage, in which some of the words you have studied in this unit appear in **boldface** type. Then complete each statement given below the passage by circling the letter of the item that is **the same** or **almost the same** in meaning as the highlighted word.*

Ahead of Her Time

(Line)

Few people today have heard of Victoria Claflin Woodhull, one of America's most **resolute** crusaders for equality and the first woman to seek the presidency. Born to a large family that ran a traveling medicine show, she met people from all walks of life. She developed progressive social, spiritual, economic, and political views and

(5)   learned to express herself well. She soon gained widespread fame—and notoriety.

In 1870, with support from railroad tycoon Cornelius Vanderbilt, Woodhull and her sister Tennessee Claflin became Wall Street's first female stockbrokers. Woodhull reasoned that her ability to earn her own money would give her lifelong independence. Also in 1870, the sisters launched a

(10)   newspaper, *Woodhull & Claflin's Weekly*. For six years, it provided Woodhull with a forum in which she **articulated** her ideas in **forthright** language.

To advance her beliefs, Victoria Woodhull took to making fiery public speeches. In 1871, Woodhull

(15)   addressed the Judiciary Committee of the House of Representatives on the subject of a woman's right to vote. In 1872, the Equal Rights Party of the National Woman Suffrage Association nominated Woodhull for U.S. president. She could not legally vote, yet no law

(20)   barred her from holding office! With noted abolitionist Frederick Douglass as her running mate, the first female presidential candidate faced Republican incumbent Ulysses S. Grant and Democrat Horace Greeley.

Woodhull had also been using her newspaper to

(25)   expose swindles and scandals. A few months before the 1872 presidential election, she revealed shocking secrets about a popular public figure. The **repercussions** were severe. Many former supporters **defected from** her cause. She faced serious legal and financial difficulties. She was, in effect, **ostracized**. Finally, in 1877, Woodhull and her sister left the United States

(30)   for England. There they succeeded in making new and prosperous lives for themselves.

Victoria Woodhull (1838–1927)

---

1. The meaning of **resolute** (line 2) is
   a. experienced
   b. popular
   c. significant
   d. determined

2. Articulated (line 11) most nearly means
   a. pondered
   b. expressed
   c. tested
   d. refined

3. Forthright (line 12) is best defined as
   a. deceitful
   b. original
   c. frank
   d. tactful

4. Repercussions (line 27) means
   a. causes
   b. origins
   c. consequences
   d. opinions

5. Defected from (line 27) means
   a. deserted
   b. questioned
   c. joined
   d. ignored

6. Ostracized (line 29) is best defined as
   a. publicized
   b. cast out
   c. welcomed
   d. criticized

Analogies *In each of the following, circle the item that best completes the comparison.*

1. coward is to **cower** as
a. champion is to ostracize
b. clown is to anguish
c. bully is to defect
d. showoff is to flaunt

2. instill is to **add** as
a. bolster is to subtract
b. oust is to add
c. purge is to subtract
d. ostracize is to add

3. forthright is to **favorable** as
a. plausible is to unfavorable
b. volatile is to favorable
c. frivolous is to unfavorable
d. plebeian is to favorable

4. assert is to **forward** as
a. obsess is to back
b. bask is to forward
c. cower is to back
d. deplore is to forward

5. proximity is to **close** as
a. recourse is to far
b. ampleness is to narrow
c. aloofness is to distant
d. premonition is to wide

6. premonition is to **before** as
a. epitaph is to back
b. repercussion is to after
c. prologue is to later
d. overture is to behind

7. pain is to **anguish** as
a. grief is to intrigue
b. appetite is to hunger
c. pleasure is to delight
d. fear is to disdain

8. aghast is to **horror** as
a. blasé is to enthusiasm
b. plausible is to resentment
c. abashed is to shame
d. aloof is to anguish

9. facetious is to **serious** as
a. solicitous is to unconcerned
b. staid is to dignified
c. volatile is to daring
d. retentive is to memorable

10. prone is to **upright** as
a. porous is to retentive
b. staid is to conservative
c. volatile is to explosive
d. resolute is to determined

11. epitaphs are to **tombstones** as
a. graffiti are to walls
b. paintings are to galleries
c. ads are to newspapers
d. words are to phrases

12. inaudible is to **hear** as
a. inflammable is to feel
b. invisible is to see
c. indiscriminate is to touch
d. inaccurate is to smell

13. pseudonym is to **writer** as
a. surname is to family
b. alias is to criminal
c. nickname is to Michael
d. stage name is to painter

14. articulate is to **voice** as
a. disdain is to nose
b. bask is to ears
c. instill is to mouth
d. peruse is to eyes

15. sequel is to **after** as
a. residue is to behind
b. proximity is to before
c. premonition is to between
d. intrigue is to beyond

16. bolster is to **undermine** as
a. rehabilitate is to control
b. disdain is to scorn
c. peruse is to struggle
d. squander is to amass

17. purge is to **oust** as
a. sustain is to support
b. instill is to remove
c. bolster is to delay
d. pulverize is to cement

18. miser is to **prodigal** as
a. scapegoat is to ornate
b. spendthrift is to frugal
c. apparition is to solicitous
d. friend is to genial

Word Associations

In each of the following groups, circle the word that is best defined or suggested by the given phrase.

1. taking pleasure in the admiration of her classmates
a. flaunt　　　　b. pulverize　　　　c. bask　　　　d. purge

2. having a good memory for facts and figures
a. retentive　　　b. solicitous　　　c. inaudible　　　d. aghast

3. had a strange feeling that something terrible was about to happen
a. purge　　　　b. repercussion　　　c. residue　　　d. premonition

4. a mother who is constantly worried about her child
a. staid　　　　b. aloof　　　　c. solicitous　　　d. aghast

5. act as though nothing impresses or pleases them
a. blasé　　　　b. resolute　　　　c. volatile　　　　d. porous

6. unable to talk or think about anything but the senior dance
a. sustained　　b. rehabilitated　　c. ousted　　　d. obsessed

7. someone or something you can turn to for help
a. plebeian　　　b. recourse　　　　c. prodigal　　　d. scapegoat

8. declare that the contract is no longer in effect
a. annul　　　　b. sustain　　　　c. deplore　　　d. pulverize

9. "I'm not at all sure I did the right thing."
a. qualms　　　b. sequels　　　　c. purges　　　d. scapegoats

10. how most people feel about prejudice
a. bolster　　　b. sustain　　　　c. assert　　　　d. deplore

11. handled the situation like a skilled diplomat
a. intrigue　　　b. proximity　　　c. disdain　　　d. finesse

12. a cliff overlooking the Pacific
a. promontory　　b. epitaph　　　c. sequel　　　d. residue

13. under the authority of a court of appeals
a. disdain　　　b. jurisdiction　　c. apparition　　d. premonition

14. the story of an elaborate conspiracy
a. proximity　　b. intrigue　　　c. jurisdiction　　d. purge

15. what little remains after all the debts have been paid
a. nonentity　　b. epitaph　　　c. anguish　　　d. residue

16. always blaming everything on poor old Pete
a. premonition　　b. scapegoat　　c. apparition　　d. sequel

17. give a boost to their drooping spirits
a. sustain　　　b. bolster　　　　c. peruse　　　　d. deplore

18. "Our new car has a faulty windshield wiper."
a. intrigue　　　b. pseudonym　　c. epitaph　　　d. defect

19. wrote under the pen name Mark Twain
a. pseudonym　　b. promontory　　c. nonentity　　d. intrigue

20. Hamlet sees the ghost of his murdered father.
a. proximity　　b. apparition　　c. qualm　　　d. bolster

Vocabulary in Context

*Read the following passage, in which some of the words you have studied in Units 4–6 appear in **boldface** type. Then complete each statement given below the passage by circling the item that is **the same** or **almost the same** in meaning as the highlighted word.*

Made for Rain or Shine

(Line)

Most people probably take the umbrella for granted. Almost everyone has one. But there was a time when the umbrella was a rare possession

(5) reserved for royalty.

Umbrellas were first used for protection from the sun. In fact, the word *umbrella* comes from the Latin *umbra*, which means "shade." The

(10) umbrella made shade portable.

The earliest known depiction of an umbrella appears on a monument to a Mesopotamian king, Sargon of Akkad, that dates from about 2400 B.C. The

(15) king is shown leading his victorious army while a **solicitous** aide walks behind him, shading him with an umbrella. Umbrellas also appear in the art of ancient Egypt, Greece,

(20) India, Rome, and China. Everywhere, the umbrella was associated with the elite, not with **plebeians**.

Umbrellas made of paper were **porous** and therefore of little use as

(25) protection in stormy weather. During the Wei dynasty (A.D. 386–535), the Chinese devised an oiled-paper umbrella for use in sun or rain. The emperor's **ornate** umbrella was red

(30) and yellow, the royal colors. The ancient Romans also developed oiled-paper umbrellas. In the fourteenth century, weavers fashioned silk fabrics sturdy enough

(35) to use for umbrellas.

In 1340, a papal envoy to India wrote of a "little tent-roof on a cane handle," which the people "open out at will as a protection against

(40) sun or rain." The envoy brought an umbrella back to Italy. However, the device was slow to gain popularity in Europe, where it was considered a woman's accessory. Men would

(45) have been **abashed** to be seen using an umbrella, even in the heaviest downpour.

The umbrella did not catch on with men until around 1750, when a British

(50) gentleman named Jonas Hanway began carrying one almost every day. He **sustained** years of public ridicule for doing so. But eventually, Hanway convinced people that carrying an

(55) umbrella in rainy London was both stylish and practical. Thanks to his persistence, it became acceptable for everyone to use the umbrella.

---

1. The meaning of **solicitous** (line 16) is
   a. tired
   b. faithful
   c. concerned
   d. smiling

2. Plebeians (line 22) most nearly means
   a. aristocrats
   b. common people
   c. professionals
   d. athletes

3. Porous (line 24) is best defined as
   a. permeable
   b. fragile
   c. colorful
   d. durable

4. The meaning of **ornate** (line 29) is
   a. elegant
   b. ample
   c. elaborate
   d. simple

5. Abashed (line 45) most nearly means
   a. embarrassed
   b. reluctant
   c. eager
   d. angered

6. Sustained (line 52) is best defined as
   a. welcomed
   b. attracted
   c. ignored
   d. suffered

Choosing the Right Meaning

Read each sentence carefully. Then circle the item that best completes the statement below the sentence.

"No, we didn't just beat our opponents," she replied scornfully, "we pulverized them, 56–zip!" (2)

1. The best meaning for the word **pulverized** in line 1 is

a. pummeled   b. ground   c. overcame   d. demolished

One of the jobs a paleontologist performs involves articulating the fossil remains of animals that have been extinct for millennia. (2)

2. The word **articulating** in line 1 most nearly means

a. fitting together   b. pronouncing   c. expressing   d. clarifying

The judge quickly sustained the defense's objection to the district attorney's question as "irrelevant and incompetent." (2)

3. In line 1 the word **sustained** most nearly means

a. nourished   b. validated   c. withstood   d. underwent

Some scholars believe that the "Catalog of Ships" in the *Iliad* reproduces the official musters of the Greek forces that actually fought at Troy. (2)

4. The word **musters** in line 2 is used to mean

a. gatherings   b. payrolls   c. rosters   d. biographies

The Food and Drug Administration regulates the manufacture, distribution, and sale of ethical drugs such as insulin and nonprescription products such as aspirin. (2)

5. In line 2 the word **ethical** is best defined as

a. legal
b. requiring a prescription

c. morally permissible
d. pure

Antonyms

*In each of the following groups, circle the word or expression that is most nearly the **opposite** of the word in **boldface** type.*

1. staid
a. movable
b. flashy
c. clean
d. pretty

2. plebeian
a. ugly
b. aristocratic
c. brave
d. safe

3. aghast
a. frightened
b. horrified
c. youthful
d. delighted

4. ornate
a. common
b. wrong
c. simple
d. kind

5. nonentity
a. officer
b. player
c. celebrity
d. victim

6. ample
a. tall
b. full
c. inadequate
d. outstanding

7. aloof
a. low
b. involved
c. careful
d. meek

8. proximity
a. dullness
b. danger
c. damage
d. distance

9. defect
a. remain faithful
b. betray
c. admire
d. organize

11. blasé
a. willful
b. enthusiastic
c. plain
d. empty

13. resolute
a. secret
b. quiet
c. hesitant
d. difficult

15. prone
a. careful
b. possible
c. unlikely
d. thoughtless

10. forthright
a. full
b. indirect
c. selective
d. ashamed

12. indiscriminate
a. haphazard
b. selective
c. prejudiced
d. incomplete

14. volatile
a. unsafe
b. helpful
c. depressed
d. stable

16. annul
a. concern
b. reduce
c. embarrass
d. confirm

Word Families

A. *On the line provided, write the word you have learned in Units 4–6 that is related to each of the following nouns.*
EXAMPLE: ornateness—**ornate**

1. defectiveness, defection _____

2. obsession, obsessiveness _____

3. rehabilitation _____

4. frivolousness, frivolity _____

5. sustenance _____

6. porousness, porosity _____

7. geniality, genialness _____

8. ampleness, amplitude, amplification _____

9. peruser, perusal _____

10. plausibleness, plausibility _____

11. annulment _____

12. articulateness, articulation _____

13. forthrightness _____

14. assertion, assertiveness _____

15. purgatory _____

16. ethic, ethicist, ethicality, ethicalness _____

17. ostracism, ostracization _____

B. *On the line provided, write the word you have learned in Units 4–6 that is related to each of the following verbs.*
EXAMPLE: abash—**abashed**

18. resolve _____

19. solicit _____

20. retain _____

Two-Word Completions

Circle the pair of words that best complete the meaning of each of the following passages.

1. Though I tried to _____ my words clearly and distinctly, my voice was all but _____ above the roar of the storm.
a. sustain . . . ample
b. bolster . . . abashed
c. articulate . . . inaudible
d. muster . . . prone

2. During the bloody _____ of the early 1930s, Joseph Stalin "liquidated" every potential rival whom he feared might one day seek to _____ him from his position as absolute master.
a. purges . . . oust
b. repercussions . . . sustain
c. premonitions . . . ostracize
d. sequels . . . intrigue

3. "Using a(n) _____ has caused me a really unexpected problem," the famous novelist remarked. "Most people only know me by my pen name. So if I introduce myself by my real name, I run the risk of being regarded as a complete _____."
a. pseudonym . . . nonentity
b. bolster . . . scapegoat
c. sequel . . . plebeian
d. epitaph . . . apparition

4. Some of my friends have remarkably _____ memories from which nothing ever seems to escape. Unfortunately, I've been blessed with a memory that is as _____ as a sieve.
a. staid . . . durable
b. retentive . . . porous
c. ample . . . volatile
d. devoid . . . prodigious

5. "His cold and distant attitude toward people clearly betrays his deep _____ for the human race," I observed. "No one who genuinely likes human beings would constantly prefer to remain so _____ from them."
a. apparition . . . solicitous
b. disdain . . . aloof
c. anguish . . . prone
d. obsession . . . abashed

6. Since her objections to the plan were clearly _____, I thought that she was being _____. After all, if she had been serious, her comments would have had more substance to them.
a. plausible . . . articulate
b. genial . . . solicitous
c. inaudible . . . forthright
d. frivolous . . . facetious

7. Elected officials cannot be too careful about their behavior while in office. If they become _____ about matters of right and wrong, they may do things that the average citizen of this country does not consider _____. Such mistakes could cost the offenders their jobs.
a. solicitous . . . plausible
b. obsessed . . . prodigal
c. blasé . . . ethical
d. resolute . . . indiscriminate

Building with Classical Roots

cur, curr, curs, cour—to run

This root appears in **recourse** (page 53). The original meaning was "a running back to," but the word now means "a turning to for help or protection" or "a source of help." Some other words based on the same root are listed below.

concourse	current	incur	recur
courier	discourse	precursor	recurrent

From the list of words above, choose the one that corresponds to each of the brief definitions below. Write the word in the blank space in the illustrative sentence below the definition.

1. occurring or appearing repeatedly; returning regularly

Most movie soundtracks are made up of several _____ musical themes.

2. a flow, movement; of the present time; in general use

My poem appears in the _____ issue of the school magazine.

3. to happen again, be repeated ("*run again*")

Disturbing thoughts that _____ frequently may cause a person to seek help from a therapist.

4. a forerunner; that which precedes and shows the way

Ancient Athens is considered the _____ of modern democracy.

5. to meet with, run into; to bring upon oneself ("*run into*")

If you do not stick to a budget, you may _____ unnecessary debts.

6. a messenger, usually on urgent or official business

To ensure their safety, the top-secret letters were sent by diplomatic _____.

7. to talk; a conversation, long discussion on some topic

The featured speaker delivered a(n) _____ on using the Internet as a research tool.

8. a crowd; a thoroughfare; a place where crowds gather ("*running together*")

We joined the _____ of people in the village square.

From the list of words above, choose the one that best completes each of the following sentences. Write the word in the space provided.

1. We listened with interest as the veteran player _____ on the relative greatness of former basketball superstars.

2. Try as I might, I could not identify a pattern in the _____ nightmares I suffered.

3. The chilly autumn breeze was a(n) _____ of the cold weather to come.

4. In recent years there has been a proliferation of _____ services specializing in the airborne transport of documents.

5. "Please bring us up to date," the reporter said pointedly, "by telling us about some of the city's _____ plans to reduce traffic congestion."

6. I still do not know what I could have done to _____ their anger.

7. Do not wait until the sharp pains _____; see the doctor now!

8. The architect planned a huge _____ in front of the city hall as an open area where the citizens could gather.

---

*Circle the **boldface** word that more satisfactorily completes each of the following sentences.*

1. Although I had the leaky faucet repaired, I knew that the problem would (**recur, incur**) eventually.

2. The Turing machine, introduced by a British mathematician in 1936, was a (**courier, precursor**) of today's computers.

3. When we reached the rapids, we had to paddle hard to keep our boat from capsizing in the swift (**current, concourse**).

4. Mercury, the (**precursor, courier**) of the gods in Roman mythology, is often portrayed as wearing a winged hat or winged sandals to symbolize the speed with which he carries out his tasks.

5. The main (**concourse, discourse**) is usually the busiest part of a shopping mall.

6. The new tenants (**incurred, recurred**) the hostility of their neighbors by repeatedly playing loud music late at night.

7. The dinner party guests (**incurred, discoursed**) on a wide variety of topics from politics to movies.

8. An athlete who has been plagued by (**current, recurrent**) injuries may eventually have no choice but to retire.

Read the following sentences, paying special attention to the words and phrases underlined. From the words in the box below, find better choices for these underlined words and phrases. Then use these choices to rewrite the sentences.

WORD BANK				
aghast	flaunt	intrigue	premonition	rehabilitate
assert	frivolous	jurisdiction	prodigal	staid
bask	genial	muster	qualm	sustain
cower	instill	plausible	resolute	volatile

Linking the Rails

1. The "Wedding of the Rails" ceremony took place at Promontory Summit, Utah, on May 10, 1869. However, reporters mistakenly <u>stated as truth</u> that the event occurred 35 miles away at Promontory Point.

_____

_____

2. The celebration marked the completion of the <u>firm</u> effort by the Central Pacific and Union Pacific companies to build the final section of the transcontinental railway.

_____

_____

3. Each company did everything it could to be the first to reach Promontory Summit. This race <u>puzzled or excited the curiosity of</u> the public.

_____

_____

4. At the ceremony, dignitaries and politicians <u>took pleasure</u> in the public's acclaim as the specially engraved golden spike was driven into the rails.

_____

_____

5. After many decades of neglect, the site has been <u>fixed up</u>. Each year, railroad enthusiasts gather at the Golden Spike National Historic Site for a reenactment of the ceremony.

_____

_____

6. A highlight of this event is the appearance of the locomotives Jupiter and 119. Experts agree that these colorful engines are <u>reasonable or believable</u> facsimiles of the originals.

_____

_____

Analogies — *In each of the following, circle the item that best completes the comparison.*

1. **audacious** is to **cower** as
a. timid is to tremble
b. obstinate is to yield
c. solicitous is to care
d. enterprising is to venture

2. **collaborators** are to **cooperate** as
a. friends are to wrangle
b. scapegoats are to obsess
c. conspirators are to intrigue
d. apparitions are to flaunt

3. **annul** is to **invalidate** as
a. purge is to purify
b. minimize is to exaggerate
c. pulverize is to vie
d. comply is to request

4. **plebeians** are to **elite** as
a. voters are to electorate
b. relatives are to family
c. industrialists are to economy
d. outcasts are to society

5. **frugal** is to **prodigal** as
a. myriad is to complex
b. wanton is to willful
c. prodigious is to legendary
d. staid is to flamboyant

6. **ample** is to **bountiful** as
a. porous is to watertight
b. lacking is to devoid
c. aloof is to solicitous
d. volatile is to hysterical

7. **churlish** is to **genial** as
a. saucy is to abashed
b. heavy is to gingerly
c. tardy is to laggard
d. relevant is to plausible

8. **citadel** is to **city** as
a. promontory is to sea
b. vigil is to night
c. rubble is to explosion
d. perspective is to painting

9. **troops** are to **muster** as
a. market is to glut
b. effort is to sustain
c. money is to amass
d. riot is to instigate

10. **inhibited** is to **qualms** as
a. retentive is to memories
b. indiscriminate is to standards
c. skittish is to reservations
d. resolute is to misgivings

Choosing the Right Meaning — *Read each sentence carefully. Then circle the item that best completes the statement below the sentence.*

Our troupe called its version of the age-old morality tale "The Prodigal" so that it would not be confused with a Prokofiev ballet on the same subject.　(2)

1. In line 1 the word **Prodigal** is best defined as
a. Genius　　b. Liberal　　c. Openhanded　　d. Wastrel

Our opponent's defense was so porous that we had little trouble scoring points against it either on the ground or in the air.　(2)

2. The word **porous** in line 1 is best defined as
a. disorganized　b. permeable　　c. inexperienced　　d. cautious

The enduring wonder of the King James Version of the Bible is that so frugal a vocabulary can express such complex ideas so memorably.　(2)

3. In line 1 the word **frugal** most nearly means

    a. ordinary   b. skimpy   c. unusual   d. limited

Unlike the "decrees" of the skittish world of high fashion, the laws of nature never change.   (2)

4. In line 1 the word **skittish** most nearly means

    a. fickle   b. bashful   c. cautious   d. coy

What would our Wild West have been without those hordes of ranch hands punching cows and wrangling horses?   (2)

5. The word **wrangling** in line 2 is best defined as

    a. rustling   b. arguing with   c. herding   d. raising

Two-Word Completions

Circle the pair of words that best complete the meaning of each of the following sentences.

1. Overproduction _____ the market with goods, which in turn caused prices to fall, lowered profit margins, and had several other severe _____ on the industry.

    a. sustained . . . residues   c. pulverized . . . sequels
    b. glutted . . . repercussions   d. congested . . . perspectives

2. Like so many moths around a lamp, team doctors and field attendants _____ anxiously over the _____ figure of the injured player sprawled on the 50-yard line.

    a. jostled . . . laggard   c. basked . . . prodigious
    b. hovered . . . prone   d. wrangled . . . dissonant

3. Modern-day teachers still use such time-honored _____ as "Early to bed and early to rise, makes a man healthy, wealthy, and wise" to _____ desirable personal qualities in the minds of their students.

    a. epitaphs . . . bolster   c. adages . . . instill
    b. excerpts . . . instigate   d. antics . . . articulate

4. As a(n) _____ enemy of all forms of social and political injustice, I believe it is my duty to _____ the rights of the downtrodden openly and without hesitation.

    a. solicitous . . . deplore   c. resolute . . . allot
    d. durable . . . venerate   d. avowed . . . assert

5. On the night before the fateful battle, the general's normally placid mind was deeply _____ by ominous _____ of disaster, which unfortunately proved to be accurate.

    a. perturbed . . . premonitions   c. anguished . . . myriads
    b. obsessed . . . vigils   d. tethered . . . apparitions

Enriching Your Vocabulary

Read the passage below. Then complete the exercise at the bottom of the page.

Olé!

Have you ever picked up a word or phrase that a friend uses and added it to your own vocabulary? Something similar happens to languages when individuals from different cultures interact.

The long history of interaction between Spanish-speaking and English-speaking peoples has had a powerful impact on the English language. Many Spanish words, such as *bonanza* (Unit 1) and *embargo* (Unit 12), have entered English with little or no change. Other familiar English words have their roots in Spanish. The English noun *breeze* comes from the Spanish *brisa*, which means "northeast wind." *Siesta* ("an afternoon nap or rest") comes from the Spanish *sexta* ("afternoon"). Still other words came to English as a result of Spanish contact with the native peoples of Central and South America. These include *barbecue*, *chocolate*, and *hurricane*.

Backyard barbecues have become an American tradition.

The *tuna*, the *armadillo*, the *mosquito*, the *alligator*, and the *cockroach* all bear names of Spanish origin. And the Latin word *armatus* ("armed") is the root not only of *armadillo* but also of *armada* ("a fleet of warships").

Many other words that English has borrowed from Spanish end with the vowel *o*. Some examples are given in the exercise below.

In Column A below are 10 more words borrowed from Spanish. With or without a dictionary, match each word with its meaning in Column B.

Column A

_____ **1.** incommunicado
_____ **2.** patio
_____ **3.** aficionado
_____ **4.** barrio
_____ **5.** cargo
_____ **6.** peccadillo
_____ **7.** silo
_____ **8.** bravado
_____ **9.** desperado
_____ **10.** tornado

Column B

a. a tall cylindrical structure used for storing fodder
b. someone who likes and is knowledgeable about an interest or activity
c. a bold or violent criminal
d. freight
e. swaggering behavior, a pretense of bravery
f. an inner courtyard; an outdoor dining area
g. a Spanish-speaking neighborhood
h. without means of communication
i. a violent, destructive whirling wind
j. a slight offense

Definitions

Note carefully the spelling, pronunciation, part(s) of speech, and definition(s) of each of the following words. Then write the word in the blank space(s) in the illustrative sentence(s) following. Finally, study the lists of synonyms and antonyms given at the end of each entry.

1. acme
(ak′ mē)

(*n.*) the highest point

A perfect game is the _____ of any pitcher's career in baseball.

SYNONYMS: summit, top, peak, pinnacle
ANTONYMS: low point, bottom, nadir

2. attribute
(*n.*, at′ trə byüt;
v., ə trib′ yət)

(*n.*) a quality or characteristic belonging to or associated with someone or something; (*v.*) to assign to, credit with; to regard as caused by or resulting from

The _____ I most admire in you is your willingness to give everyone's opinions a fair hearing.

The doctor _____ my runny nose and itchy eyes to multiple allergies.

SYNONYMS: (*n.*) trait; (*v.*) ascribe

3. belittle
(bi lit′ əl)

(*v.*) to make something appear smaller than it is; to refer to in a way that suggests lack of importance or value

Candidates for public office may resort to negative ads that _____ their opponents' records.

SYNONYMS: minimize, underrate, disparage
ANTONYMS: exaggerate, magnify, overestimate

4. convey
(kən vā′)

(*v.*) to transport; to transmit; to communicate, make known; to transfer ownership or title to

Please _____ our best wishes to your parents on their twenty-fifth wedding anniversary.

SYNONYMS: carry, send, impart

5. doctrine
(däk′ trin)

(*n.*) a belief, principle, or teaching; a system of such beliefs or principles; a formulation of such beliefs or principles

No two religions see eye to eye on every fine detail of

_____ .

6. excise
(*v.*, ek sīz′;
n., ek′ sīz)

(*v.*) to remove by cutting; (*n.*) an indirect tax on the manufacture, sale, or distribution of a commodity or service

If you _____ that irrelevant remark, you will improve your essay.

The _____ imposed on such potentially dangerous products as tobacco and alcohol have skyrocketed.

SYNONYMS: (*v.*) cut out, delete, expunge
ANTONYMS: (*v.*) put in, insert, interpolate

7. exotic
(ig zät′ ik)

(*adj.*) foreign; charmingly unfamiliar or strikingly unusual

A recipe may call for _____ herbs and spices that are difficult to obtain.

SYNONYMS: strange, alien, picturesque, colorful
ANTONYMS: native, indigenous, familiar, commonplace

8. haggard
(hag′ ərd)

(*adj.*) thin, pale, and careworn as a result of worry or suffering; wild-looking

The _____ refugees were given food, clothing, and temporary shelter.

SYNONYMS: drawn, gaunt, wasted
ANTONYMS: healthy, glowing, radiant, hale and hearty

9. jaunty
(jôn′ tē)

(*adj.*) lively, easy, and carefree in manner; smart or trim in appearance

I bought a _____ straw hat.

SYNONYMS: unconcerned, lighthearted
ANTONYMS: downcast, dejected, glum

10. juncture
(jungk′ chər)

(*n.*) a joining together; the point at which two things are joined; any important point in time

Our property ends at the _____ of the two stone walls.

SYNONYMS: union, seam, joint, turning point

11. menial
(mē′ nē əl)

(*adj.*) lowly, humble, lacking importance or dignity; (*n.*) a person who does the humble and unpleasant tasks

During the Great Depression, people were thankful to have work of any kind, no matter how _____.

New immigrants may find jobs as _____ in hotels and restaurants.

SYNONYMS: (*n.*) underling, scullion, servant
ANTONYMS: (*adj.*) lofty, elevated; (*n.*) boss, master

12. parry
(par′ ē)

(*v.*) to ward off, fend off, deflect, evade, avoid; (*n.*) a defensive movement in fencing and other sports

An effective press secretary can _____ almost any question a reporter asks.

The challenger's swift _____ caught the champion completely off guard.

13. predatory
(pred′ ə tôr ē)

(*adj.*) preying on, plundering, or piratical

Owls and other _____ birds play an important role in maintaining the balance of nature.

SYNONYMS: looting, pillaging, ravenous, rapacious

14. ravage
(rav′ ij)

(v.) to destroy, lay waste, ruin; (n.) ruinous damage, destruction

Swarms of locusts _____ the farmer's fields and orchards.

No one can escape the _____ of time.

SYNONYMS: (v.) wreck, devastate
ANTONYM: (v.) spare

15. stance
(stans)

(n.) a way of holding the body; an attitude or position on an issue

A fashion model's _____ is calculated to show off a designer's clothing to best advantage.

SYNONYMS: posture, bearing

16. tawdry
(tô′ drē)

(adj.) showy and flashy but lacking in good taste

An excess of gold braid and glittery beads gave the costumes a _____ look.

SYNONYMS: loud, garish, gaudy, tacky, vulgar
ANTONYMS: refined, tasteful, subdued, muted

17. turncoat
(tərn′ kōt)

(n.) a person who switches to an opposing side or party

Strikers generally consider those workers who cross the picket lines to be _____ .

SYNONYMS: traitor, quisling, deserter, renegade
ANTONYMS: loyalist, diehard

18. unassuming
(ən ə sü′ miŋ)

(adj.) not putting on airs, unpretentious; modest

Many celebrities remain _____ despite their fame and wealth.

ANTONYMS: conceited, pretentious, self-important

19. wallow
(wäl′ ō)

(v.) to roll about in a lazy, clumsy, or helpless way; to overindulge in; to have in abundance; (n.) a wet, muddy, or dusty area used by animals as a sort of bath; a state of moral or physical collapse

After a strenuous hike, I was too tired to do anything but _____ blissfully in a hot bath.

On the Serengeti Plain, _____ offer animals much-needed relief from the sun's scorching rays.

SYNONYMS: (v.) delight in, bask in

20. waver
(wā′ vər)

(v.) to move to and fro, become unsteady; to show lack of firmness or decision

The committee _____ for several days before choosing the winner of the essay contest.

SYNONYMS: hesitate, falter
ANTONYMS: stand firm, be resolute

Completing the Sentence

From the words for this unit, choose the one that best completes each of the following sentences. Write the word in the space provided.

1. Her happy expression and the _____ way she walked down the street gave the impression of someone "on top of the world."

2. Two of our divisions were marching rapidly toward each other and hoped to effect a(n) _____ before the enemy attacked.

3. Since my boss has, as they say, "a short fuse," patience cannot be considered one of her outstanding _____.

4. Most Americans think of Australia as a strange and wonderful continent full of _____ plants and animals.

5. Because of his ability to _____ his opponents' blows, he was rarely hurt in his many fights in the ring.

6. Disease had so _____ his once-handsome face that I could scarcely recognize him!

7. In her most celebrated novels, such as *Pride and Prejudice* and *Emma,* Jane Austen reached the _____ of her literary art.

8. A baseball player who improves his _____ at the plate usually also improves his batting average.

9. In the early nineteenth century, Thomas Bowdler attempted to "clean up" the works of Shakespeare by _____ all words and phrases that he felt were coarse or offensive.

10. She sat there staring at the menu, _____ between the steak sandwich and the chef's salad.

11. When he switched parties, people called him a(n) _____, but he said that he had just had an honest change of opinion.

12. The room was so overcrowded with gaudy furnishings that the overall effect was cheap and _____.

13. I agree that we should not exaggerate her achievements, but we should not _____ them either.

14. Though many _____ creatures prefer to hunt at night, lions and leopards are active during the daytime.

15. The author's first published work was a rather _____ little pamphlet on the joys of fly fishing.

16. The Monroe _____ sought to prevent the colonization of the American continents by European powers.

17. During our trip through Kenya, we took many pictures of hippos as they _____ in a mudhole.

18. The drawn and _____ faces of the rescued miners showed clearly the terrible strain of the ordeal they had undergone.

19. We will need several trucks to _____ all the books to the new library building.

20. Even though you are starting at a(n) _____ job, you will gain valuable experience and knowledge of how the company works.

Synonyms

*Choose the word from this unit that is **the same** or **most nearly the same** in meaning as the **boldface** word or expression in the given phrase. Write the word on the line provided.*

1. a closet filled with **garish** outfits   _____

2. denounced as a **traitor**   _____

3. **transported** supplies to the front lines   _____

4. struck a **carefree** pose   _____

5. **devastated** by a series of storms   _____

6. seldom **falters** under pressure   _____

7. took an unpopular **position**   _____

8. left the cleaning up to the **underlings**   _____

9. the **principle** of equal justice for all   _____

10. sought to **deflect** the force of the assault   _____

11. saw something decidedly **rapacious** in their eyes   _____

12. have many **traits** in common   _____

13. **basked** in the attention of the media   _____

14. a critical **turning point** in the nation's history   _____

15. **minimized** the importance of the polls   _____

Antonyms

*Choose the word from this unit that is **most nearly opposite** in meaning to the **boldface** word or expression in the given phrase. Write the word on the line provided.*

16. **insert** the word *frequently*   _____

17. chose **familiar** destinations   _____

18. at the **nadir** of their fame   _____

19. a thoroughly **conceited** individual   _____

20. a **radiant** expression on their faces   _____

Choosing the Right Word

*Circle the **boldface** word that more satisfactorily completes each of the following sentences.*

1. Our system of justice is based on the (**doctrine, acme**) that defendants are presumed innocent unless the prosecution can prove them guilty.

2. The immigrants never (**excised, wavered**) in their determination to become American citizens.

3. The general (**belittled, attributed**) our failure to win the battle to a lack of sufficient forces rather than to a lack of courage.

4. Even after pitching two no-hit games this season, Stan was the same quiet and (**exotic, unassuming**) boy we had always known.

5. For many years the towns and villages along the Normandy coast of France showed the (**ravages, doctrines**) of the great invasion of 1944.

6. He hoped that election to the presidency would be the (**acme, juncture**) of his long and brilliant career in public service.

7. We were infuriated by the (**unassuming, tawdry**) speech in which he tried to portray himself as a great national leader.

8. Americans expect candidates to take a definite (**stance, parry**) on each of the important issues in a national election.

9. No matter how (**menial, tawdry**) the assignment may be, take pride in your work, and do your best.

10. Instead of answering my question, the skillful debater (**parried, ravaged**) by asking a question of her own.

11. During our trip to China, we sampled such (**exotic, predatory**) dishes as thousand-year-old eggs and bird's nest soup.

12. When I arrived at the critical (**juncture, stance**) in my career, I realized that my whole future would depend on the decision I was about to make.

13. History teaches us that in any great conflict, there will be some (**turncoats, menials**) willing to go over to the enemy.

14. Thieves are essentially a (**predatory, jaunty**) class of criminals because they live off what they can take from others.

15. I am thoroughly disgusted by people who try to make themselves seem more important than they really are by (**conveying, belittling**) others.

16. "If we are to keep the body politic healthy," the senator remarked, "we must (**excise, attribute**) the cancer of racial prejudice entirely from it."

17. I could see that the captain was deeply worried, even though he tried hard to appear confident and (**haggard, jaunty**) to the passengers.

18. He is so conceited that it is hard to (**convey, wallow**) to him the simple idea that we don't want him as a member of our group.

19. After waiting for news of her loved ones for several days, the woman looked careworn and (**haggard, menial**).

20. So long as you continue to (**waver, wallow**) in self-pity, you will lack the strength needed to solve your problems.

*Read the following passage, in which some of the words you have studied in this unit appear in **boldface** type. Then complete each statement given below the passage by circling the letter of the item that is **the same** or **almost the same** in meaning as the highlighted word.*

Cool!

(Line)

You probably don't think there is anything **exotic** about ice. Today, most homes have freezers, automatic ice-making machines, and other gadgets that provide a ready supply of ice. All you have to do is go to your refrigerator to get some ice cubes to cool off a beverage. But there was a time when only nature could provide ice. (5)

In ancient Rome, when excess was at its **acme**, lavish banquets and elaborate parties were common among the upper classes. The best and wealthiest hosts would provide great quantities of ice or snow for guests to add to their goblets.

Ice was a luxury item in ancient Rome.

Not everyone approved of the Roman appetite for cold drinks. Philosophers saw (10) the growing popularity of consuming snow and ice as a sure sign that Roman culture was declining. Doctors **attributed** all sorts of physical ailments to chilled food and drink. But this did not stop those who could afford (15) ice and snow. For example, one emperor ordered workers to build an enormous mountain of snow in the garden of his villa to cool him during hot Roman summers!

How did Romans get such large quantities of (20) the cold stuff? They imported it from high mountains that were snowcapped all year long. Containers of fresh mountain snow were painstakingly **conveyed** by donkey to local "snow shops" and ice cellars, where they were insulated with straw for protection from the intense Roman heat. (25) Eventually, the snow would melt; but it would conveniently freeze into ice when it dripped into deeper, colder layers of the ice cellars. This simple technology called for large teams of **menials** both to gather and transport the snow and to tend the ice cellars. Their bosses enjoyed great profits because rich Romans would pay almost any price for these cool products. Snow and ice were the hottest things in town. (30)

---

1. The meaning of **exotic** (line 1) is
  a. lofty   c. strange
  b. familiar   d. tacky

2. Acme (line 6) most nearly means
  a. best   c. worst
  b. bottom   d. peak

3. Attributed (line 13) is best defined as
  a. attracted   c. diagnosed
  b. ascribed   d. treated

4. Conveyed (line 24) most nearly means
  a. melted   c. expunged
  b. carved   d. carried

5. Menials (line 28) is best defined as
  a. farmers   c. artisans
  b. servants   d. nobles

Definitions

Note carefully the spelling, pronunciation, part(s) of speech, and definition(s) of each of the following words. Then write the word in the blank space(s) in the illustrative sentence(s) following. Finally, study the lists of synonyms and antonyms given at the end of each entry.

1. abut
(ə bət')

(*v.*) to join at one end or be next to; to support, prop up

Land that _____ a river or lake is considered a highly desirable location on which to build a summer home.

SYNONYMS: border on, bolster

2. attire
(ə tīr')

(*n.*) clothes, apparel, garb; (*v.*) to dress, adorn, or bedeck

The special _____ that firefighters wear helps to protect them from flames and smoke.

The children happily _____ their stuffed animals in holiday outfits and accessories.

SYNONYM: (*n.*) clothing

3. avail
(ə vāl')

(*v.*) to be of use or benefit to; to make use of; to take advantage of; to profit or benefit; (*n.*) use, benefit, or value

Be sure to _____ yourself of all the services that the school library has to offer.

I tried repeatedly to contact my neighbor by phone, but to absolutely no _____ .

4. crony
(krō' nē)

(*n.*) a very close friend, pal, chum, buddy

We have been _____ ever since we met in the second grade.

ANTONYMS: enemy, rival

5. cryptic
(krip' tik)

(*adj.*) puzzling, mystifying, or enigmatic

The letter to the editor was so _____ that I couldn't be certain what the writer had actually intended to say.

ANTONYMS: crystal clear, unambiguous

6. divergent
(də vər' jənt)

(*adj.*) going in different directions; different from each other; departing from convention, deviant

Two people may be close friends despite their having very _____ interests and beliefs.

SYNONYMS: not in agreement, differing, unorthodox, unconventional
ANTONYMS: merging, intersecting, converging, orthodox, conventional

7. enmity
(en′ mə tē)

(*n.*) hatred, ill-will

Despite a long, close, and tense match, the defeated player felt no _____ toward the new champion.

SYNONYMS: hostility, animosity, antagonism
ANTONYMS: friendship, amity

8. fervent
(fər′ vənt)

(*adj.*) very earnest, emotional, passionate; extremely hot

The president delivered a _____ plea for tolerance and unity.

SYNONYMS: enthusiastic, ardent, burning, blazing, scorching
ANTONYMS: blasé, apathetic, restrained, emotionless

9. gaunt
(gônt)

(*adj.*) thin and bony, starved looking; bare, barren

We left food and water for the _____ alley cat.

SYNONYMS: lean, scrawny, lanky, all skin and bones
ANTONYMS: plump, chubby, stout, corpulent

10. infiltrate
(in′ fil trāt)

(*v.*) to pass through or gain entrance to gradually or stealthily

Some of our men _____ the enemy's camp and captured their leader.

SYNONYMS: slip into, creep into, penetrate

11. nullify
(nəl′ ə fī)

(*v.*) to make of no value or consequence, cancel, wipe out

After seven days, you cannot _____ the contract without being charged a penalty.

SYNONYMS: invalidate, annul
ANTONYMS: confirm, endorse, ratify, sanction

12. perceptible
(pər sep′ tə bəl)

(*adj.*) capable of being grasped by the senses or mind

There was no _____ improvement in the patient's condition despite the doctors' best efforts to treat the infection.

SYNONYMS: noticeable, discernible, observable
ANTONYMS: invisible, unnoticeable, indiscernible

13. plummet
(pləm′ ət)

(*v.*) to plunge straight down; (*n.*) a weight fastened to a line

Gannets and other seabirds _____ headfirst into the ocean to catch small fish and squid.

Experts think the pierced round stones found at the site served as _____ to weight fishing nets.

SYNONYM: (*v.*) take a nosedive
ANTONYMS: (*v.*) soar, skyrocket

14. proclaim
(prō klām')

(v.) to declare publicly or officially

We _____ our loyalty to our country when we recite the Pledge of Allegiance.

SYNONYMS: announce, promulgate
ANTONYMS: conceal, cover up

15. proxy
(präk' sē)

(n.) an agent, substitute; a written permission allowing one person to act in another's place

The vice president may be called upon to be the president's _____ at the funeral of a foreign leader.

SYNONYMS: deputy, representative

16. rankle
(raŋ' kəl)

(v.) to cause anger, irritation, or bitterness (with the suggestion that the pain grows worse with time)

Insults may _____ a person for many years.

SYNONYMS: irritate, vex, nettle, irk, gall
ANTONYMS: please, delight, gratify

17. scavenger
(skav' ən jər)

(n.) a person who collects or removes usable items from waste materials; an animal that feeds on refuse or dead bodies

A few _____ such as catfish and other bottom feeders will help to keep a fish tank clean.

SYNONYM: rummager

18. stint
(stint)

(v.) to limit, be sparing or frugal; (n.) a limit or restriction; a fixed share of work or duty; a period of activity

Good hosts never _____ on food and drink for the guests who attend their parties.

A _____ as the guest host of a popular talk show may be a big career break for a young comedian.

SYNONYMS: (v.) restrict, scrimp, economize
ANTONYMS: (v.) splurge, squander, lavish

19. stoical
(stō' i kəl)

(adj.) self-controlled, not showing feeling in response to pleasure or pain

The refugees' _____ acceptance of their plight was deeply moving.

SYNONYMS: unresponsive, impassive
ANTONYMS: excitable, emotional, hotheaded

20. unflagging
(ən flag' iŋ)

(v.) tireless, continuing with vigor

After the votes were counted, the candidates paid tribute to the _____ loyalty of their supporters.

SYNONYMS: steady, undiminished, unremitting
ANTONYMS: diminishing, drooping, sagging

Completing the Sentence

From the words for this unit, choose the one that best completes each of the following sentences. Write the word in the space provided.

1. The statements by witnesses are so _____ that it's hard to know how the accident actually happened.

2. All her efforts to get more business for her troubled company proved to be of no _____, and the store had to close down.

3. Even after he retired and we expected him to slow down, his efforts in support of his beloved school remained _____.

4. Each year the president _____ the last Thursday in the month of November as a day of national thanksgiving.

5. As a teenager, she developed a(n) _____ interest in biology that led to a lifelong career.

6. Shakespeare said that Cassius had a "lean and hungry look," but I would describe him by the single word _____.

7. Over a period of years, words and phrases used in the field of computer science _____ everyday speech.

8. Although the vulture has a decidedly poor reputation, it does a useful job as a(n) _____, clearing away decaying materials.

9. Their parents had _____ for many years to save the money needed to send the children to college.

10. In our community, people of many ethnic backgrounds work together without jealousy or _____.

11. Instead of giving us a clear answer, the speaker confined himself to the _____ prophecy that "time will tell."

12. His failure to win the election _____ in his mind until it caused him a complete emotional breakdown.

13. To prepare for the job interview, she _____ herself in a neat, simple navy blue suit.

14. We watched in dismay as our new model airplane suddenly went out of control and _____ to the ground.

15. We decided not to buy the house, mainly because the property it stands on unfortunately _____ the noisy main highway.

16. Since I will not be able to attend the meeting, I hereby appoint Ms. Brown to act as my _____.

17. My father has three _____ who go with him each year on a camping trip in the High Sierras.

18. I didn't think she would have the nerve to ask me for a loan, but she did it—and with no _____ embarrassment.

19. He tried to appear _____ when he heard the bad news, but I realized that he was deeply hurt.

20. The rise in the cost of living _____ my efforts to save some money from my small salary.

Synonyms

*Choose the word from this unit that is **the same** or **most nearly the same** in meaning as the **boldface** word or expression in the given phrase. Write the word on the line provided.*

1. hackers who **penetrate** computer databases _____

2. an **ardent** advocate for the poor _____

3. selected to act as my **representative** _____

4. a lack of respect that **galls** _____

5. packed **clothes** suitable for all kinds of weather _____

6. plan to visit an old **pal** _____

7. lingering **antagonism** despite the settlement _____

8. forced to **economize** even on necessities _____

9. **announced** my intention to run for office _____

10. remedies that are of no **benefit** _____

11. a barely **discernible** defect in the workmanship _____

12. as **scrawny** as a skeleton _____

13. left out for **rummagers** to sift through _____

14. tolerant of **differing** opinions _____

15. the place where the borders of four states **join** _____

Antonyms

*Choose the word from this unit that is **most nearly opposite** in meaning to the **boldface** word or expression in the given phrase. Write the word on the line provided.*

16. **diminishing** enthusiasm for the task at hand _____

17. left **unambiguous** instructions _____

18. a person of **excitable** temperament _____

19. watched the candidate's approval ratings **soar** _____

20. **ratify** the agreement _____

Choosing the Right Word

*Circle the **boldface** word that more satisfactorily completes each of the following sentences.*

1. During the prolonged dry spell, the farmers' (**fervent, perceptible**) prayers for rain were seldom answered.

2. We honor this wonderful woman tonight for her (**unflagging, divergent**) devotion to every good cause in our community.

3. If we had a good civil service system in this town, the mayor wouldn't be able to put his (**cronies, enmities**) on the public payroll.

4. It is a sad fact of experience that postwar political blunders can often (**nullify, infiltrate**) or even reverse the results of battlefield triumphs.

5. It didn't take me long to master the (**fervent, cryptic**) greetings, signs, and handclasps that were part of the club's rituals.

6. Before going to college, my brother did a (**stint, proxy**) as an apprentice radio operator on an oceangoing tanker.

7. The two candidates are working hard to get the voters' support, but in my opinion there is no (**cryptic, perceptible**) difference between them.

8. In a democracy, we expect people to have (**gaunt, divergent**) views and to express them openly.

9. In the unforgettable words of the Declaration of Independence, Jefferson (**proclaimed, rankled**) to the world that a new nation had been born.

10. The (**unflagging, gaunt**) and leafless trees seemed to add to the gloom of that wintry scene.

11. The senator shocked the nation with charges that Communists had (**infiltrated, proclaimed**) the various branches of our government.

12. All the heroism of our men could not (**abut, avail**) against the enemy's superior forces.

13. President Kennedy bore his pain in such a (**perceptible, stoical**) manner that few people realized how much he suffered from his World War II back injury.

14. I pretended that being ignored by the "best people in town" meant nothing to me, but actually those snubs (**rankled, nullified**) deeply.

15. Our hopes for a winning touchdown (**availed, plummeted**) in the last minute when Jim fumbled and South High recovered the ball.

16. Let me state my unchanging (**stoicism, enmity**) for those who seek to bring about political change by violent means.

17. Every day, the homeless go through all the litter baskets on our street, trying to make a living as (**plummets, scavengers**).

18. Large numbers of stockholders sent in (**proxies, cronies**) giving their voting power to the directors of the corporation.

19. After the big snowstorm, the trees seemed to be (**attired, scavenged**) in white lace.

20. When we were kids, our lives pretty much (**stinted, abutted**); but after high school, we went our separate ways.

8

Vocabulary in Context

*Read the following passage, in which some of the words you have studied in this unit appear in **boldface** type. Then complete each statement given below the passage by circling the letter of the item that is **the same** or **almost the same** in meaning as the highlighted word.*

Old Eggs, New Discoveries

(Line)

The dry, windy plains of Patagonia, in central Argentina, are as beautiful as they are barren. But did they once teem with life? Paleontologists (scientists who study fossils) have proved that this rugged region is a rich repository of reptile remains. Camped out in the field for weeks at a time, these scientific **scavengers** search with
(5) **unflagging** curiosity and dedication for new clues to some of the mysteries of the long-extinct dinosaurs. Their tools are rock hammers, brushes, and hand lenses.

Being on a dig is not easy for the members of a research team, even if they are rewarded with exciting results. To endure the primitive conditions in the field, the
(10) scientists need to have a **stoical** attitude and a good sense of humor. Even the most experienced and hardy dinosaur hunters limit their fieldwork to a **stint** of about a month. They then return to their
(15) laboratories, where they record, classify, and analyze their latest specimens. But most paleontologists eventually feel the strong urge to explore again despite the physical hardships.
(20) Digs in Patagonia have revealed the existence of a dozen previously unknown dinosaur species, including

Fossilized eggs found in mud flats

Argentinosaurus, the largest plant eater ever found, and *Giganotosaurus*, the newest monarch of meat eaters. The arid conditions of the region, so hostile to life today,
(25) have preserved the prehistoric past. Recently, in an area where rocky cliffs **abut** ancient mud flats, researchers made a remarkable find: hundreds of thousands of fossilized dinosaur eggs. In just three days, they harvested eighty undamaged eggs, all nestled together in regularly spaced clusters. Scientists consider this find **perceptible** evidence of dinosaur behavior. They think that mothers may have dug
(30) bowl-shaped nests, carefully spaced apart to protect the precious eggs. What other wonders remain hidden in the dusty Patagonian desert?

1. The meaning of **scavengers** (line 4) is
a. doctors
b. climbers
c. campers
d. rummagers

2. Unflagging (line 5) most nearly means
a. tireless
b. thorough
c. occasional
d. diminishing

3. Stoical (line 10) is best defined as
a. emotional
b. self-controlled
c. scientific
d. cryptic

4. The meaning of **stint** (line 13) is
a. splurge
b. period
c. agenda
d. vacation

5. Abut (line 25) most nearly means
a. border on
b. separate
c. tower over
d. obstruct

6. Perceptible (line 29) is best defined as
a. abstract
b. reliable
c. observable
d. invisible

Unit 8 ■ 97

Definitions

Note carefully the spelling, pronunciation, part(s) of speech, and definition(s) of each of the following words. Then write the word in the blank space(s) in the illustrative sentence(s) following. Finally, study the lists of synonyms and antonyms given at the end of each entry.

1. apt
(apt)

(*adj.*) suitable, fitting, likely; quick to learn

The appropriate greeting card for a particular occasion is one that expresses _____ sentiments.

SYNONYMS: appropriate, fit, proper, liable
ANTONYMS: inappropriate, unlikely, slow

2. awry
(ə rī′)

(*adj., adv.*) in a turned or twisted position or direction; wrong, out of the right or hoped-for course

After running to catch the bus, I realized that my clothing was all _____ .

When something goes _____ during a countdown, NASA officials will cancel a shuttle launch.

SYNONYMS: (*adj.*) crooked, askew, amiss
ANTONYMS: (*adj.*) straight, symmetrical

3. bludgeon
(bləj′ ən)

(*n.*) a short club used as a weapon; (*v.*) to strike with a heavy club; to use force or strong arguments to gain some point

Early humans fashioned _____ from the thick limbs of trees.

Heavy-handed writers tend to _____ readers with explanations of their characters' motives.

SYNONYMS: (*n.*) cudgel; (*v.*) clobber, clout

4. capitulate
(kə pich′ ə lāt)

(*v.*) to end resistance, give up, surrender, throw in the towel

When I saw that I had been outmaneuvered by my opponent, I had no choice but to _____ .

ANTONYMS: hold out, persist

5. chafe
(chāf)

(*v.*) to warm by rubbing; to wear sore by rubbing; to feel annoyance or dissatisfaction, annoy, irk; to strain or press against; (*n.*) a sore or injury caused by rubbing

The American colonists _____ under the many unjust laws imposed on them by King George II.

To keep that raw _____ from becoming infected, you should put a clean bandage on it.

SYNONYMS: (*v.*) irritate, scrape, abrade
ANTONYMS: (*v.*) soothe, mollify, please, elate

6. defile
(di fīl′)

(*v., trans.*) to make unclean or dirty, destroy the purity of; (*v., intrans.*) to march in a single line or in columns; (*n.*) a narrow passage; gorge, canyon

Those who _____ a house of worship will be punished to the full extent of the law.

The victorious troops _____ past the reviewing stand.

The weary hikers paused to rest before proceeding through the steep and rocky _____ .

SYNONYMS: (*v., trans.*) pollute, contaminate, desecrate
ANTONYMS: (*v., trans.*) cleanse, purify

7. dire
(dīr)

(*adj.*) dreadful, causing fear or suffering; warning of trouble to come; demanding immediate action to avoid disaster

Environmentalists warn of the _____ consequences of the destruction of the world's rain forests.

SYNONYMS: disastrous, ominous, sinister, urgent
ANTONYMS: favorable, auspicious, beneficial

8. disarming
(dis ärm′ iŋ)

(*adj.*) charming, tending to get rid of unfriendliness or suspicion

My best friend has a most _____ smile.

SYNONYMS: endearing, winning
ANTONYMS: alarming, troubling, disquieting

9. disgruntled
(dis grənt′ əld)

(*adj., part*) in bad humor, discontented, annoyed

When flights are delayed because of bad weather, airline passengers may become extremely _____ .

SYNONYMS: displeased, grumpy, surly
ANTONYMS: pleased, satisfied, content

10. encroach
(en krōch′)

(*v.*) to advance beyond the usual or proper limits, trespass

Where suburbs _____ on unspoiled forests or wetlands, delicate ecosystems may be disrupted.

SYNONYMS: intrude, infringe

11. endow
(en daù′)

(*v.*) to furnish, equip, provide with funds or some other desirable thing or quality

Wealthy individuals often make provisions in their wills to _____ their favorite charities.

SYNONYMS: grant, bestow, present, bequeath
ANTONYMS: take away, deprive

12. fend
(fend)

(*v.*) to ward off, resist; to get along, manage

A novel's heroine may have to _____ off the proposals of unappealing suitors.

SYNONYMS: stave off, cope

13. impunity
(im pyü′ nə tē)

(*n.*) freedom from punishment

Bullies must be made to realize that they cannot push other people around with _____ .

SYNONYMS: exemption from penalty, immunity

14. mien
(mēn)

(*n.*) air, manner; appearance; expression

A person may adopt a cheerful _____ in an attempt to conceal sorrow or anger.

SYNONYMS: look, bearing, demeanor

15. penal
(pē′ nəl)

(*adj.*) having to do with punishment

Devil's Island, off the coast of French Guiana, was once the site of an infamous _____ colony.

SYNONYMS: correctional, disciplinary

16. pertinent
(pər′ tə nənt)

(*adj.*) related to the matter at hand, to the point

The joke you told was very amusing, but I fail to see how it was _____ to the conversation.

SYNONYMS: relevant, germane, apropos
ANTONYMS: unrelated, irrelevant, immaterial

17. predominant
(pri däm′ ə nənt)

(*adj.*) the greatest in strength or power; most common

Cy Young, for whom the coveted pitching award is named, was once the _____ pitcher in baseball.

SYNONYMS: chief, major, paramount, prevalent
ANTONYMS: secondary, minor, subsidiary, rare

18. prodigy
(präd′ ə jē)

(*n.*) something wonderful or marvelous; something monstrous or abnormal; an unusual feat; a child or young person with extraordinary ability or talent

The careers of some musical _____ have turned out to be short-lived.

SYNONYMS: marvel, wonder, freak, genius
ANTONYMS: dumbbell, dunce, dullard

19. recluse
(re′ klüs)

(*n.*) a person who leads a life shut up or withdrawn from the world

An individual who has suffered a great emotional loss may become something of a _____ .

SYNONYMS: loner, hermit

20. renown
(ri naůn′)

(*n.*) fame, glory

Some writers earn acclaim during their lifetime, but others win _____ only after their death.

SYNONYMS: reputation, celebrity, prestige
ANTONYMS: obscurity, infamy, notoriety

Completing the Sentence

From the words for this unit, choose the one that best completes each of the following sentences. Write the word in the space provided.

1. Even before Martin Luther King, Jr., won the Nobel Peace Prize in 1964, his _____ had spread throughout most of the world.

2. The Scottish poet Robert Burns reminds us that no matter how carefully we plan, things may still go _____.

3. As the jurors filed back into the courtroom, their stern _____ alarmed the defendants.

4. Shoes that will not _____ your feet are the most important part of the equipment you will need for a hike.

5. The couple's parents promised that they would not be the kind of meddling in-laws who _____ on the privacy of their married children.

6. When his efforts to _____ off the angry bill collectors proved unsuccessful, my uncle was forced to declare bankruptcy.

7. It is up to you to make good use of the talents with which nature has seen fit to _____ you.

8. The brave soldiers defending the fort _____ only when they realized that further resistance was useless.

9. Even though you are _____ because the candidate you favored did not win the nomination, you should still vote in the election.

10. In your answers, try to limit yourself to giving us only the details that you know are _____ to this investigation.

11. Do you believe that the crime rate will go down if the _____ code is made more severe?

12. We were amazed that the large, fierce-looking dog allowed the child to pull its tail with _____.

13. Some people have a decidedly unpleasant habit of using facts and figures like a(n) _____ to beat down their opponents in an argument.

14. To carry out his great work, he chose to separate himself from society and live the solitary life of a(n) _____.

15. Let us hope that scientists are wrong in their _____ predictions that there will be a major earthquake in our region.

16. True, I wanted to make some money, but my _____ reason for taking the job was that I needed practical work experience.

17. Sideshow exhibits at the circus usually include mermaids, wolf-men, and other so-called _____ of nature.

18. We were prepared to make an angry complaint to the salesclerk, but her _____ manner soon put us in a friendlier mood.

19. There's an old saying which tells us that if you walk like a duck and talk like a duck, people are _____ to take you for a duck.

20. In my opinion, the countryside is _____ by billboards that block our view of the beauties of nature.

Synonyms

*Choose the word from this unit that is **the same** or **most nearly the same** in meaning as the **boldface** word or expression in the given phrase. Write the word on the line provided.*

1. further **irritated** our already strained nerves _____

2. a gruff **demeanor** but a kindly heart _____

3. a **paramount** concern for parents and teachers _____

4. paid a **fitting** tribute _____

5. had a reputation for being a **loner** _____

6. trespassed with apparent **freedom from punishment** _____

7. **surrendered** after a long and exhausting struggle _____

8. a crime that **desecrates** the nation's honor _____

9. fought all attempts to **infringe** on our freedom _____

10. beat the victim with a **cudgel** _____

11. unable to **ward** off the blow _____

12. left the curtains hanging **askew** _____

13. sent the defendant to a **correctional** facility _____

14. **equip** a new research laboratory _____

15. obtain all the **relevant** documents _____

Antonyms

*Choose the word from this unit that is **most nearly opposite** in meaning to the **boldface** word or expression in the given phrase. Write the word on the line provided.*

16. achieved considerable **notoriety** _____

17. another **satisfied** customer _____

18. thought by some to be a **dullard** _____

19. behaved in a **troubling** fashion _____

20. a **favorable** forecast for the economy _____

Choosing the Right Word

*Circle the **boldface** word that more satisfactorily completes each of the following sentences.*

1. His plain clothing and quiet (**prodigy, mien**) were not what we expected in a famous Hollywood director.

2. Some great composers, such as Mozart and Mendelssohn, have shown an amazing (**pertinence, aptitude**) for music at a very early age.

3. The lecturer is a man who served ten years in prison and is now devoting his life to bringing about reforms in our (**penal, predominant**) system.

4. When the featured singer failed to appear, the (**disgruntled, apt**) fans demanded their money back.

5. Yes, we are still friends, but not as close as we used to be; something has gone (**awry, dire**) in our relationship.

6. The injured quarterback (**chafed, defiled**) at sitting on the bench while his team was being badly beaten on the field.

7. A team as determined to win as ours is will never (**capitulate, endow**), no matter how many points behind it is in the final moments of a game.

8. Alvin York performed such (**impunities, prodigies**) on the battlefields of France that he was awarded this nation's highest honors.

9. During the winter the wind usually blows from the north in that area, but during the summer southerly currents are (**predominant, awry**).

10. What bad taste it is for her to approach people she scarcely knows and (**bludgeon, capitulate**) her way into private conversations!

11. The message of a great work of literature may be as (**pertinent, disgruntled**) today as it was when it was first written.

12. Do you understand how someone can live as a (**mien, recluse**) even in the midst of a great city?

13. My problem was to (**fend, bludgeon**) off their unwelcome attentions without being openly insulting.

14. The college my sister attends is a small one, but it has gained a great deal of (**recluse, renown**) for the quality of its faculty.

15. As we use up the earth's fossil-fuel supplies, we are faced with an increasingly (**disarming, dire**) need to develop new energy sources.

16. The rights guaranteed us by the U.S. Constitution do not permit us to (**fend, encroach**) on the rights of others.

17. The Declaration of Independence mentions a number of "unalienable rights" with which all people "are (**endowed, chafed**) by their Creator."

18. Nature is kind to us in many ways, but we must learn that we cannot violate nature's laws with (**impunity, renown**).

19. I was so (**disarmed, chafed**) by the way in which he asked for a loan that almost to my surprise I found myself giving him the money.

20. He claims to be a patriot, but his appeals to racism are (**encroaching, defiling**) the great ideals on which this nation was built.

Vocabulary in Context

*Read the following passage, in which some of the words you have studied in this unit appear in **boldface** type. Then complete each statement given below the passage by circling the letter of the item that is **the same** or **almost the same** in meaning as the highlighted word.*

A Quiet Voice for Freedom

(Line)

The great **renown** that Rosa Parks has earned as the "mother of the civil rights movement" often overwhelms this modest woman. She changed the course of American life; yet her simple refusal to **capitulate** to racism was unplanned. She explains that she was "just one of many who fought for freedom." (5)

Rosa Parks riding a Montgomery bus, 1956

On December 1, 1955, Parks took a city bus home from her job at a store in downtown Montgomery, Alabama. According to the segregation laws of the day, Parks, an African American, was required to sit in the back of the bus. She was accused of **encroaching** (10) on the whites-only section, and the bus driver tried to convince her to obey the law. Instead, Parks kept both her dignified **mien** and her seat. At last, the driver warned her that he would send for the police. "Go ahead and call them," Parks answered. (15)

Rosa Parks was arrested, jailed, tried, convicted, and fined. She refused to pay. Her experience set off a 382-day boycott of Montgomery city buses. When her case reached the U.S. Supreme Court, the justices declared the segregation of Montgomery's public (20) transportation to be unconstitutional.

Rosa Parks's courage inspired all those struggling for their civil rights, but her life was seriously disrupted. She was constantly harassed and received threats, some of them **dire**. In 1957, she and her husband moved to Detroit to escape (25) persistent ill will. There she founded the Rosa and Raymond Parks Institute for Self-Development, a school for teens, and continued her work for racial equality. In 1999, Rosa Parks was awarded the Congressional Gold Medal, the highest honor given by the American government.

---

1. The meaning of **renown** (line 1) is
  a. rewards   c. infamy
  b. praise   d. fame

2. Capitulate (line 3) most nearly means
  a. complain   c. convert
  b. surrender   d. respond

3. Encroaching (line 10) is best defined as
  a. demonstrating   c. encamping
  b. performing   d. intruding

4. The meaning of **mien** (line 13) is
  a. temper   c. bearing
  b. beliefs   d. attire

5. Dire (line 25) most nearly means
  a. auspicious   c. ominous
  b. anonymous   d. subtle

Analogies

In each of the following, circle the item that best completes the comparison.

1. parry is to **blow** as
a. bludgeon is to club
b. fend off is to attack
c. chafe is to neck
d. ravage is to scavenger

2. traitor is to **turncoat** as
a. hermit is to recluse
b. musician is to prodigy
c. enemy is to crony
d. judge is to criminal

3. tawdry is to **unfavorable** as
a. predatory is to favorable
b. unflagging is to unfavorable
c. apt is to favorable
d. pertinent is to unfavorable

4. defile is to **purify** as
a. capitulate is to give up
b. waver is to stand fast
c. nullify is to make clear
d. proclaim is to hold out

5. acme is to **high** as
a. menial is to low
b. stance is to high
c. mien is to low
d. stint is to high

6. soar is to **plummet** as
a. attire is to adorn
b. ratify is to nullify
c. fend is to parry
d. stint is to abut

7. batter is to **stance** as
a. patron is to endowment
b. scavenger is to refuse
c. menial is to drudgery
d. candidate is to position

8. vulture is to **scavenger** as
a. globe is to explorer
b. orchestra is to conductor
c. goldfish is to aquarium
d. hawk is to predator

9. sweater is to **attire** as
a. road is to juncture
b. writer is to doctrine
c. scavenger is to jackal
d. bludgeon is to weapon

10. crony is to **friendship** as
a. proxy is to enmity
b. turncoat is to betrayal
c. recluse is to renown
d. scapegoat is to impunity

11. belittle is to **less** as
a. plummet is to more
b. abut is to less
c. encroach is to more
d. convey is to less

12. thin is to **gaunt** as
a. dire is to weak
b. careless is to awry
c. tired is to exhausted
d. clear is to cryptic

13. spy is to **infiltrate** as
a. sheep is to bleat
b. pig is to wallow
c. mole is to tunnel
d. horse is to trot

14. edible is to **eaten** as
a. manual is to automated
b. perceptible is to seen
c. tangible is to sensed
d. visual is to blinded

15. suffering is to **haggard** as
a. enmity is to disarming
b. hesitation is to unflagging
c. contentment is to disgruntled
d. starvation is to gaunt

16. neck is to **chafe** as
a. knife is to bludgeon
b. boredom is to yawn
c. sandpaper is to defile
d. shoe is to scuff

17. jaunty is to **good mood** as
a. disgruntled is to bad mood
b. irritated is to good mood
c. content is to bad mood
d. frustrated is to good mood

18. penal is to **punishment** as
a. judicial is to justice
b. stoical is to education
c. liable is to impunity
d. fervent is to apathy

Word Associations

In each of the following groups, circle the word that is best defined or suggested by the given phrase.

1. a change that everyone noticed
   a. perceptible   b. exotic   c. predominant   d. predatory

2. so pleasant that we couldn't be angry with him
   a. gaunt   b. disarming   c. jaunty   d. tawdry

3. cause constant irritation or bitterness
   a. endow   b. capitulate   c. rankle   d. convey

4. make use of strong arguments to overcome all objections
   a. abut   b. bludgeon   c. encroach   d. endow

5. an important new idea in our foreign policy
   a. doctrine   b. wallow   c. attribute   d. enmity

6. with her hat twisted to one side
   a. awry   b. disarming   c. apt   d. predatory

7. cheered our team with undiminished enthusiasm
   a. stoical   b. unflagging   c. fervent   d. apt

8. a remark that can be interpreted in several different ways
   a. cryptic   b. unflagging   c. exotic   d. unassuming

9. explained her position on a critical issue
   a. waver   b. proxy   c. stance   d. doctrine

10. has a way of making other people feel unimportant
   a. nullify   b. belittle   c. parry   d. fend

11. the point at which the head and the neck meet
   a. renown   b. acme   c. juncture   d. bludgeon

12. the disastrous consequences of their actions
   a. haggard   b. dire   c. cryptic   d. divergent

13. efforts that proved to be of no use
   a. enmity   b. stint   c. renown   d. avail

14. has no respect for the privacy of others
   a. capitulate   b. encroach   c. waver   d. rankle

15. an amazing ability to get away with anything
   a. renown   b. impunity   c. prodigy   d. stint

16. cities destroyed by an earthquake
   a. attired   b. conveyed   c. excised   d. ravaged

17. will join any side that he thinks is going to win
   a. recluse   b. menial   c. crony   d. turncoat

18. the kind of person who doesn't "put up a big front"
   a. unassuming   b. dire   c. menial   d. exotic

19. has the manner and bearing of an aristocrat
   a. mien   b. enmity   c. attire   d. renown

20. gave my lawyer the right to act for me
   a. enmity   b. impunity   c. attribute   d. proxy

Vocabulary in Context

*Read the following passage, in which some of the words you have studied in Units 7–9 appear in **boldface** type. Then complete each statement given below the passage by circling the item that is **the same** or **almost the same** in meaning as the highlighted word.*

To Be Continued . . .

(Line)

A new literary form known as the *serial novel* developed in England around 1840. It was made famous by Charles Dickens, William Makepeace
(5) Thackeray, and a number of other writers. The stories were peopled with a lively array of characters, from **unassuming** heroes and **disarming** heroines to **predatory** villains. They
(10) were faced with realistic and heart-wrenching dilemmas. The story lines were complex, and each episode had a cliff-hanging ending that left readers hungry for more.
(15) Serial novels were usually published over a period of a year or more. Each new installment was printed as the author finished it. The serial form gave nineteenth-century
(20) novelists the freedom to make up their stories as they went along. This allowed them to take the public's reaction into account. Loyal readers vigorously **proclaimed** their views in
(25) letters to publishers and at open literary discussions.
These writers were not able to **avail themselves of** the kinds of sophisticated market research
(30) techniques that today's writers can

turn to, but they knew how to satisfy their readers. Depending on the reaction to each new episode, a writer might decide to soften a
(35) planned harsh ending or provide a long-lost wealthy relative to come to the rescue of a poor character.
Today's daily soap operas and weekly television series owe much to
(40) serial novels. An individual episode stands on its own but is also part of an ongoing saga. Viewers and readers regard recurring characters almost as members of the family.
(45) They await each new episode to see how the story will unfold.
The serial novels of Charles Dickens were enormously popular, attracting **fervent** fans on both sides
(50) of the Atlantic. In Boston, for example, thousands of readers flocked to the harbor to greet the ships that brought each new installment from London. The phrase
(55) "hot off the press" really meant something to readers eager to know what would become of the characters who had won their hearts.

---

1. The meaning of **unassuming** (line 8) is
a. boastful   c. modest
b. foolish   d. friendly

2. Disarming (line 8) most nearly means
a. alarming   c. charming
b. tearful   d. tragic

3. Predatory (line 9) is best defined as
a. rapacious   c. proud
b. snarling   d. clever

4. The meaning of **proclaimed** (line 24) is
a. declared   c. repeated
b. concealed   d. changed

5. Avail themselves of (line 28) means
a. read about   c. look up
b. make use of   d. pay for

6. Fervent (line 49) is best defined as
a. stoical   c. loyal
b. enthusiastic   d. critical

Read each sentence carefully. Then circle the item that best completes the statement below the sentence.

"Although my distinguished colleague's research clearly abuts my own," the famous archaeologist replied, "the conclusions we have drawn are very different." (2)

1. In line 1 the word **abuts** most nearly means

a. argues against   b. leans against   c. connects with   d. diverges from

Academic freedom guarantees that all views—both the conventional and the divergent—will be given a fair hearing free of outside interference. (2)

2. The best definition for the words **the divergent** in line 2 is

a. those departing from the normal   c. those going off in different directions
b. those that are mistaken   d. those differing from each other

As soon as our regulars in their scarlet jackets began to defile through the pass, the hill tribesmen of the area opened fire on them from the heights above. (2)

3. The best definition for **defile** in line 1 is

a. double-time it   b. straggle   c. thread their way   d. proceed

To shield their sensitive skin from sunburn, hippopotamuses will often use an old streambed as a wallow in which to coat themselves with a protective layer of mud. (2)

4. In line 2 the word **wallow** most nearly means

a. place to eat   b. place to roll   c. place to rest   d. place to sleep

In an upper-class Victorian kitchen, both the cooks and the menials who assisted them were usually under the direct authority of the housekeeper. (2)

5. The word **menials** in line 1 may best be defined as

a. field hands   b. scullions   c. domestic staff   d. parlormaids

Antonyms

In each of the following groups, circle the word or expression that is most nearly the **opposite** of the word in **boldface** type.

1. haggard
a. secret
b. rosy-cheeked
c. sweet
d. kind

2. unassuming
a. worn
b. arrogant
c. happy
d. steady

3. fervent
a. near
b. cool
c. lowly
d. fresh

4. renown
a. danger
b. newness
c. obscurity
d. justice

5. impunity
a. bigness
b. praise
c. acceptance
d. liability

6. predominant
a. strong
b. severe
c. secondary
d. crooked

7. perceptible
a. unprepared
b. unmerciful
c. unnoticeable
d. unintentional

8. jaunty
a. ugly
b. gloomy
c. loud
d. thin

9. exotic
a. clumsy
b. agreeable
c. familiar
d. stately

11. awry
a. lopsided
b. curved
c. straight
d. upside-down

13. belittle
a. hire
b. lower
c. enjoy
d. exaggerate

15. enmity
a. bottom
b. love
c. belief
d. top

10. excise
a. take out
b. hold up
c. go under
d. put in

12. stint
a. employ
b. attempt
c. squander
d. reveal

14. pertinent
a. tired
b. unrelated
c. abolished
d. quiet

16. stoical
a. close
b. excitable
c. distant
d. hidden

Word Families

A. On the line provided, write the word you have learned in Units 7–9 that is related to each of the following nouns.
EXAMPLE: predominance—**predominant**

1. abutment, abuttal, abutter _____

2. stoicalness, stoic, stoicism _____

3. attribution _____

4. proclaimer, proclamation _____

5. disgruntlement _____

6. tawdriness _____

7. encroacher, encroachment _____

8. penalty, penalization _____

9. endowment _____

10. aptness, aptitude _____

11. ferventness, fervency, fervor _____

12. conveyance, conveyor(-er) _____

13. predator, predation _____

14. capitulator, capitulation _____

15. nullifier, nullification _____

B. On the line provided, write the word you have learned in Units 7–9 that is related to each of the following verbs.
EXAMPLE: penalize—**penal**

16. indoctrinate _____

17. disarm _____

18. scavenge _____

19. diverge _____

20. predominate _____

Two-Word Completions

Circle the pair of words that best complete the meaning of each of the following passages.

1. During the deciding game, the challenger, a 12-year-old _____ by the name of Mikie, _____ the moves of the champion, herself a grandmaster and noted chess authority, with all the skill and expertise of an accomplished veteran.

a. prodigy . . . parried
b. crony . . . belittled

c. recluse . . . nullified
d. acme . . . fended off

2. The old adage that clothes often _____ the man simply means that a person's _____ is frequently a kind of public statement about his or her personality.

a. convey . . . renown
b. attribute . . . mien

c. defile . . . stance
d. proclaim . . . attire

3. At first, I was perfectly content to do the rather _____ tasks that my summer job involved. But as time went on, I became thoroughly _____ with such undemanding and oftentimes unpleasant assignments.

a. exotic . . . obsessed
b. unassuming . . . endowed

c. menial . . . disgruntled
d. tawdry . . . intrigued

4. Though they never seem to think alike on any subject, there isn't even the slightest hint of _____ between them. I find that somewhat surprising. Usually, two people whose views _____ so sharply dislike one another intensely.

a. juncture . . . abut
b. enmity . . . diverge

c. impunity . . . encroach
d. doctrine . . . nullify

5. For a while the politician stood high in public favor, but then his reputation suddenly _____ to earth. One day he was basking in the sunshine of popular approval; the next he found himself _____ under the yoke of universal disfavor.

a. plummeted . . . chafing
b. wavered . . . encroaching

c. parried . . . wallowing
d. belittled . . . rankling

6. A dreadful disease had reduced my friend to a pale shadow of her former self. For that reason, I did not at first recognize the _____ figure that lay in the bed before me. Indeed, it took me some time to find the happy, carefree girl that I had known in the drawn and _____ face that I was looking at.

a. cryptic . . . jaunty
b. ravaged . . . disarming

c. gaunt . . . haggard
d. stinted . . . fervent

chron—time; **cryph, crypt**—hidden, secret

Building with Classical Roots

The root **chron** appears in **crony** (page 91), "a very close friend, pal, chum." The root **cryph** or **crypt** appears in **cryptic** (page 91), "puzzling or mystifying." Some other words based on these roots are listed below.

anachronism	**chronic**	**chronological**	**synchronize**
apocryphal	**crypt**	**cryptogram**	**encrypt**

From the list of words above, choose the one that corresponds to each of the brief definitions below. Write the word in the blank space in the illustrative sentence below the definition.

1. arranged in the order of time of occurrence

A ship captain's log provides a(n) _____ record of a voyage.

2. of long duration, continuing; constant

Drought is a _____ problem in many parts of the world.

3. to convert a message into a code or cipher

Prisoners sometimes try to _____ pleas for help in their letters.

4. to occur at the same time

Pairs skaters must _____ their movements so that they execute their routines in unison.

5. something written in a code to conceal its meaning, a cipher

Army intelligence intercepted an enemy _____ .

6. something that is out of its proper time

A telephone would be a(n) _____ in a movie set in colonial times.

7. of questionable authorship or authenticity, false, counterfeit

Many tales of the exploits of Daniel Boone and Davy Crockett are probably

_____ .

8. an underground vault or chamber, often used for burial

Colorful paintings adorned the walls of the pharaoh's _____ .

From the list of words above, choose the one that best completes each of the following sentences. Write the word in the blank space provided.

1. A huge mainframe computer of the type so common in the 1960s would be a(n)

_____ in today's offices.

2. At many Fourth of July celebrations, fireworks are _____ with patriotic music.

3. A message in which the words are written backwards is probably the simplest form of _____ to decode.

4. Many people suffer from some type of _____ pain.

5. The documents in the newspaper's archives are organized by subject and filed in _____ order.

6. As time passes, more and more _____ tales attach themselves to the reputations of the rich and famous.

7. Some Beatles fans believed that secret messages were _____ in the lyrics of some of the group's songs.

8. Members of many generations may be buried in a family _____.

---

*Circle the **boldface** word that more satisfactorily completes each of the following sentences.*

1. People eventually grow tired of listening to the grievances of a (**chronological, chronic**) complainer.

2. Writers of historical fiction need to do careful research to make sure there are no (**cryptograms, anachronisms**) to mar the authenticity of their books.

3. Computer viruses (**encrypted, synchronized**) in e-mail attachments can be very destructive.

4. Most new parents keep a (**chronic, chronological**) record of their child's first year of development.

5. In one of Edgar Allan Poe's stories, noises are heard coming from a (**crypt, cryptograph**) in which a supposedly dead family member has just been interred.

6. The planners of the D-Day invasion had to (**encrypt, synchronize**) the landing of thousands of troops on the beaches of Normandy.

7. Some scholars believe that a recently discovered poem supposedly written by Shakespeare is in fact (**apocryphal, chronic**).

8. "Once I decipher this (**anachronism, cryptogram**)," said the famous detective, "I will know who committed this heinous crime."

Writer's Challenge

Read the following sentences, paying special attention to the words and phrases underlined. From the words in the box below, find better choices for these underlined words and phrases. Then use these choices to rewrite the sentences.

WORD BANK

acme	endow	jaunty	predatory	renown
attribute	enmity	mien	prodigy	stoical
convey	fervent	parry	rankle	unassuming
divergent	haggard	perceptible	recluse	unflagging

A Musical Phenomenon

1. Doctors and other scientists have long been familiar with individuals <u>furnished</u> with amazing abilities despite severe limitations in other areas of their lives.

_____

_____

2. One such <u>child with extraordinary ability or talent</u> was Thomas Greene Bethune, later known as Blind Tom Wiggins. Born to slave parents in 1849, Tom, who was totally blind, was a sickly child.

_____

_____

3. From early childhood, Tom displayed a love of sounds of all kinds, especially music. He was able to mimic any sound that was <u>capable of being grasped by the senses</u> and to play the piano with remarkable skill.

_____

_____

4. He began to play in public when he was only eight years old and continued to do so until the age of fifty-five. During this time, he gained great <u>fame and reputation and celebrity.</u>

_____

_____

5. Tom's amazing musical gift fascinated all who saw and heard him, including Mark Twain. Perhaps the <u>highest point and peak</u> of his long career was a command performance for President James Buchanan.

_____

_____

6. Experts today would most likely identify Thomas Bethune as an autistic savant. But during his lifetime, many people <u>assigned and credited</u> his musical genius to some form of divine inspiration.

_____

_____

Analogies In each of the following, circle the item that best completes the comparison.

1. belittle is to **minimize** as
a. nullify is to invalidate
b. abut is to encroach
c. venerate is to deplore
d. attire is to undress

2. perceptible is to **notice** as
a. unflagging is to waver
b. enterprising is to venture
c. plausible is to doubt
d. audible is to hear

3. relevant is to **pertinent** as
a. volatile is to explosive
b. penal is to painful
c. staid is to tawdry
d. predominant is to menial

4. nonentity is to **renown** as
a. laggard is to perspective
b. recluse is to emotion
c. prodigy is to finesse
d. plebeian is to status

5. disgruntled is to **satisfaction** as
a. aghast is to horror
b. abashed is to composure
c. audacious is to courage
d. articulate is to premonition

6. fervent is to **enthusiasm** as
a. smug is to discontent
b. unassuming is to pride
c. blasé is to boredom
d. clumsy is to finesse

7. distraught is to **anguish** as
a. predatory is to impunity
b. stoical is to enmity
c. ethical is to longevity
d. haughty is to disdain

8. task is to **menial** as
a. appearance is to frugal
b. attitude is to servile
c. mien is to jaunty
d. mood is to haggard

9. awry is to **straight** as
a. oblique is to direct
b. wanton is to bent
c. gaunt is to crooked
d. devoid is to level

10. resolute is to **waver** as
a. frivolous is to banter
b. prodigal is to stint
c. skittish is to cower
d. solicitous is to veer

Choosing the Right Meaning Read each sentence carefully. Then circle the item that best completes the statement below the sentence.

On that fervent day in the desert, the temperature rose to 120°F, and every particle of sand seemed to glow like a hot coal underfoot. (2)

1. The word **fervent** in line 1 can best be defined as
a. enthusiastic   b. scorching   c. passionate   d. earnest

So Scrooge concludes, while in the corner poor Bob Cratchit chafes his hands in a furious attempt to keep some semblance of the divine spark alive in him. (2)

2. In line 1 the word **chafes** most nearly means
a. irritates   b. torments   c. rubs   d. claps

Under the year 1229 it is recorded that Henry III conveyed the earldom of Leicester to his faithful retainer Simon de Montfort by deed of gift. (2)

3. In line 1 the word **conveyed** most nearly means

a. communicated   b. transported   c. imported   d. transferred

As I stepped from the plane, I noticed that the great metropolis was once again attired in its gloomy blanket of fog.   (2)

4. The best meaning for **attired** in line 2 is

a. shimmering   b. spruced up   c. draped   d. decked out

And just who is that elegant incognito dancing with the marquise?" Claudia inquired casually of Lestat as they sauntered through the Palais-Royal.   (2)

5. The most satisfactory definition for **incognito** in line 1 is

a. disguised   b. bearded   c. glamorous   d. clever
   person   hermit   celebrity   student

Two-Word Completions

Circle the pair of words that best complete the meaning of each of the following sentences.

1. "Like an indulgent parent, Nature has been truly _____ in the gifts with which she has _____ this part of the country," I observed.

a. indiscriminate . . . infiltrated   c. wanton . . . stinted
b. bountiful . . . endowed   d. staid . . . allotted

2. Even though he had _____ a series of crushing defeats, King Alfred steadfastly refused to _____ to the apparently unbeatable enemy.

a. parried . . . incapacitate   c. instilled . . . rehabilitate
b. proclaimed . . . pulverize   d. sustained . . . capitulate

3. The tornado had _____ the area with such devastating effect that in places whole towns had been reduced to nothing more than piles of twisted

_____ .

a. precluded . . . residue   c. ravaged . . . rubble
b. incapacitated . . . detriment   d. maimed . . . glut

4. During that unusual winter warm spell, temperatures _____ for days around the 70-degree mark, but they _____ to record-breaking lows when the next cold front passed through.

a. hovered . . . plummeted   c. mustered . . . wallowed
b. basked . . . jostled   d. evolved . . . reverted

5. On almost any day of the week, "Pops" Rafferty can be found at the local social club, swapping wisecracks with one of his _____ or engaging in a bit of good-natured _____ with a perfect stranger.

a. proxies . . . doctrine   c. cronies . . . banter
b. recluses . . . wrangling   d. apparitions . . . intrigue

Enriching Your Vocabulary

Read the passage below. Then complete the exercise at the bottom of the page.

From the Bible

Of all the books ever published, the Bible is the world's most enduring best-seller. The Bible was first written in Hebrew and then in Greek. Later it was translated into many other languages, including Latin, Coptic, and Syriac.

The first complete translation of the Bible into English was published by Miles Coverdale in 1535. Over the centuries, there have been many other English-language translations of the Old and New Testaments. The King James Version, for example, was written in the English of Shakespeare's time. In recent decades, the Bible has been translated into the English of our own time.

This Gutenburg Bible, the first book printed in movable type, belongs to the Library of Congress.

Many words and expressions that enrich the English language have biblical origins. Some words have come into the language directly from Hebrew or Greek. One such word is *seraph*, a type of angel, which comes directly from Hebrew. *Scapegoat* (Unit 6) comes from the Old Testament story of the escaped goat. In Leviticus 16:10, a high priest confesses the sins of his people over a goat, which is then allowed to escape into the desert, symbolically bearing away those sins. Someone who is the "salt of the earth" (Matthew 5:13) is worthy and honest, one of the best. A "Good Samaritan" (Luke 10:30–37) is someone who is ready to help those in distress.

In Column A below are 8 more words with biblical origins. With or without a dictionary, match each word with its meaning in Column B.

Column A

_____ **1.** manna
_____ **2.** sabbatical
_____ **3.** cherub
_____ **4.** antediluvian
_____ **5.** apocalypse
_____ **6.** jeremiad
_____ **7.** behemoth
_____ **8.** shibboleth

Column B

a. of the time before the great biblical flood; very old

b. a winged, rosy-faced angel; a person with an innocent-looking, rosy face

c. a huge, powerful animal; something of monstrous power or size

d. a recurring period of rest, originally every seven years

e. food miraculously provided to the Israelites wandering in the desert; something valuable that suddenly falls one's way

f. symbolic story of the triumph of good over evil; a revelation or prophetic disclosure

g. a password or secret phrase that distinguishes members of a group; a commonplace saying

h. a long complaint or lamentation; an angry speech

Definitions

Note carefully the spelling, pronunciation, part(s) of speech, and definition(s) of each of the following words. Then write the word in the blank space(s) in the illustrative sentence(s) following. Finally, study the lists of synonyms and antonyms given at the end of each entry.

1. accord
(ə kôrd')

(*n.*) agreement, harmony; (*v.*) to agree, be in harmony or bring into harmony; to grant, bestow on

The labor union reached an _____ with management before the midnight deadline.

The Nobel Committee _____ the Peace Prize to the Red Cross in 1917, 1944, and 1963.

SYNONYM: (*n.*) mutual understanding
ANTONYMS: (*n.*) disagreement, conflict, friction

2. barter
(bär' tər)

(*n.*) an exchange in trade; (*v.*) to exchange goods

By definition, _____ does not involve the exchange of money in any form.

According to the Bible, Esau _____ away his birthright for a hot meal.

SYNONYMS: (*v.*) trade, swap
ANTONYMS: (*v.*) sell, buy, purchase

3. curt
(kərt)

(*adj.*) short, rudely brief

Tour guides are trained to give complete and polite answers to questions, not _____ responses.

SYNONYMS: rude, brusque, terse, summary
ANTONYMS: civil, courteous, lengthy, detailed

4. devise
(di vīz')

(*v.*) to think out, plan, figure out, invent, create

The advertising agency _____ clever television commercials promoting the new car.

SYNONYMS: concoct, contrive, work out, design

5. dexterous
(dek' strəs)

(*adj.*) skillful in the use of hands or body; clever

The _____ movements of those master chefs we see on TV took years of practice to perfect.

SYNONYMS: agile, handy, deft
ANTONYMS: clumsy, awkward, ungainly

6. engross
(en grōs')

(*v.*) to occupy the complete attention, absorb fully

The exciting new film _____ every member of the audience.

SYNONYMS: immerse, preoccupy
ANTONYMS: bore, stultify, put to sleep

7. entail
(v., en tāl';
n., en' tāl)

(v.) to put a burden on, impose, require, involve; to restrict ownership of property by limiting inheritance; (n.) such a restriction

Reaching your goals will _____ both hard work and sacrifice.

By tradition, an _____ requires that our family home must pass to the eldest child.

SYNONYM: (v.) necessitate
ANTONYMS: (v.) exclude, rule out, preclude

8. ferret
(fer' ət)

(n.) a kind of weasel; (v.) to search or hunt out; to torment, badger

_____ were once used to chase rabbits and other pests from their burrows.

No matter how long it takes, we'll keep asking questions until we _____ out the true story.

SYNONYMS: (v.) track down, sniff out

9. habituate
(hə bich' ü āt)

(v.) to become used to; to cause to become used to

Rookies who quickly _____ themselves to discipline can make important contributions to a team.

SYNONYMS: acclimate, inure, get used to
ANTONYMS: deprogram, brainwash

10. impending
(im pen' diŋ)

(adj., part.) about to happen, hanging over in a menacing way

If you have studied hard, you will have no reason to worry about your _____ final exams.

SYNONYMS: imminent, upcoming
ANTONYMS: distant, remote

11. personable
(pərs' nə bəl)

(adj.) pleasing in appearance or personality, attractive

A group of very _____ and enthusiastic teens volunteered to help senior citizens with daily chores.

SYNONYMS: charming, agreeable, likable
ANTONYMS: unpleasant, disagreeable, obnoxious

12. rue
(rü)

(v.) to regret, be sorry for; (n.) a feeling of regret

It is only natural to _____ mistakes and missed opportunities.

My heart was filled with _____ when I realized how thoughtlessly I had behaved.

SYNONYMS: (v.) lament, repent
ANTONYM: (v.) cherish

13. scoff
(skäf)

(v.) to make fun of; to show contempt for

People once _____ at the notion that the use of personal computers would become widespread.

SYNONYMS: ridicule, laugh at, jeer at
ANTONYMS: take seriously, admire, revere

14. transition
(tran zish' ən)

(*n.*) a change from one state or condition

Because of a change in leadership, the country is
undergoing a period of political _____.

SYNONYMS: changeover, conversion, switch, passage

15. trepidation
(trep ə dā' shən)

(*n.*) fear, fright, trembling

Even veteran actors experience _____
just before they go on stage.

SYNONYMS: dread, anxiety, apprehension
ANTONYMS: confidence, self-assurance, poise

16. upbraid
(əp brād')

(*v.*) to blame, scold, find fault with

The police officer _____ the
driver for blocking the crosswalk.

SYNONYMS: bawl out, reprimand
ANTONYMS: praise, pat on the back

17. veritable
(ver' ə tə bəl)

(*adj.*) actual, true, real

Those dusty old boxes in my grandparents' attic contained
a _____ treasure trove of rare books
and antiques.

ANTONYMS: false, specious

18. vex
(veks)

(*v.*) to annoy, anger, exasperate; to confuse, baffle

The annual task of filling out federal and state income tax
returns _____ many people.

SYNONYMS: irritate, irk, puzzle, distress
ANTONYMS: please, delight, soothe, mollify

19. vitality
(vī tal' ə tē)

(*n.*) strength, energy, liveliness; the capacity to live and develop;
the power to endure or survive

To win a marathon, a runner must have patience, speed,
and exceptional _____.

SYNONYMS: vigor, stamina
ANTONYMS: lifelessness, torpor, lethargy

20. whimsical
(whim' zə kəl)

(*adj.*) subject to odd ideas, notions, or fancies; playful;
unpredictable

Rube Goldberg was famous for _____
drawings of wildly impractical contraptions.

SYNONYMS: odd, peculiar, quaint, fanciful
ANTONYMS: serious, sober, matter-of-fact, realistic

Completing the Sentence

From the words for this unit, choose the one that best completes each of the following sentences. Write the word in the space provided.

1. Although the salesclerk didn't seem to know the stock very well, he was so pleasant and _____ that we were very glad to have him serving us.

2. I don't expect long explanations, but why must his answers to my questions be so _____?

3. Every time I go to the dentist, she _____ me for eating things that are bad for my teeth.

4. Before you make fun of my new automatic back scratcher, remember how people _____ at Edison and the Wright brothers.

5. It is the job of a gossip columnist to _____ out the "secrets of the stars."

6. Although I have read *Peter Pan* many times, the _____ characters and imaginative story never fail to amuse me.

7. The project I am working on _____ me so thoroughly that I forgot to stop for lunch.

8. During the twentieth century, many countries in Africa and Asia made the _____ from colonial status to national independence.

9. Her early years on her family's farm _____ her to long hours and hard manual labor.

10. The _____ fingers of the great violinist were guided by his deep understanding of the music.

11. Before applying for that job, you should know that it _____ the use of a computer.

12. At a well-known theater in Virginia, playgoers could _____ various kinds of food for the price of admission.

13. The purpose of this meeting is to _____ a plan for encouraging recycling in our community.

14. You should try not to allow petty annoyances to _____ you so much.

15. One doesn't have to be a weather specialist to know that a darkening sky is a sign of a(n) _____ storm.

16. When I think of all the things that could go wrong, I view the task ahead with great _____.

17. I assure you that you will _____ the day you challenged us to a jogging contest.

18. Since the artist seems to have known everyone of importance in her time, her diaries read like a(n) _____ *Who's Who* of the period.

19. During those difficult years, the state was in the hands of a do-nothing administration completely lacking in _____ and direction.

20. The firefighters who made that daring rescue from a burning building fully deserve all the honors _____ them.

Synonyms

*Choose the word from this unit that is **the same** or **most nearly the same** in meaning as the **boldface** word or expression in the given phrase. Write the word on the line provided.*

1. nearly overcome with **dread**   _____

2. the **changeover** to daylight saving time   _____

3. could not have been more **charming**   _____

4. **lament** our long separation   _____

5. a **peculiar** sense of humor   _____

6. prepared for the **imminent** battle   _____

7. the **vigor** with which they compete   _____

8. **requires** a thorough knowledge of math   _____

9. **tracked down** the information   _____

10. persistent barking that **irritated** the neighbors _____

11. never **jeered** at my attempts to sing   _____

12. **swapped** housekeeping chores for room and board _____

13. thoroughly **acclimated** to city life   _____

14. a **true** friend in need   _____

15. **concoct** a convincing alibi   _____

Antonyms

*Choose the word from this unit that is **most nearly opposite** in meaning to the **boldface** word or expression in the given phrase. Write the word on the line provided.*

16. their **clumsy** handling of the problem   _____

17. a conversation that **bored** us both   _____

18. felt it was unnecessary to **praise** us   _____

19. **friction** among the club's members   _____

20. never expected such **courteous** treatment   _____

Choosing the Right Word

Circle the **boldface** word that more satisfactorily completes each of the following sentences.

1. Our science teacher (**engrossed, upbraided**) us when we failed to follow proper safety precautions in the lab.

2. Instead of trying to (**rue, devise**) an elaborate excuse, why not tell them frankly just what happened and hope for the best?

3. A long series of minor illnesses sapped his (**vitality, transition**), leaving him unable to work.

4. "And fools, who came to (**scoff, barter**), remained to pray."

5. Despite my best efforts, I was unable to (**habituate, ferret**) out the time and place of the meeting.

6. In spite of my (**vitality, trepidation**) about making a speech at the assembly, I actually found it a rather enjoyable experience.

7. Although we all long for world peace, we should not allow ourselves to (**barter, entail**) away our liberties to secure it.

8. Presidents need capable assistants who will shield them from minor problems that may (**vex, devise**) them.

9. Millions of people, not only in India but in all parts of the world, came to regard Gandhi as a (**veritable, dexterous**) saint.

10. The mayor warned of a(n) (**whimsical, impending**) crisis unless measures are taken immediately to conserve the city's water supply.

11. During the oil crisis of the 1970s, Americans had to (**habituate, vex**) themselves to lower indoor temperatures and decreased use of private transportation.

12. The telegram contained a(n) (**impending, curt**) message ordering me to return home as soon as possible.

13. My uncle told me that dropping out of school at an early age was a decision he has always (**rued, ferreted**).

14. I wouldn't describe our hostess as just (**personable, veritable**); I think she is a truly captivating woman.

15. You may find it hard to become (**engrossed, upbraided**) in the study of irregular verbs, but you'll have to master them if you want to learn French.

16. Representatives from many countries are meeting to try to work out some kind of (**accord, trepidation**) on reducing air pollution.

17. Good office managers must be (**dexterous, curt**) in using their powers to accomplish what they want with the least possible upset to everyone.

18. When we moved from an apartment to a house, we found that being homeowners (**entails, scoffs**) more responsibilities than we had imagined.

19. The years of adolescence mark the (**transition, accord**) from childhood to adulthood.

20. My cousin is full of (**personable, whimsical**) ideas that may not be practical but are a lot of fun to discuss.

Vocabulary in Context

Read the following passage, in which some of the words you have studied in this unit appear in **boldface** type. Then complete each statement given below the passage by circling the letter of the item that is **the same** or **almost the same** in meaning as the highlighted word.

Disappearing Data

(Line)

There are a great many ways to record and preserve data. When the digital method of storage was **devised**, people believed that their documents and memories would be preserved permanently. Unfortunately, scientists now realize that this belief was mistaken. The problem is real, and no one should **scoff** at dire predictions of data
(5) loss. That videotape of your first steps as a baby or your family's summer vacation may not last long enough to **engross** your children or grandchildren.

Many things can cause data to disappear. Tapes may eventually dry out, break, or lose their magnetic
(10) charge. Even if tapes survive, the machines on which they are played may become obsolete. Technology changes so rapidly that both the data formats and the machines
(15) needed to access the information are vulnerable. For example, documents that you saved on a 5 1/4-inch floppy disk may be lost to you when you trade in your old
(20) computer for a model that does not have the appropriate disk drive. In a high-tech lab at the National Archives

Some widely used data storage formats

in Washington, D.C., out-of-date recording machines of all types are preserved in working order. Technicians are laboring to transfer priceless information from old
(25) formats to more stable ones. However, despite great care, the **transition** from one format to another is not always perfect. Errors may creep in, making the original information unintelligible or unreliable. Long-term solutions have not yet been found.

This possibility of the **impending** loss of data **vexes** all those who want to preserve memories and information. Sooner or later, scientists will solve this
(30) problem. In the meantime, the best thing that you can do is save your valuable data in the simplest possible form.

---

1. The meaning of **devised** (line 2) is
a. rejected   c. changed
b. invented   d. spoiled

2. Scoff (line 4) most nearly means
a. tremble   c. shrug
b. cry   d. laugh

3. Engross (line 6) is best defined as
a. amuse   c. absorb
b. distract   d. annoy

4. The meaning of **transition** (line 25) is
a. conversion   c. diversion
b. repetition   d. complication

5. Impending (line 28) most nearly means
a. imminent   c. sudden
b. remote   d. complete

6. Vexes (line 28) is best defined as
a. soothes   c. bores
b. interests   d. distresses

Definitions

Note carefully the spelling, pronunciation, part(s) of speech, and definition(s) of each of the following words. Then write the word in the blank space(s) in the illustrative sentence(s) following. Finally, study the lists of synonyms and antonyms given at the end of each entry.

1. appease
(ə pēz')

(*v.*) to make calm, soothe; to relieve, satisfy; to yield to

A snack of fresh fruit should ＿＿＿＿＿＿＿＿＿＿ your hunger until mealtime.
SYNONYMS: pacify, mollify, placate, propitiate
ANTONYMS: enrage, provoke, irritate

2. belated
(bi lā' tid)

(*adj.*) late, tardy

The ＿＿＿＿＿＿＿＿＿＿ arrival of the party's guest of honor put the hosts in an awkward position.
SYNONYMS: delayed, behindhand
ANTONYMS: early, ahead of time

3. calamitous
(kə lam' it əs)

(*adj.*) causing great misfortune

In 1906, a ＿＿＿＿＿＿＿＿＿＿ earthquake and fire leveled much of the city of San Francisco.
SYNONYMS: disastrous, catastrophic, ruinous, fatal
ANTONYMS: fortunate, beneficial, salutary

4. cite
(sīt)

(*v.*) to quote; to mention; to summon to appear in court; to commend, recommend

Be sure to ＿＿＿＿＿＿＿＿＿＿ your sources when you write a research paper.
SYNONYMS: refer to, enumerate, subpoena
ANTONYMS: ignore, disregard

5. conventional
(kən ven' shə nəl)

(*adj.*) in line with accepted ideas or standards; trite

Many people have rather ＿＿＿＿＿＿＿＿＿＿ taste in clothing.
SYNONYMS: ordinary, commonplace, orthodox
ANTONYMS: outlandish, bizarre, unorthodox

6. decoy
(*v.*, di koi';
n., dē' koi)

(*v.*) to lure into a trap; (*n.*) a person or thing used to lure into a trap

The Pied Piper ＿＿＿＿＿＿＿＿＿＿ all the children away from the town of Hamelin by playing his flute.

Painted wooden ＿＿＿＿＿＿＿＿＿＿ are prized by collectors of folk art as well as by hunters.
SYNONYMS: (*v.*) entice, entrap; (*n.*) lure, bait

7. delve
(delv)

(v.) to dig; to search deeply and thoroughly into

Scholars continue to _____ into all aspects of America's Civil War.

SYNONYMS: probe, investigate

8. ensue
(en sü')

(v.) to follow in order, come immediately after and as a result

When an airplane crashes, both investigations and lawsuits can be expected to _____.

SYNONYM: result
ANTONYMS: precede, come before

9. gallantry
(gal' ən trē)

(n.) heroic courage; respect and courtesy; an act or statement marked by a high level of courtesy

The Medal of Honor is awarded by Congress to those who perform acts of "conspicuous _____" in combat.

SYNONYMS: chivalrousness, valor, daring
ANTONYMS: cowardice, boorishness

10. impart
(im pärt')

(v.) to make known, tell; to give, pass something on

All over the world, elders _____ the traditions of their culture to the younger generation.

SYNONYMS: transmit, bestow, grant
ANTONYMS: withhold, keep back, conceal

11. judicious
(jü dish' əs)

(adj.) using or showing good judgment, wise, sensible

Cautious and _____ people consider all their options before making important decisions.

SYNONYMS: thoughtful, prudent, shrewd, astute
ANTONYMS: foolish, thoughtless, ill-considered

12. mediate
(v., mē' dē āt;
adj., mē' dē ət)

(v.) to bring about an agreement between persons or groups, act as a go-between; (adj.) occupying a middle position; indirect, acting through an intermediary

A neutral third party often _____ contract talks between labor and management.

The name of the _____ star in Orion's Belt is Alnilam.

SYNONYMS: (v.) settle, arbitrate, umpire, referee

13. milieu
(mēl yü')

(n.) the setting, surroundings, environment

An authentic _____ is an essential ingredient in a good historical novel.

14. outlandish
(aut land′ ish)

(*adj.*) strange, freakish, weird, foreign-looking; out-of-the-way, geographically remote; exceeding reasonable limits

Imaginative and _____ outfits are popular attire at a costume party.

SYNONYMS: peculiar, bizarre, odd, unorthodox, unconventional
ANTONYMS: conventional, orthodox, staid, sober

15. overbearing
(ō vər bâr′ iŋ)

(*adj.*) domineering, haughty, bullying; overpowering, predominant

An _____ person has a strong need to be in charge all the time.

SYNONYMS: high-handed, overriding
ANTONYMS: meek, unassuming, self-effacing

16. pert
(pərt)

(*adj.*) high-spirited; lively; bold, saucy; jaunty

Most adults are willing to tolerate a certain amount of _____ behavior in children.

SYNONYMS: vivacious, impudent, fresh
ANTONYMS: sullen, gloomy, morose, peevish

17. quirk
(kwərk)

(*n.*) a peculiar way of acting; a sudden twist or turn

A writer may be famous for creating characters who are full of interesting _____ .

SYNONYMS: peculiarity, oddity, eccentricity

18. regale
(ri gāl′)

(*v.*) to feast, entertain agreeably

Most people are eager to _____ their friends with accounts of their vacation adventures.

SYNONYMS: amuse, divert

19. shiftless
(shift′ ləs)

(*adj.*) lazy, lacking in ambition and energy; inefficient

How can anyone lead a _____ life when there are so many interesting things to learn and to see?

SYNONYMS: careless, sloppy, lackadaisical
ANTONYMS: energetic, hardworking, ambitious

20. taint
(tānt)

(*n.*) a stain or spot; a mark of corruption or dishonor; (*v.*) to stain or contaminate

The _____ of bribery or other corrupt practices can put an end to the career of a public official.

When toxic chemicals _____ lakes and rivers, many fish and other animals die.

SYNONYMS: (*n.*) blot; (*v.*) soil, tarnish, pollute
ANTONYMS: (*v.*) purify, decontaminate, cleanse

Completing the Sentence

From the words for this unit, choose the one that best completes each of the following sentences. Write the word in the space provided.

1. Two of the youngsters acted as _____ while a third tried to swipe a few apples from the unguarded bin.

2. Having grown up in a(n) _____ where children were supposed to be "seen and not heard," my grandfather finds it hard to understand the more outspoken behavior of young people today.

3. Without trying to _____ deeply into the reasons for their conduct, just describe accurately what they did.

4. Giv..ıg up your bus seat to a pretty girl is showing off, but giving it up to a tired old lady is true _____.

5. Some people will never do the _____ thing when it is possible to behave in an unusual or shocking way.

6. When the American people learned of the bombing of Pearl Harbor in December 1941, they realized that war must _____.

7. Although I know I should have written long before now, I hope you will accept my _____ thanks for the beautiful gift you sent me.

8. In spite of all that has been reported about pollution, some people still do not grasp its _____ effects on the environment.

9. After many years of public service, she has a splendid record without the slightest _____ of wrongdoing.

10. We all know that our coach is strict, but can you _____ a single instance in which he has been unfair?

11. When we were upset and confused, it was only your _____ advice that prevented us from doing something foolish.

12. As my friend became older, the _____ in his behavior grew stranger and more difficult to deal with.

13. After our bitter quarrel, my brother tried to _____ me by offering to lend me his bicycle.

14. After seven owners had made additions to the house, all in different styles, the building looked so _____ that no one would buy it.

15. He _____ us with food, drink, and endless stories of his seafaring days.

16. I don't like listening to two people quarrel, but I like even less being the person to _____ their disagreements.

17. A good supervisor is one who can be firm and efficient without giving the impression of being _____.

18. A good teacher can give you knowledge and skills, but no teacher can _____ the wisdom that comes only with experience.

19. His devil-may-care attitude toward his job eventually earned him quite a reputation for being _____ and unreliable.

20. "In that smart new outfit, you look as _____ and stylish as a model," I said to my sister.

Synonyms

*Choose the word from this unit that is **the same** or **most nearly the same** in meaning as the **boldface** word or expression in the given phrase. Write the word on the line provided.*

1. raised in a rough-and-tumble **environment** _____

2. a **jaunty** little hat _____

3. cannot explain such **peculiar** behavior _____

4. a **lackadaisical** attitude toward studying _____

5. resent their **high-handed** attitude _____

6. a memorable show of **valor** _____

7. actions that **tarnished** the company's image _____

8. tried to **settle** arguments between neighbors _____

9. **diverted** us with jokes and silly antics _____

10. tolerant of personal **eccentricities** _____

11. did not stop to think about what might **result** _____

12. set out a **lure** to catch the thieves _____

13. **commended** the volunteers for their dedication _____

14. received a **late** invitation to the dance _____

15. **investigate** the cause of the accident _____

Antonyms

*Choose the word from this unit that is **most nearly opposite** in meaning to the **boldface** word or expression in the given phrase. Write the word on the line provided.*

16. makes **foolish** remarks _____

17. **withheld** crucial information _____

18. **unorthodox** ways of getting things done _____

19. tried to **provoke** the crowd _____

20. a series of **fortunate** events _____

Choosing the Right Word

Circle the **boldface** word that more satisfactorily completes each of the following sentences.

1. The best way to (**mediate, impart**) a spirit of patriotism to young people is to teach them about the ideals on which this nation is built.

2. The more I (**regale, delve**) into mythology, the more clearly I see how these ancient stories help us understand the basic truths of life.

3. When he finally made his (**belated, outlandish**) repayment of the money he owed me, he acted as though he was doing me a big favor.

4. Our neighbor came over this morning to (**regale, delve**) us with all the gossip that we had missed during our two-week trip.

5. The company has called in an efficiency expert to increase productivity and root out (**judicious, shiftless**) work habits.

6. Foolishly, Neville Chamberlain attempted to avoid a second world war by (**citing, appeasing**) Hitler's demands for territory in Europe.

7. By careful planning and (**belated, judicious**) investments, she greatly increased the fortune her parents had left her.

8. Instead of relying on a (**calamitous, conventional**) textbook, our social studies teacher has us using many different materials and media.

9. I am taking this step with my eyes open, and I will accept full responsibility for whatever may (**ensue, impart**).

10. Though some people believe that we should make more use of nuclear power, others insist that such a decision would be (**calamitous, pert**).

11. If you believe a story as (**outlandish, conventional**) as that, I think you will believe anything!

12. One of the chief functions of the United Nations is to (**appease, mediate**) disputes between member nations.

13. Though Benedict Arnold originally fought for the American cause, his name is forever (**tainted, ensued**) by his ultimate act of treachery.

14. Although some may consider such happenings silly fairy tales, I can (**cite, appease**) many true stories of poor young men who became president.

15. Language that seems appropriate in the (**milieu, taint**) of the locker room may be totally out of place in the classroom.

16. She is not a particularly pretty young woman, but her high spirits and (**overbearing, pert**) personality make her very attractive.

17. As every baseball player knows, a knuckleball is extremely hard to hit because its flight is full of unexpected (**quirks, milieus**) called *breaks*.

18. We will not allow ourselves to be (**decoyed, imparted**) into supporting candidates who try to mislead the voters.

19. In debate she has the (**overbearing, shiftless**) manner of one who believes firmly that she is never wrong.

20. Whatever his later failures, let us remember that he won the nation's highest military decoration for (**gallantry, decoy**) in action.

Read the following passage, in which some of the words you have studied in this unit appear in **boldface** type. Then complete each statement given below the passage by circling the letter of the item that is **the same** or **almost the same** in meaning as the highlighted word.

An American Tragedy

(Line)

History is full of **calamitous** events. Some of these events are caused by nature; others are caused by human actions. The flood that destroyed much of Johnstown, Pennsylvania, in 1889 was caused by a combination of nature's fury and human failure.

The South Fork Dam, located 14 miles above Johnstown, was built in the early 1800s to block the Conemaugh River for a reservoir. A **judicious** plan for the maintenance of the enormous earth-filled dam was never formulated. The dam (5)

began to weaken even before the reservoir was full. Repairs were inadequate.

In 1879, a developer purchased the (10) dam, the lake, and the surrounding land. The property was turned into the South Fork Fishing and Hunting Club, a private resort for the wealthy. Little attention was given to the worsening (15) condition of the dam.

In the spring of 1889, extremely heavy snows and rains put an enormous strain on the dam. The club's managing engineers spotted (20) problems, but their **belated** attempt to shore up the dam failed. At 3:10 on

Buildings devastated by fire and flood

the afternoon of May 31, the dam gave way with a thunderous roar. Tons of water swept down the valley into Johnstown in a towering, unstoppable wave. As the flood roared through the town, debris and bodies piled up at the Stoneycreek (25) Bridge. Railcars filled with chemicals ignited, and a terrible fire **ensued**.

Despite the **gallantry** of hundreds of horrified volunteers who tried to pull victims from the water, 2,209 people died. Clara Barton herself led the relief work of a team from the American Red Cross. It took five years for the stunned survivors to rebuild their city and their lives. (30)

---

1. The meaning of **calamitous** (line 1) is
a. memorable   c. catastrophic
b. infamous   d. beneficial

2. Judicious (line 5) most nearly means
a. prudent   c. costly
b. detailed   d. foolish

3. Belated (line 21) is best defined as
a. clumsy   c. prompt
b. early   d. tardy

4. The meaning of **ensued** (line 26) is
a. raged   c. started
b. resulted   d. preceded

5. Gallantry (line 27) most nearly means
a. daring   c. cowardice
b. folly   d. effort

Definitions

Note carefully the spelling, pronunciation, part(s) of speech, and definition(s) of each of the following words. Then write the word in the blank space(s) in the illustrative sentence(s) following. Finally, study the lists of synonyms and antonyms given at the end of each entry.

1. abdicate
(ab′ də kāt)

(*v.*) to resign, formally give up an office or a duty; to disown, discard

Of all England's monarchs, Edward VIII was the only one to _____ the throne voluntarily.

SYNONYMS: step down, relinquish, renounce
ANTONYM: retain

2. bestow
(bi stō′)

(*v.*) to give as a gift; to provide with lodgings

The nation will _____ its highest civilian honor on the noted educator.

SYNONYMS: grant, confer, lodge, put up
ANTONYMS: receive, take, take back, take away

3. capacious
(kə pā′ shəs)

(*adj.*) able to hold much, roomy

Whenever I go beach-combing, I take along a backpack with _____ compartments and pockets.

SYNONYMS: spacious, commodious
ANTONYMS: cramped, confined, restricted, narrow

4. caustic
(kô′ stik)

(*adj.*) able to burn or eat away by chemical action; biting, sarcastic

All _____ household liquids, such as drain cleaners, must be kept out of the reach of children.

SYNONYMS: burning, corrosive, sharp
ANTONYMS: bland, mild, sugary, saccharine

5. crusade
(krü sād′)

(*n.*) a strong movement to advance a cause or idea; (*v.*) to campaign, work vigorously

Rachel Carson's landmark book *Silent Spring* sparked the _____ to ban the use of DDT.

The people who _____ for civil rights in America during the 1960s came from all walks of life.

SYNONYMS: (*n.*) campaign, organized movement

6. deface
(di fās′)

(*v.*) to injure or destroy the surface or appearance of; to damage the value, influence, or effect of; to face down, outshine

In many towns, those who _____ walls with graffiti must pay a fine and clean up the mess.

SYNONYMS: mar, disfigure
ANTONYMS: repair, restore, renovate, recondition

7. embargo
(em bär′ gō)

(*n.*) an order forbidding the trade in or movement of commercial goods; any restraint or hindrance; (*v.*) to forbid to enter or leave port; to forbid trade with

The U.S. Congress may impose an _____ against a country that violates trade agreements.

In wartime, the president may _____ goods from countries that trade with the nation's enemies.

SYNONYMS: (*n.*) stoppage, ban, boycott

8. fallacy
(fal′ ə sē)

(*n.*) a false notion or belief; an error in thinking

Reviewers cited several major _____ in the controversial author's newest book.

SYNONYM: misconception
ANTONYMS: sound reasoning, logic

9. levity
(lev′ ə tē)

(*n.*) a lack of seriousness or earnestness, especially about things that should be treated with respect; buoyancy, lightness in weight

A bit of _____ may help you to cope with difficult people or situations.

SYNONYMS: giddiness, flippancy, frivolity, fickleness
ANTONYMS: seriousness, humorlessness, solemnity

10. mendicant
(men′ də kənt)

(*n.*) beggar; (*adj.*) depending on begging for a living

People who have fallen on hard times may have no choice but to become _____ .

_____ friars roamed the streets of medieval towns and cities, asking for coins.

SYNONYM: (*n.*) panhandler
ANTONYMS: (*n.*) millionaire, philanthropist

11. nauseate
(nô′ zē āt)

(*v.*) to make sick to the stomach; to fill with disgust

The fumes that _____ everyone in the building were traced to a faulty heating system.

SYNONYMS: sicken, disgust
ANTONYMS: delight, tickle pink

12. negate
(ni gāt′)

(*v.*) to nullify, deny, bring to nothing

One offensive remark may well _____ the goodwill a politician has built up among voters.

SYNONYMS: cancel, invalidate, annul
ANTONYMS: affirm, confirm, corroborate, buttress

13. pivotal
(piv′ ət əl)

(*adj.*) vitally important, essential

The D day invasion was _____ to the Allies' eventual victory in Europe in World War II.

SYNONYMS: crucial, critical, decisive, seminal
ANTONYMS: unimportant, insignificant

14. recipient
(ri sip′ ē ənt)

(*n.*) one who receives; (*adj.*) receiving; able or willing to receive

The first American _____ of the Nobel Prize for literature was the novelist Sinclair Lewis.

A long list of _____ charities may benefit from a wealthy individual's generosity.

SYNONYMS: (*n.*) receiver, beneficiary
ANTONYMS: (*n.*) donor, benefactor, contributor

15. ruse
(rüz)

(*n.*) an action designed to confuse or mislead, a trick

Thieves employ a variety of _____ to gain entrance to homes and apartments.

SYNONYMS: stratagem, subterfuge, dodge

16. teem
(tēm)

(*v.*) to become filled to overflowing; to be present in large quantities

Our national parks _____ with visitors during the summer months.

SYNONYMS: abound, swarm, overflow
ANTONYMS: lack, be wanting

17. tenet
(ten′ ət)

(*n.*) an opinion, belief, or principle held to be true

One of the primary _____ of medicine is to do no harm to the sick and injured.

SYNONYMS: doctrine, precept

18. tractable
(trak′ tə bəl)

(*adj.*) easily managed, easy to deal with; easily wrought, malleable

A _____ colleague is preferable to one who is unwilling to cooperate or compromise.

SYNONYMS: submissive, docile, yielding, amenable
ANTONYMS: unruly, obstreperous, refractory

19. ungainly
(ən gān′ lē)

(*adj.*) clumsy, awkward; unwieldy

The first time I tried to ice-skate, my movements were hesitant and _____.

SYNONYM: graceless
ANTONYMS: nimble, agile, supple, graceful

20. voracious
(vô rā′ shəs)

(*adj.*) having a huge appetite, greedy, ravenous; excessively eager

Newly hatched caterpillars are _____ eaters of leafy green plants.

SYNONYMS: gluttonous, insatiable, avid
ANTONYMS: indifferent, apathetic

Completing the Sentence

From the words for this unit, choose the one that best completes each of the following sentences. Write the word in the space provided.

1. It was not hard for his opponents to shoot holes in his argument because the
_____ it contained were as plain as day.

2. I have never seen a car with a trunk _____ enough to hold all the
luggage you want to take on any trip.

3. The president placed a(n) _____ on the sale of arms to the two
nations at war.

4. A ruler who has lost the support of the people may choose to _____
and live in exile.

5. The horse was often hard to manage, but he was _____ as long
as he was headed in the direction of the barn.

6. Your attempts at _____ during the most serious moments of the
dedication ceremony were decidedly out of place.

7. Whenever I pass a group of homeless _____ huddled in a doorway,
I give them my spare change.

8. San Francisco is a city that _____ with color and places of
historical interest.

9. Dad said that he liked the fig-banana pie I had concocted, but the funny look on his
face as he tasted it _____ his words.

10. If any of the _____ substance gets on your clothing, wash it off
with lukewarm water to prevent it from eating away the fabric.

11. Early in this century, reform-minded journalists called *muckrakers* _____
vigorously against corruption in government.

12. Don't expect a wealthy old lady to _____ a fortune on you for
helping her across the street, particularly if she doesn't want to cross it.

13. She is such a(n) _____ reader that she often has a book propped
up in front of her while she is eating.

14. A fundamental _____ of democracy is that all people are equal
before the law.

15. Although seals and sea lions are _____ on land, they are extremely
graceful in the water.

16. Though a number of people may be nominated for a particular Oscar each year,
usually only one of them is the actual _____ of it.

17. The noise in the crowded train station gave me a headache, and the foul odor
_____ me.

18. For thousands of years, thoughtless tourists have _____ monuments of the past by writing or carving their initials on them.

19. Since the Greeks could not capture Troy by force, they resorted to the celebrated _____ of the wooden horse to take the city.

20. Our hard-fought victory over South High was the _____ game of the season because it gave us the self-confidence we needed to win the championship.

Synonyms

*Choose the word from this unit that is **the same** or **most nearly the same** in meaning as the **boldface** word or expression in the given phrase. Write the word on the line provided.*

1. a **doctrine** that we live by   _____

2. acts of cruelty that **sickened** us all   _____

3. possesses a **biting** wit   _____

4. the **campaign** to end poverty   _____

5. had good reason to **cancel** the agreement   _____

6. a group of ragged **beggars**   _____

7. **bans** on counterfeit designer goods   _____

8. the oldest **trick** in the book   _____

9. a theory based entirely on **misconceptions**   _____

10. their **insatiable** thirst for knowledge   _____

11. took a series of **awkward** steps   _____

12. a **crucial** moment in the nation's history   _____

13. sole **beneficiary** of a sizable fortune   _____

14. forced to **step down**   _____

15. a place that **swarms** with insects   _____

Antonyms

*Choose the word from this unit that is **most nearly opposite** in meaning to the **boldface** word or expression in the given phrase. Write the word on the line provided.*

16. surprised by the **seriousness** of your remarks   _____

17. a thoroughly **unruly** individual   _____

18. housed in **cramped** quarters   _____

19. **repaired** the priceless antique   _____

20. **received** many special favors and privileges   _____

Choosing the Right Word

Circle the **boldface** word that more satisfactorily completes each of the following sentences.

1. The fact that she is not a member of the Board of Education does not (**negate, abdicate**) her criticisms of the school system.

2. I am willing to become a veritable (**mendicant, recipient**) in order to raise money for that most worthy cause.

3. One guiding (**levity, tenet**) of our energy program is that it is just as important to avoid wasting energy as it is to increase its production.

4. The tall boy who appeared so (**ungainly, caustic**) as he walked through the school corridors was agile and coordinated on the basketball court.

5. It is a (**fallacy, tenet**) to say that because no woman has ever been elected president, no woman is qualified to serve in that office.

6. Although the students made jokes about the coming exams, we knew that beneath the (**levity, ruse**) they were quite worried.

7. When the United States gives out foreign aid, are the (**pivotal, recipient**) nations supposed to make repayment?

8. She is a very severe critic, and the (**capacious, caustic**) comments in her reviews have made her many enemies.

9. As soon as the new highway extension was built, the sleepy town began to (**teem, bestow**) with activity.

10. She has the kind of (**capacious, voracious**) mind that seems able to hold endless information and ideas on any subject.

11. Weather and pollution had so (**defaced, nauseated**) the statue that its original expression was no longer distinguishable.

12. We will not allow you to (**embargo, abdicate**) your responsibilities as a leading citizen of this community.

13. "All that I have to (**negate, bestow**) on you," said the elderly father to his son, "is an honorable family name."

14. Instead of launching a great (**crusade, fallacy**) to save the world, why not try to help a few people in your own neighborhood?

15. Although the play is named *Julius Caesar*, I think that the (**pivotal, ungainly**) character, on whom all the action depends, is Mark Antony.

16. It's good to be open to new ideas, but don't try to become so (**mendicant, tractable**) that you have no firm opinions of your own.

17. His mind is closed, as though he had placed a(n) (**embargo, crusade**) on new information and ideas.

18. Has anyone ever measured how many hours of TV time are needed to satisfy a small child's (**voracious, tractable**) appetite for cartoons?

19. A favorite bedtime (**ruse, tenet**) of small children is to keep asking for a glass of water to delay having to go to sleep.

20. I can forgive most human weaknesses, but I am (**nauseated, defaced**) by hypocrisy.

Vocabulary in Context

*Read the following passage, in which some of the words you have studied in this unit appear in **boldface** type. Then complete each statement given below the passage by circling the letter of the item that is **the same** or **almost the same** in meaning as the highlighted word.*

Playing It Again

(Line)

"So, Mom, now that we've loaded that **ungainly** old jukebox into the back of the van, where are we taking it?" I asked.

"The lucky **recipient** is going to be the Musical Museum in Deansboro. That's in upstate New York, near Utica," Mom answered.

(5) "Musical Museum? You know I love music," I said. "But what fun is looking at a bunch of antique instruments locked away in display cases? And besides, this old piece of junk doesn't even work anymore."

"I expect that they'll be able to fix it," replied Mom.

(10) "This isn't a stuffy, formal museum. It **teems** with odd instruments and mechanical music-making devices. Most have been repaired and restored so that interested visitors can actually play them."

"Yeah, right," I said with a **caustic** tone. "I suppose

(15) people just waltz into the place, grab an instrument, and start making beautiful music, just like that." I snapped my fingers in the air.

"Just about! Most of the items in the collection are automatic instruments that work with the help of

(20) gears, motors, magnets, and switches. They play themselves," said Mom. "The Musical Museum was originally a local man's collection of unusual contraptions that make music. He was a **voracious** collector, and soon his house was filled to overflowing

(25) with musical gizmos. Eventually, he found a space **capacious** enough to hold his growing collection. Today, the museum has seventeen rooms devoted to the display of music boxes, jukeboxes, melodeons and harmoniums, old record players, player pianos,

(30) and other devices. I think you'll really like it."

Classic "dometop" jukebox

"So—hit the road, Jack!" I sang, grinning broadly.

Mom was delighted. "Ah, that's music to my ears," she said.

1. The meaning of **ungainly** (line 1) is
a. unwieldy
b. colorful
c. battered
d. costly

2. Recipient (line 3) mostly nearly means
a. donor
b. owner
c. customer
d. receiver

3. Teems (line 10) is best defined as
a. plays
b. sings
c. overflows
d. starts

4. Caustic (line 14) most nearly means
a. sugary
b. sarcastic
c. solemn
d. silly

5. Voracious (line 23) most nearly means
a. avid
b. dedicated
c. occasional
d. smart

6. Capacious (line 26) is best defined as
a. narrow
b. sunny
c. inexpensive
d. roomy

Analogies

In each of the following, circle the item that best completes the comparison.

1. judicious is to **favorable** as
a. capacious is to unfavorable
b. ungainly is to favorable
c. curt is to unfavorable
d. caustic is to favorable

2. teeming is to **quantity** as
a. gigantic is to size
b. overbearing is to manner
c. abundant is to position
d. belated is to time

3. quirk is to **eccentric** as
a. fallacy is to erroneous
b. thimble is to capacious
c. comment is to caustic
d. transition is to impending

4. mule is to **tractable** as
a. fox is to sly
b. mouse is to meek
c. ox is to intelligent
d. otter is to aquatic

5. ungainly is to **handle** as
a. deaf is to hear
b. tractable is to control
c. veritable is to believe
d. dim is to see

6. overbearing is to **unfavorable** as
a. personable is to favorable
b. whimsical is to unfavorable
c. shiftless is to favorable
d. tractable is to unfavorable

7. scoff is to **contempt** as
a. engross is to vulgarity
b. mediate is to anger
c. negate is to levity
d. rue is to sorrow

8. milieu is to **setting** as
a. beaver is to ferret
b. accord is to friction
c. tenet is to belief
d. appetite is to voracity

9. shovel is to **delve** as
a. cup is to pour
b. water is to boil
c. knife is to cut
d. kitchen is to cook

10. mendicant is to **beg** as
a. recipient is to bestow
b. librarian is to borrow
c. deserter is to crusade
d. host is to regale

11. juggler is to **dexterous** as
a. coward is to gallant
b. spy is to devious
c. diplomat is to curt
d. banker is to financial

12. hunter is to **decoy** as
a. inventor is to device
b. magician is to ruse
c. policeman is to traffic
d. trader is to embargo

13. donor is to **bestow** as
a. believer is to scoff
b. teacher is to impart
c. judge is to ensue
d. thief is to barter

14. hero is to **gallantry** as
a. bully is to transition
b. recipient is to vitality
c. mendicant is to levity
d. coward is to trepidation

15. personable is to **charm** as
a. overbearing is to wealth
b. judicious is to foolishness
c. pert is to trepidation
d. energetic is to vitality

16. disaster is to **calamitous** as
a. ruse is to veritable
b. quirk is to peculiar
c. fallacy is to correct
d. crusade is to pert

17. ensue is to **after** as
a. precede is to before
b. entail is to after
c. impend is to after
d. engross is to before

18. king is to **abdicate** as
a. president is to resign
b. author is to cite
c. salesclerk is to barter
d. employee is to dismiss

Word Associations

In each of the following groups, circle the word that is best defined or suggested by the given phrase.

1. a blot on a once-promising political career
a. crusade   b. embargo   c. fallacy   d. taint

2. "I don't like his sarcastic, critical remarks."
a. conventional   b. calamitous   c. caustic   d. pivotal

3. scolded them for their rude behavior
a. entailed   b. cited   c. decoyed   d. upbraided

4. "If you will mow my lawn, I'll wash your car."
a. mediate   b. regale   c. barter   d. impart

5. cut off trade with certain nations
a. barter   b. devise   c. embargo   d. abdicate

6. final exams coming up next week
a. pivotal   b. calamitous   c. belated   d. impending

7. "You are a true friend in need."
a. dexterous   b. caustic   c. veritable   d. pivotal

8. constantly cracking your knuckles or pulling your ear
a. taint   b. gallantry   c. quirk   d. ruse

9. saucy in a cute, winning way
a. overbearing   b. pert   c. curt   d. tractable

10. reached an agreement on the limitation of nuclear arms
a. embargo   b. accord   c. decoy   d. fallacy

11. cleverly misled the enemy into thinking we were about to retreat
a. crusade   b. ruse   c. quirk   d. embargo

12. a book that fully absorbs my attention
a. entail   b. engross   c. appease   d. abdicate

13. the principle of separation of powers in government
a. tenet   b. milieu   c. fallacy   d. recipient

14. helped to settle the quarrel between two people
a. mediate   b. negate   c. vex   d. upbraid

15. concoct an excuse for not attending a meeting
a. negate   b. devise   c. delve   d. rue

16. like a supertanker or a jumbo jet
a. personable   b. capacious   c. outlandish   d. shiftless

17. known for her playful humor
a. judicious   b. dexterous   c. caustic   d. whimsical

18. the gradual change from a rural to an urban nation
a. transition   b. gallantry   c. taint   d. ruse

19. spring floods following the quick melting of heavy snows
a. ensue   b. entail   c. engross   d. embargo

20. organized a great national effort to find a cure for cancer
a. trepidation   b. crusade   c. taint   d. accord

Vocabulary in Context

*Read the following passage, in which some of the words you have studied in Units 10–12 appear in **boldface** type. Then complete each statement given below the passage by circling the item that is **the same** or **almost the same** in meaning as the highlighted word.*

A Theatrical Spectacle

(Line)

About 400 years ago, a spectacular type of theater developed in the ancient Japanese capital city of Kyoto. It is called *Kabuki*, from the
(5) words *ka*, which means "song"; *bu*, which means "dance"; and *ki*, which means "skill." Kabuki actors must excel in all these arts. They undergo many years of rigorous
(10) training that usually begins when they are small children.

Over the centuries, Kabuki has developed into a highly stylized art form that **regales** audiences with
(15) an exciting blend of song, dance, speech, and mime. With its gorgeous costumes and spectacular stage effects, Kabuki is a **veritable** feast for the eyes and ears.
(20) The inventor of Kabuki was a shrine attendant named Okuni. She began by performing her plays, which were based on Buddhist themes, in Kyoto's dry riverbeds. Okuni recruited other
(25) women performers, and their dance plays quickly became very popular. However, the government considered it improper for women to take part in theatrical performances. In 1629, it
(30) banned women from the stage. Since then, the performers in Kabuki have all been men.

Kabuki was the first Japanese theater art that was designed to
(35) appeal to the common people, rather than the royal court or the warrior class (the samurai). As the merchant class and farmers grew more prosperous during the seventeenth century,
(40) Kabuki's popularity increased.

The plays performed by Kabuki troupes include historical sagas, love stories, ghost stories, and tales of domestic tragedy. Comic interludes
(45) that portray the foolish **quirks** of human nature are interspersed to add a note of **levity** to the program. And while the plays are intended to entertain, they also **impart** moral
(50) lessons. The virtuous are rewarded, and the wicked are punished.

Though Kabuki is hundreds of years old, it is not a dusty relic. It retains tremendous **vitality** and
(55) continues to delight audiences wherever it is performed.

---

1. The meaning of **regales** (line 14) is
a. bores
b. entertains
c. pacifies
d. annoys

2. Veritable (line 18) most nearly means
a. tawdry
b. specious
c. meager
d. true

3. Quirks (line 45) is best defined as
a. oddities
b. faults
c. fantasies
d. sorrows

4. The meaning of **levity** (line 47) is
a. solemnity
b. frivolity
c. piety
d. sanity

5. Impart (line 49) most nearly means
a. transmit
b. repeat
c. conceal
d. ignore

6. Vitality (line 54) is best defined as
a. timeliness
b. seriousness
c. conflict
d. liveliness

Choosing the Right Meaning

Read each sentence carefully. Then circle the item that best completes the statement below the sentence.

After the successful defense of Rorke's Drift, eleven members of the Twenty-Fourth Regiment were cited for gallantry and received the Victoria Cross. (2)

1. In line 2 the word **cited** is best defined as

a. commended   b. subpoenaed   c. quoted   d. summoned

"This holy [time] of Christmas
All others doth deface." ("God Rest Ye Merry, Gentlemen") (2)

2. The best meaning for the word **deface** in line 2 is

a. mar   b. outshine   c. disfigure   d. erase

In Europe the use of the ferret to drive rats and other kinds of vermin out of their underground burrows has been practiced since Roman times. (2)

3. The best meaning for **ferret** in line 1 is

a. bird dog   b. weasel   c. badger   d. nettle

Though the Misses Bennet were indeed their father's daughters, they did not come into his landed property because, centuries before, inheriting it had been entailed on the male line. (2)

4. In line 3 the phrase **entailed on** most nearly means

a. required of   b. involved with   c. restricted to   d. necessitated by

"Time doth transfix the flourish set on youth
And delves the parallels in beauty's brow."
(Shakespeare, Sonnet 60, 9–10) (2)

5. The word **delves** in line 2 most nearly means

a. investigates   b. searches out   c. ransacks   d. digs

Antonyms

In each of the following groups, circle the word or expression that is most nearly the **opposite** of the word in **boldface** type.

1. nauseate
a. try
b. mislead
c. please
d. begin

2. veritable
a. cute
b. false
c. late
d. small

3. personable
a. unattractive
b. unreasonable
c. direct
d. beautiful

4. fallacy
a. success
b. danger
c. truth
d. height

5. levity
a. simplicity
b. sarcasm
c. commonness
d. seriousness

6. tractable
a. clumsy
b. stubborn
c. slow
d. sharp

7. negate
a. remove
b. affirm
c. aid
d. deny

8. shiftless
a. successful
b. overdressed
c. thoughtful
d. hardworking

9. caustic
a. saccharine
b. secondary
c. unkind
d. slow

11. vex
a. play
b. charm
c. give
d. know

13. cite
a. oppose
b. join
c. hear
d. fail to mention

15. ungainly
a. odd
b. serious
c. clean
d. graceful

10. trepidation
a. importance
b. confidence
c. end
d. answer

12. recipient
a. doubter
b. giver
c. runner
d. seeker

14. taint
a. find
b. attack
c. cleanse
d. return

16. engross
a. divide
b. bore
c. remove
d. depart

Word Families

A. *On the line provided, write the word you have learned in Units 10–12 that is related to each of the following nouns.*
EXAMPLE: pivot—**pivotal**

1. judiciousness _____

2. vexation, vexatiousness _____

3. citation _____

4. dexterousness, dexterity _____

5. habituation, habit, habitude _____

6. conventionality, convention _____

7. calamitousness, calamity _____

8. capaciousness, capacity _____

9. nausea, nauseousness _____

10. abdicator, abdication _____

11. voraciousness, voracity _____

12. negator, negation, negative, negativeness, negativity _____

13. whimsicalness, whim, whimsy, whimsicality _____

14. bestowal, bestowment, bestower _____

15. appeasement, appeaser _____

B. *On the line provided, write the word you have learned in Units 10–12 that is related to each of the following verbs.*
EXAMPLE: rue—**rueful**

16. overbear _____

17. receive _____

18. pivot _____

19. impend _____

20. vitalize _____

Two-Word Completions

Circle the pair of words that best complete the meaning of each of the following passages.

1. Long overdue though it surely was, his _____ apology was sufficient to soothe my ruffled feelings and _____ my anger.

a. belated . . . appease
b. dexterous . . . vex
c. curt . . . negate
d. caustic . . . mediate

2. Despite the _____ of a few brave men, whose daring deeds on that fateful day are still remembered by history, imperial Rome suffered a(n) _____ defeat that brought a once-mighty empire to its knees.

a. trepidation . . . veritable
b. gallantry . . . calamitous
c. vitality . . . whimsical
d. dexterity . . . impending

3. "My ability to hold on to this job will pretty much depend on the answer to one _____ question," I thought. "Will I prove to be truly hardworking and reliable, or _____ and irresponsible?"

a. pivotal . . . shiftless
b. whimsical . . . personable
c. impending . . . tractable
d. caustic . . . dexterous

4. "That rock group's strange antics, _____ costumes, and weird songs don't really impress me," Clara remarked. "Frankly, I prefer musicians who are much more _____."

a. caustic . . . whimsical
b. pert . . . overbearing
c. bartered . . . tainted
d. outlandish . . . conventional

5. "I certainly don't view the upcoming scholarship examination with any _____," I asserted confidently. "Still, it's a serious matter, and I'm not treating it with undue _____ either."

a. gallantry . . . vitality
b. nausea . . . dexterity
c. curtness . . . vexation
d. trepidation . . . levity

6. The speaker did not _____ many examples to back up her argument, but those that she did provide were extremely well chosen. A larger but less _____ selection of illustrations probably would not have made such a powerful impression on the audience.

a. devise . . . ungainly
b. impart . . . outlandish
c. cite . . . judicious
d. bestow . . . capacious

7. "Though I'd spent all my life in a rural environment, I didn't think I'd have any trouble adjusting to city life," Ted said to his friend. "But making the _____ to an urban _____ proved to be much more difficult than I had imagined."

a. crusade . . . recipient
b. tenet . . . embargo
c. transition . . . milieu
d. ruse . . . tenet

Building with Classical Roots

ven, vent—to come

This root appears in **conventional** (page 124). Literally, the word means "referring to or resulting from a coming together." It now has the meaning "customary, familiar, lacking in originality." Some other words based on the same root are listed below.

circumvent	eventful	intervene	revenue
convene	eventual	inventive	venue

From the list of words above, choose the one that corresponds to each of the brief definitions below. Write the word in the blank space in the illustrative sentence below the definition.

1. happening at an unspecified time in the future, ultimate

If you stick to an exercise program, you will see _____ improvement in your strength and fitness.

2. to get around or avoid; to defeat, overcome

The pilot was able to _____ the storm by flying farther west.

3. to assemble, come together; to call together

The new book discussion group plans to _____ once a month.

4. full of events or incidents; important

Someone who has led a very _____ life may decide to write an autobiography.

5. the place where a crime or cause of legal action occurs; a locality from which a jury is called and in which a trial is held; the scene or locale of any action or event

A defense attorney may sometimes request a change of _____ in order to assure a client a fair trial.

6. to come between; to enter to help settle a dispute

I refuse to _____ in their argument because I do not want to take sides.

7. income; the income of a government; the yield from property or investment

_____ from the new product line has exceeded the company's expectations.

8. good at making or thinking up new ideas or things; imaginative

The notebooks of Leonardo da Vinci contain abundant evidence of his remarkably inquisitive and _____ intellect.

From the list of words above, choose the one that best completes each of the following sentences. Write the word in the space provided.

1. The _____ she receives from her investments is not sufficient to support her taste for luxury.

2. His "big news" was about nothing more _____ than catching a five-pound bluefish.

3. I am positive that your _____ mind will come up with something more interesting than a better kind of mousetrap.

4. The coaches _____ before the battling players could seriously hurt one another.

5. Unfortunately, there will always be people who will try to _____ rules and laws.

6. I cannot accept the theory that predicts the _____ end of all life on Earth.

7. The mayor quickly ordered all department heads to _____ in the conference room to prepare for the expected emergency.

8. The _____ of the political gathering was carefully chosen to guarantee a friendly audience for the candidate.

---

*Circle the **boldface** word that more satisfactorily completes each of the following sentences.*

1. The (**venue, revenue**) generated by the tax increase will be used to build new schools.

2. If we put our minds to the task, we will find (**inventive, eventual**) solutions to long-standing problems.

3. Each year, the Supreme Court (**circumvents, convenes**) to begin its new term on the first Monday in October.

4. The doctor is confident of the patient's (**eventual, eventful**) recovery from her long illness.

5. We have remained friends since childhood despite the years that have (**intervened, convened**) and the long distances that have separated us.

6. There is some uncertainty about the appropriate (**revenue, venue**) in which to present the concert.

7. The children were tired after an (**eventful, inventive**) day at the amusement park.

8. The resourceful commander used a combination of skill and daring to (**intervene, circumvent**) the enemy.

Read the following sentences, paying special attention to the words and phrases underlined. From the words in the box below, find better choices for these underlined words and phrases. Then use these choices to rewrite the sentences.

WORD BANK

accord	deface	habituate	quirk	transition
calamitous	delve	impart	scoff	trepidation
cite	fallacy	milieu	shiftless	vex
conventional	gallantry	outlandish	teem	whimsical

Jackal Myths, Jackal Reality

1. The lands of ancient Egypt <u>became filled to overflowing</u> with jackals. Thus, it is not surprising that the jackal figures prominently in Egyptian mythology and art.

_____

_____

2. Anubis, the Egyptian god of the dead, is portrayed as having the head of a jackal. Anubis guided the dead in their <u>changeover or switch</u> into the next world, where their souls would be judged.

_____

_____

3. Throughout history, many have viewed jackals with <u>fear and trembling</u>.

_____

_____

4. Some cultures have associated jackals with <u>really bad</u> events, probably because of their skulking movements and their eerie howls, yelps, and yips.

_____

_____

5. But it is a <u>false notion or belief</u> to associate jackals with catastrophes.

_____

_____

6. Scientists who <u>search deeply and thoroughly</u> into the behavior of jackals in the wild recognize that these noisy scavengers are also clever, cooperative hunters.

_____

_____

7. Experts have discovered that the members of jackal family groups live together in remarkable <u>mutual understanding</u>. This greatly enhances their ability to adapt to changing environments.

_____

_____

Analogies

In each of the following, circle the item that best completes the comparison.

1. willful is to **tractable** as
a. prone is to apt
b. voracious is to retentive
c. staid is to outlandish
d. whimsical is to frivolous

2. shiftless is to **enterprising** as
a. wavering is to unflagging
b. pertinent is to relevant
c. gingerly is to ungainly
d. ample is to bountiful

3. capacious is to **room** as
a. oblique is to direction
b. laggard is to time
c. prodigious is to size
d. jaunty is to attitude

4. wrangle is to **accord** as
a. ostracize is to favor
b. vie is to rivalry
c. comply is to agreement
d. collaborate is to competition

5. chain is to **tether** as
a. ladder is to grope
b. feather is to pulverize
c. spade is to delve
d. screwdriver is to grapple

6. taint is to **defile** as
a. qualm is to hesitate
b. defect is to repair
c. quirk is to habituate
d. detriment is to harm

7. plausible is to **scoff at** as
a. commendable is to upbraid
b. perceptible is to observe
c. audible is to hear
d. durable is to wear

8. sequel is to **ensue** as
a. prologue is to precede
b. preface is to follow
c. aftermath is to introduce
d. finale is to impend

9. scavenger is to **ferret** as
a. recipient is to endow
b. mendicant is to beg
c. scapegoat is to preclude
d. turncoat is to ravage

10. tenet is to **doctrine** as
a. banter is to rubble
b. repercussion is to backlash
c. anguish is to intrigue
d. crony is to enemy

Choosing the Right Meaning

Read each sentence carefully. Then circle the item that best completes the statement below the sentence.

The levity of some gases in respect to air ideally suits them to use in dirigibles, weather balloons, and other such devices. (2)

1. The word **levity** in line 1 most nearly means
a. fickleness   b. lightness   c. frivolity   d. mildness

As Great Britain pushed its colonial empire to the limit in the late nineteenth century, English men and women began to turn up in the most inaccessible and outlandish places. (2)

2. The word **outlandish** in line 3 can best be defined as
a. out-of-the-way   b. unconventional   c. freakish   d. foreign-looking

Writing may have come to ancient Egypt directly from Sumer, or it may have arrived by some mediate process involving Syria and Palestine. (2)

3. The best definition of the word **mediate** in line 2 is

a. indirect   b. casual   c. middle   d. agreed

As Dickens points out, the fierceness with which Mr. Boythorn expresses his
opinions hardly accords with his overall mildness of temperament.   (2)

4. The best meaning for the phrase **accords with** in line 2 is

a. bestows on   b. approves of   c. adapts to   d. harmonizes with

Once young Mr. Sedley, whose sweet tooth was decidedly pronounced, had glutted
himself on chocolates, he fell asleep, much to the annoyance of his sister and Miss Sharp.   (2)

5. In line 1 the word **glutted** most nearly means

a. flooded   b. overstuffed   c. choked   d. sickened

Two-Word Completions

Circle the pair of words that best complete the meaning of each of the following sentences.

1. With all the fervor of the _____ Knights of the Round Table and
other fabled heroes of old, Don Quixote embarked on his hilarious personal
_____ to right the wrongs of the world.

a. elite . . . embargo   c. myriad . . . juncture
b. legendary . . . crusade   d. renowned . . . ruse

2. Though _____ like the mountain lion and the lynx have entirely
disappeared from the settled parts of this country, they can still be found in areas
that _____ with wildlife.

a. predators . . . teem   c. milieus . . . wallow
b. scavengers . . . bask   d. decoys . . . cower

3. "Certain misguided students may think that they can _____ school
property with _____, but I assure them that such acts of vandalism
will not go unpunished," the principal warned.

a. maim . . . longevity   c. incapacitate . . . nonentity
b. bestow . . . incognito   d. deface . . . impunity

4. When labor and management cannot arrive at an agreement through collective
bargaining or some other means, they sometimes have _____ to
outside _____ to settle a dispute.

a. proximity . . . infiltration   c. recourse . . . mediation
b. transition . . . intrigue   d. proxy . . . jurisdiction

5. Since he derived no pleasure from the more serious pursuits of life, the fun-loving prince
_____ himself with hunts, balls, and other _____
entertainments.

a. bolstered . . . solicitous   c. regaled . . . frivolous
b. glutted . . . ethical   d. asserted . . . conventional

Enriching Your Vocabulary

Read the passage below. Then complete the exercise at the bottom of the page.

What's in a Name?

When you order a sandwich with mayonnaise, have you ever wondered how those popular food items got their names? The sandwich was named for British diplomat John Montagu, the fourth earl of Sandwich, who lived in the 1700s. While spending hour upon hour playing games of chance, he would appease his hunger by eating slices of meat between pieces of bread. Over the centuries, this convenient and versatile combination of ingredients has become a favorite of millions of people. Mayonnaise is said to have been invented by a French nobleman's chef. In the eighteenth century, the duke of Richelieu set out to capture the port town of Mahon on Minorca, Spain. During the long siege, the cook strove to make an interesting sauce for the duke, who was accustomed to fine dining. Not much was available on the island except eggs and olive oil. The chef beat these two ingredients together, added vinegar, and created "la sauce mahonnaise," named in honor of the place where he invented it.

This kind of sandwich has many names: *hero*, *hoagie*, *submarine*, and *poor boy*.

Many other English words are derived from the names of people, fictional characters, or places. Sometimes the exact name is used. For example, *braille*, the system of raised dots that enables the visually impaired to read, is named for its inventor, Louis Braille. Sometimes a name has been altered to form a new word. For instance, the adjective *tawdry* (Unit 7) comes from *tawdry lace*, a contraction of *Saint Audrey's lace*, which was a type of scarf named after a seventh-century Northumbrian queen. When these scarves were mass-produced, their quality deteriorated, and *tawdry* came to mean cheap or flashy.

In Column A below are 10 more words derived from names. With or without a dictionary, match each word with its meaning in Column B.

Column A

_____ **1.** boycott
_____ **2.** martinet
_____ **3.** gargantuan
_____ **4.** bowdlerize
_____ **5.** maverick
_____ **6.** maudlin
_____ **7.** charlatan
_____ **8.** mesmerize
_____ **9.** spoonerism
_____ **10.** philippic

Column B

a. the transposition of the initial sounds of two or more words

b. of enormous size or volume

c. to alter a text by removing material regarded as vulgar

d. a speech filled with bitter condemnation

e. a refusal to deal with someone or something as a means of protest

f. to hypnotize; to fascinate or hold spellbound

g. weakly and excessively sentimental

h. a strict disciplinarian; a stickler for the rules

i. a quack; someone who makes a showy pretense to ability or knowledge

j. a person who is independent, someone who does not go along with a group or political party

Definitions

Note carefully the spelling, pronunciation, part(s) of speech, and definition(s) of each of the following words. Then write the word in the blank space(s) in the illustrative sentence(s) following. Finally, study the lists of synonyms and antonyms given at the end of each entry.

1. adapt
(ə dapt')

(*v.*) to adjust or change to suit conditions

As anyone who moves to a new home or starts a new job can tell you, it takes time to _____ to new surroundings.

SYNONYMS: regulate, alter, acclimate
ANTONYM: remain unchanged

2. attest
(ə test')

(*v.*) to bear witness, affirm to be true or genuine

I can _____ to the truth of her story because I, too, saw what happened.

SYNONYMS: witness, verify, confirm, corroborate
ANTONYMS: deny, disprove, refute, rebut

3. dovetail
(dəv' tāl)

(*v.*) to fit together exactly; to connect so as to form a whole; (*n.*) a carpentry figure resembling a dove's tail

We may be able to _____ our activities with theirs if we all plan ahead.

We examined the fine _____ the carpenter used to construct the antique chest.

SYNONYMS: (*v.*) mesh, jive, harmonize
ANTONYMS: (*v.*) clash, be at odds

4. enormity
(i nôr' mə tē)

(*n.*) the quality of exceeding all moral bounds; an exceedingly evil act; huge size, immensity

The _____ of the disaster shocked and saddened the nation.

SYNONYMS: atrociousness, heinousness, atrocity, vastness
ANTONYMS: mildness, harmlessness, innocuousness

5. falter
(fôl' tər)

(*v.*) to hesitate, stumble, lose courage; to speak hesitatingly; to lose drive, weaken, decline

The newscaster's voice _____ as he announced to the nation that the president was dead.

SYNONYM: waver
ANTONYMS: persevere, plug away at

6. foreboding
(fôr bō' diŋ)

(*n.*) a warning or feeling that something bad will happen; (*adj.*) marked by fear, ominous

As the hurricane neared, residents of towns along the coast were filled with _____.

All through that long and sleepless night, I was troubled by
_____ thoughts.

SYNONYMS: (*n.*) misgiving, presentiment, premonition

7. forlorn
(fôr lôrn′)

(*adj.*) totally abandoned and helpless; sad and lonely; wretched
or pitiful; almost hopeless

When my best friend moved to another state halfway across
the country, I felt extremely _____.

SYNONYMS: woebegone, forsaken, bereft, pathetic
ANTONYMS: jaunty, buoyant, blithe, chipper

8. haughty
(hô′ tē)

(*adj.*) chillingly proud and scornful

The _____ tone of voice in which
you refused my invitation offended me deeply.

SYNONYMS: disdainful, supercilious
ANTONYMS: meek, humble, unassuming, modest

9. impediment
(im ped′ ə mənt)

(*n.*) a physical defect; a hindrance, obstacle

You must not let _____ in your path
keep you from pursuing your dreams.

SYNONYMS: obstruction, stumbling block
ANTONYMS: help, advantage, asset, plus

10. imperative
(im per′ ə tiv)

(*adj.*) necessary, urgent; (*n.*) a form of a verb expressing a
command; that which is necessary or required

If a tick bites you, it is _____ that
you see a doctor as soon as possible.

The writing of a thank-you note to acknowledge a gift or act
of kindness is a social _____.

SYNONYMS: (*adj.*) essential, indispensable, mandatory
ANTONYMS: (*adj.*) nonessential, unnecessary, optional

11. loiter
(loi′ tər)

(*v.*) to linger in an aimless way, hang around, dawdle, tarry

Some students always _____ in the
school yard long after classes are over for the day.

ANTONYM: hurry along

12. malinger
(mə liŋ′ gər)

(*v.*) to pretend illness to avoid duty or work, lie down on the job

If you _____ too often, no one will
believe you when you really do fall ill.

SYNONYMS: goof off, shirk

13. pithy
(pith′ ē)

(*adj.*) short but full of meaning and point

A good editorial should be _____.

SYNONYMS: terse, short and sweet, meaty, telling
ANTONYMS: wordy, verbose, long-winded, foolish, inane

14. plunder
(plən' dər)

(v.) to rob by force, especially during wartime; to seize wrongfully; (n.) property stolen by force

In the Old West, rustlers _____ ranches and farms for cattle and horses.

Thieves often use a third party called a *fence* to sell jewelry and other _____ .

SYNONYMS: (v.) pillage, loot, sack; (n.) spoils, pelf

15. simper
(sim' pər)

(v.) to smile or speak in a silly, forced way; (n.) a silly, forced smile

Strangers may find it easier to _____ about trivial matters than to have a serious conversation.

The camera caught me with a _____ on my face.

SYNONYMS: (v.) snicker, smirk, titter, giggle

16. steadfast
(sted' fast)

(adj.) firmly fixed; constant, not moving or changing

I urge you to be _____ in your efforts to achieve your goals in life.

SYNONYMS: loyal, faithful, unwavering
ANTONYMS: inconstant, fickle, unreliable, vacillating

17. vaunted
(vônt' id)

(adj.) much boasted about in a vain or swaggering way

The rookie's _____ strength was no match for the veteran's skill and experience.

SYNONYMS: trumpeted, heralded
ANTONYMS: downplayed, soft-pedaled, de-emphasized

18. vilify
(vil' ə fī)

(v.) to abuse or belittle unjustly or maliciously

Voters have become thoroughly disgusted with candidates who _____ their rivals' reputations.

SYNONYMS: malign, defame, denigrate, traduce
ANTONYMS: glorify, extol, lionize

19. waif
(wāf)

(n.) a person (usually a child) without a home or friend; a stray person or animal; something that comes along by chance, a stray bit

The spunky _____ who triumphs over many hardships is a popular character in film and fiction.

SYNONYMS: stray, ragamuffin, street urchin

20. wry
(rī)

(adj.) twisted, turned to one side; cleverly and often grimly humorous

Charles Addams was famous for _____ cartoons chronicling the adventures of a ghoulish family.

SYNONYMS: dryly amusing, ironic, droll
ANTONYMS: humorless, solemn, straight

Completing the Sentence

From the words for this unit, choose the one that best completes each of the following sentences. Write the word in the space provided.

1. Why is it that people tend to _____ in groups in the middle of the sidewalk, blocking the flow of pedestrian traffic?

2. During our absence, a group of hungry bears broke into the cabin and _____ our food supply.

3. After the official had fallen from power, his policies were ridiculed, his motives questioned, and his character _____.

4. The comedian specialized in the kind of _____ humor that gets quiet chuckles from an audience, rather than loud bursts of laughter.

5. Unless you take steps now to correct your speech _____, it will be a serious hindrance to you throughout your life.

6. It is _____ for us to produce automobiles that will give us better gas mileage and cause less pollution.

7. When we missed those early foul shots, I had a(n) _____ that the game was going to be a bad one for our team.

8. The _____ of the crimes that the Nazis committed in the concentration camps horrified the civilized world.

9. Her _____ manner said more clearly than words that she could never associate as an equal with a "peasant" like me.

10. Great skill is required to _____ a novel or short story for the silver screen.

11. Through all the shocks and trials of the Civil War, Abraham Lincoln never _____ in his determination to save the Union.

12. A fearful young recruit may _____ in an attempt to avoid dangerous duty.

13. When she attempted to order the meal in French, we discovered that her much _____ knowledge of that language made no impression at all on the waiter.

14. They remained my _____ friends, even at a time when it might have been to their advantage to have nothing to do with me.

15. The _____ expressions on the faces of the starving children moved TV audiences to pity and indignation at their plight.

16. In every war, many children are separated from their parents and become homeless _____, begging for food and shelter.

17. I appreciate the fact that when I asked you for your opinion, you gave it to me in a few clear, direct, and _____ sentences.

18. The testimony of all the witnesses _____ neatly, forming a strong case against the accused.

19. The quick recovery of so many patients _____ to the skill of the hospital staff.

20. When he was caught red-handed in the act of going through my papers, all he did was to stand there and _____ foolishly.

Synonyms *Choose the word from this unit that is **the same** or **most nearly the same** in meaning as the **boldface** word or expression in the given phrase. Write the word on the line provided.*

1. not permitted to **tarry** after dark _____

2. **unwavering** devotion to the struggle for equality _____

3. the **heralded** excellence of the new software _____

4. **verified** the effectiveness of the medication _____

5. **looted** the enemy's camp _____

6. a collection of **droll** poems _____

7. **denigrated** the achievements of a bitter enemy _____

8. when complete bed rest is **mandatory** _____

9. worried about the **immensity** of the task _____

10. often **smirks** when embarrassed _____

11. when all the elements **harmonize** _____

12. told us they had grave **misgivings** _____

13. needed time to **acclimate** to the altitude _____

14. no tolerance for those who **goof off** _____

15. distributed warm clothing to the **ragamuffins** _____

Antonyms *Choose the word from this unit that is **most nearly opposite** in meaning to the **boldface** word or expression in the given phrase. Write the word on the line provided.*

16. in an unexpectedly **jaunty** mood _____

17. delivered a **long-winded** welcome address _____

18. **persevered** when things got tough _____

19. an extremely **modest** person _____

20. a number of minor **advantages** _____

Choosing the Right Word

*Circle the **boldface** word that more satisfactorily completes each of the following sentences.*

1. Many ad campaigns deliberately (**loiter, vaunt**) the superiority of a product over all its competition.

2. People who migrate from the suburbs to the city often find it difficult to (**adapt, dovetail**) to the noise and more crowded conditions.

3. No matter how well qualified you may be, an inability to get on well with other people will prove a serious (**imperative, impediment**) in any field of work.

4. The (**pithy, haughty**) advice given by Ben Franklin in *Poor Richard's Almanac* has rarely been equaled for its good common sense.

5. Ample food supplies in the United States (**attest, vilify**) to the abilities of American farmers.

6. In the opening scene of Shakespeare's *Macbeth*, there is a strong sense of (**foreboding, enormity**) that something terrible is going to happen.

7. Political leaders should feel free to change their minds on specific issues while remaining (**steadfast, wry**) in their support of their principles.

8. Monday morning seems to be a favorite time for practicing the fine art of (**foreboding, malingering**).

9. To (**simper, falter**) now, at the very threshold of victory, would mean that all our earlier struggles and sacrifices had been in vain.

10. Mutual respect and understanding among all racial and ethnic groups remains a(n) (**imperative, waif**) in the life of this nation.

11. When she learned that she had not been chosen for the job, she made a (**wry, forlorn**) joke, but this did not conceal her deep disappointment.

12. The director told him to smile like a "dashing man about town," but all he could do was to (**simper, adapt**) like a confused freshman.

13. Most people know the story of Cinderella, a poor, mistreated (**waif, malingerer**) who marries a prince and lives happily ever after.

14. Hordes of savage barbarians swept into the province, committing one (**impediment, enormity**) after another on the defenseless population.

15. Thinking it no crime to borrow from the past, Elizabethan dramatists often (**vilified, plundered**) ancient writers for suitable plots for their plays.

16. The police sometimes use laws against (**faltering, loitering**) to prevent the gathering of unruly crowds.

17. His (**haughty, steadfast**) attitude toward those he considered "beneath him" was a sure sign of lack of breeding and simple good manners.

18. Despite our own exhaustion, we made one final, (**forlorn, pithy**) attempt to save the drowning swimmer, but our efforts were of no avail.

19. "I did what I thought best at the time," the president replied, "and I deeply resent their cowardly attempts to (**vilify, plunder**) my actions."

20. The temperaments of the partners in the business (**dovetail, attest**) so well that they can work together without the slightest friction or conflict.

*Read the following passage, in which some of the words you have studied in this unit appear in **boldface** type. Then complete each statement given below the passage by circling the letter of the item that is **the same** or **almost the same** in meaning as the highlighted word.*

A Huge Job

(Line)

The building of the Hoover Dam on the Colorado River during the Great Depression **attests to** the U.S. government's ability to undertake a massive project

for the common good in hard times. The **enormity** of the construction project meant that a large workforce was needed. Unemployment was (5) widespread at the time, and people from all over the country flocked to the region, hoping to get a job on the dam. Native Americans and African Americans were among those who found employment on the project. Working conditions were very difficult. The (10) land around the site was so hot and dry in the summer and so cold and windy in the winter that no one lived there. In addition, the jobs were both exhausting and dangerous. Yet for those who needed work, these factors were not **impediments**. (15)

Hoover Dam illuminated at night

Work on the site began in 1931. Loose rock and earth had to be cleared away. Then tunnels were built to divert the flow of the river around the dam site. Finally work began on the dam itself. The pouring of the concrete alone went on almost (20) nonstop for nearly two years (1933–1935). Five thousand workers had to operate in a four-thousand-foot canyon. The supervisors and foremen had to **dovetail** all the jobs in just the right sequence. Work continued around the clock. It was a truly monumental undertaking. (25)

President Franklin D. Roosevelt dedicated the dam on September 30, 1935. The dam's irrigation water helped turn the desert into fertile agricultural land. Lake Mead, which was created by the dam, became a popular recreation area. Over the years, the sale of hydroelectric power generated by the dam repaid the construction costs. But perhaps most important, the Hoover Dam gave hope to a (30) **forlorn** nation, weary of the depression.

---

1. The meaning of **attests to** (line 2) is
  a. denies   c. describes
  b. challenges   d. confirms

2. Enormity (line 3) most nearly means
  a. huge size   c. huge risk
  b. high quality   d. high cost

3. Impediments (line 15) is best defined as
  a. questions   c. obstacles
  b. advantages   d. answers

4. The meaning of **dovetail** (line 24) is
  a. clash   c. define
  b. schedule   d. mesh

5. Forlorn (line 31) most nearly means
  a. woebegone   c. confused
  b. buoyant   d. divided

Definitions

Note carefully the spelling, pronunciation, part(s) of speech, and definition(s) of each of the following words. Then write the word in the blank space(s) in the illustrative sentence(s) following. Finally, study the lists of synonyms and antonyms given at the end of each entry.

1. amplify
(am′ plə fī)

(*v.*) to make stronger, larger, greater, louder, or the like

Some court rulings _____ the authority of the individual states.

SYNONYMS: increase, augment, fill out, supplement
ANTONYMS: lessen, diminish, abbreviate, shorten

2. armistice
(är′ mə stis)

(*n.*) a temporary peace, halt in fighting

Diplomats hope to negotiate an _____ between the warring nations.

SYNONYMS: cease-fire, truce

3. arrogant
(ar′ ə gənt)

(*adj.*) haughty, too convinced of one's own importance

An _____ individual is likely to find it difficult to work as part of a team.

SYNONYMS: high-handed, overbearing, presumptuous
ANTONYMS: meek, humble, modest, unassuming

4. bland
(bland)

(*adj.*) gentle, soothing, mild; lacking interest or taste

Some people prefer to live in a place where the climate is _____ and unchanging all year round.

SYNONYMS: dull, insipid
ANTONYMS: harsh, irritating, pungent, spicy, piquant

5. disclaim
(dis klām′)

(*v.*) to deny interest in or connection with; to give up all claim to

Both candidates _____ any ties to special-interest groups.

SYNONYMS: disavow, disown, repudiate
ANTONYMS: admit, acknowledge, avow, confess

6. epoch
(ep′ ək)

(*n.*) a distinct period of time, era, age

The mapping of the human genetic code marked the beginning of a promising new _____ in medicine.

7. estrange
(e strānj′)

(*v.*) to drift apart or become unfriendly; to cause such a separation; to remove or keep at a distance

A long and bitter feud may _____ a family that was once close-knit.

SYNONYMS: part company, alienate
ANTONYMS: bring together, reunite, reconcile

8. gratify
(grat′ ə fī)

(v.) to please, satisfy; to indulge or humor

Experts advise parents not to _____ a child's every whim.

SYNONYM: delight
ANTONYMS: disappoint, dissatisfy, frustrate, thwart

9. infinite
(in′ fə nit)

(adj.) exceedingly great, inexhaustible, without limit, endless; (n., preceded by *the*) an incalculable number, the concept of infinity; (cap. *I*) a name for God

It may take _____ patience to be a parent, but the rewards are equally great.

A belief in the _____ is a source of comfort and hope to many people who are in distress.

SYNONYMS: (adj.) unlimited, boundless
ANTONYMS: (adj.) limited, restricted, measurable

10. irascible
(ir as′ ə bəl)

(adj.) easily made angry, hot-tempered

Working for an _____ boss can be very difficult indeed.

SYNONYMS: irritable, quarrelsome, cantankerous
ANTONYM: even-tempered

11. kindred
(kin′ drəd)

(n.) a person's relatives; a family relationship; (adj.) related by blood; like, similar

If you have any long-lost _____ , you may be able to use the Internet to locate them.

People who feel that they are _____ spirits usually have many interests in common.

SYNONYMS: (n.) kin, relations
ANTONYMS: (adj.) unlike, dissimilar, contrasting

12. naive
(na ēv′)

(adj.) innocent, unsophisticated, showing lack of worldly knowledge and experience

A _____ person may be easily taken in by get-rich-quick schemes.

SYNONYMS: green, wet behind the ears
ANTONYMS: sophisticated, knowing, urbane, suave, blasé

13. niche
(nich)

(n.) a decorative recess in a wall; a suitable place or position for a person or thing

That _____ in the hallway is a perfect spot for a vase of fresh flowers.

SYNONYMS: nook, alcove

14. obliterate
(ə blit′ ə rāt)

(v.) to blot out completely, destroy utterly

An earthquake can _____ large portions of a major city in a matter of minutes.

SYNONYMS: wipe out, erase, expunge, efface
ANTONYMS: foster, promote, create

15. ramshackle
(ram' shak əl)

(*adj.*) appearing ready to collapse, loose and shaky

A few _____ buildings are all that remain of the old mining town.

SYNONYMS: rickety, unsteady, run-down, dilapidated
ANTONYMS: well built, well maintained, shipshape, trim

16. ransack
(ran' sak)

(*v.*) to search or examine thoroughly; to rob, plunder

Robbers _____ the house for cash and other valuables.

SYNONYMS: rummage, scour
ANTONYM: spot-check

17. rote
(rōt)

(*n.*) unthinking routine or repetition, a fixed or mechanical way of doing something; (*adj.*) based on a mechanical routine

Most people learn to type by _____.

_____ memorization can be helpful when you begin to study a foreign language.

18. solvent
(säl' vənt)

(*adj.*) able to meet one's financial obligations; having the power to dissolve other substances; (*n.*) a liquid used to dissolve other substances; something that solves, explains, eliminates, or softens

If you want to remain _____, set a budget and stick to it.

You will need to use a _____ to remove tar or paint from your hands.

SYNONYMS: financially sound, in the black
ANTONYMS: bankrupt, flat broke, in the red

19. tedious
(tē' dē əs)

(*adj.*) long and tiresome

Sometimes I find it hard to pay close attention to a _____ lecture.

SYNONYMS: boring, monotonous
ANTONYMS: stimulating, interesting, short and sweet

20. vendor
(ven' dər)

(*n.*) a person who sells something

If the appliance you purchased turns out to be defective, you should return it to the _____.

SYNONYMS: peddler, hawker, dealer, merchant
ANTONYMS: buyer, purchaser, customer

Completing the Sentence

From the words for this unit, choose the one that best completes each of the following sentences. Write the word in the space provided.

1. He used to be a modest, likable fellow, but now that he has come into some money, his manner has become exceedingly _____ and offensive.

2. The tinkling bell of the ice-cream _____, as he makes his way through the streets, is a pleasant sound on a summer evening.

3. Now that a(n) _____ has finally been arranged, the even more difficult job of making a lasting peace must begin.

4. After eating so much highly spiced food while on vacation, I craved some pleasantly _____ home cooking.

5. Along the walls of the church, there were _____ in which statues of saints had been placed.

6. "Unless we learn to control nuclear weapons," the speaker said, "they may _____ the human race."

7. We want to buy components that will _____ our CDs without distorting their sound.

8. The Declaration of Independence's assertion that "all men are created equal" marked a new _____ in world history.

9. "A dinner that is truly well prepared _____ the eye as well as the palate," a famous chef once remarked.

10. "You should understand the reason for all the steps in the problem," our math teacher said, "not simply carry them out by _____."

11. Although she had been separated from her family for years, in that hour of need, all her _____ came to her aid.

12. Since I was obeying all traffic regulations at the time that the accident occurred, I _____ responsibility for it.

13. Increasing dissatisfaction with the direction her political party was taking slowly _____ her from it.

14. When the electric power failed, we _____ the kitchen to find candles and matches.

15. I've been broke for so long that I'm afraid I won't know how to behave when I find myself _____ again.

16. After four hours of doing the same small task over and over again, I began to find my new job on the assembly line _____.

17. Most religions rest on faith in a Supreme Being of _____ power and goodness.

18. I think that the vivid phrase "having a short fuse" aptly describes my neighbor's _____ temperament.

19. How could you have been so _____ and foolish as to take their compliments seriously!

20. We did not realize how poor the people in that isolated region were until we saw the _____ huts in which they were living.

Synonyms *Choose the word from this unit that is **the same** or **most nearly the same** in meaning as the **boldface** word or expression in the given phrase. Write the word on the line provided.*

1. unwilling to **alienate** supporters _____

2. a **merchant** with an old-fashioned pushcart _____

3. a surprisingly **dull** account of the event _____

4. **expunged** the evidence _____

5. did the job **in a mechanical way** _____

6. found the music **monotonous** _____

7. **scoured** the apartment for my keys _____

8. during a **time** of peace and prosperity _____

9. makes **presumptuous** demands _____

10. forced to deal with **quarrelsome** neighbors _____

11. a significant **position** in the retail market _____

12. agreed to the terms of the **truce** _____

13. **satisfied** my dearest wish _____

14. **increases** the echo effect _____

15. had few close **relatives** _____

Antonyms *Choose the word from this unit that is **most nearly opposite** in meaning to the **boldface** word or expression in the given phrase. Write the word on the line provided.*

16. realize that the possibilities are **limited** _____

17. surrounded by a **well-maintained** fence _____

18. a report that the company is **bankrupt** _____

19. **acknowledged** involvement in the scheme _____

20. a **sophisticated** view of the world _____

Choosing the Right Word

*Circle the **boldface** word that more satisfactorily completes each of the following sentences.*

1. He found a comfortable (**niche, rote**) for himself at a bank and worked there quite happily for more than forty years.

2. We are now learning the hard way that our energy sources are not (**infinite, ramshackle**) and that we will have to use them carefully.

3. The spirit of the new law to protect consumers is not "Let the buyer beware" but, rather, "Let the (**vendor, epoch**) beware."

4. Although I was furiously angry, I faced my accusers with a (**tedious, bland**) smile.

5. I am willing to forgive you, but I don't know if I can ever (**obliterate, estrange**) the memory of your dishonesty from my mind.

6. I (**ransacked, gratified**) my brain feverishly, but I was unable to find any way out of the difficulty.

7. Whenever my supervisor gets into one of his (**bland, irascible**) moods, I know that I'm in for some heavy weather before the day is out.

8. A person who behaves with (**kindred, arrogant**) disregard for the feelings of others is likely to have very few friends."

9. What is important for the children is not a(n) (**infinite, rote**) recital of the Pledge of Allegiance but an understanding of what the words really mean.

10. Can anyone be so (**naive, irascible**) as to believe that all famous people who endorse products on TV actually use those products?

11. The job of a mediator is to help (**kindred, estranged**) parties find a basis for settling their differences.

12. Over the years, the vigorous foreign policy that this country has pursued has greatly (**amplified, ransacked**) our role in world affairs.

13. The beginning of commercial television in the 1940s marked a revolutionary (**niche, epoch**) in the history of mass communications.

14. The business had been losing money for years; but thanks to careful new management, it is once again (**bland, solvent**).

15. Every week she meets with a small circle of (**naive, kindred**) souls whose greatest interest in life is the music of Johann Sebastian Bach.

16. They claim to have "buried the hatchet," but I fear that they have only declared a temporary (**vendor, armistice**) in their feud.

17. The excuse that he offered for his absence was so (**solvent, ramshackle**) and improbable that it fell apart as soon as we looked into it.

18. You will learn that nothing is more (**amplifying, gratifying**) than to face a problem squarely, analyze it clearly, and resolve it successfully.

19. My next-door neighbor is a(n) (**tedious, arrogant**) individual, with a remarkable talent for boring me out of my wits.

20. Rather than (**disclaim, obliterate**) their religious faiths, many Catholics, Protestants, and Jews left Europe to settle in the New World.

Vocabulary in Context

*Read the following passage, in which some of the words you have studied in this unit appear in **boldface** type. Then complete each statement given below the passage by circling the letter of the item that is **the same** or **almost the same** in meaning as the highlighted word.*

Thin Slices

(Line)

Today, potato chips are generally considered to be junk food. But they once occupied a **niche** on the menus of elegant restaurants. It all started in the 1700s, when Thomas Jefferson brought a recipe for French fries to America from France. French fries came to be regarded as serious food. By the mid-1800s, they could be

(5) found among the side dishes on restaurant menus. Then, in 1853, the demands of an **irascible** diner and a chef's annoyance ushered in a new **epoch** in eating.

George Crum, a Native American, worked as a chef at Moon Lake Lodge, a stylish restaurant at a resort in Saratoga

(10) Springs, New York. One evening, a customer complained that Crum's usual French fries were too thick. Crum prepared a new batch, this time sliced more thinly. But the **arrogant** diner sent

(15) the second batch back, too.

Crum was upset. He recognized that it was his job to **gratify** the wishes of the customer, but he was frustrated. He decided to slice a third batch of potatoes

(20) wafer-thin. The slices were so thin, in fact, that after they were fried, they could not be jabbed with a fork.

To Crum's surprise, the finicky customer

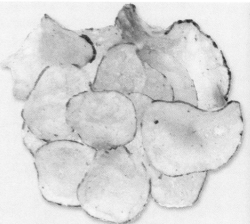

Potato chips are still a popular snack.

pronounced the crisp, crunchy, thin potatoes delicious! Other diners begged to try

(25) Crum's new "chips." Soon, George Crum opened his own restaurant. The specialty of the house was, of course, potato chips.

Although the chips soon became popular restaurant fare, they did not become a common snack until much later. It was **tedious** work to peel and cut potatoes by hand—the only option in George Crum's day. But in the 1920s, the mechanical

(30) potato peeler was invented, which made the widespread commercial manufacture of potato chips possible.

---

1. The meaning of **niche** (line 2) is
a. place   c. line
b. alcove   d. section

2. Irascible (line 6) is best defined as
a. foreign   c. irritable
b. wealthy   d. famous

3. Epoch (line 6) most nearly means
a. moment   c. chapter
b. trend   d. era

4. The meaning of **arrogant** (line 14) is
a. humble   c. high-handed
b. horrified   d. hungry

5. Gratify (line 17) is best defined as
a. anger   c. disappoint
b. please   d. ignore

6. Tedious (line 28) most nearly means
a. tiresome   c. difficult
b. hazardous   d. amusing

UNIT 15

Definitions

Note carefully the spelling, pronunciation, part(s) of speech, and definition(s) of each of the following words. Then write the word in the blank space(s) in the illustrative sentence(s) following. Finally, study the lists of synonyms and antonyms given at the end of each entry.

1. abyss
(ə bis′)

(*n.*) a deep or bottomless pit

Mountain climbers must take great care lest they slip and fall into an _____.

SYNONYMS: chasm, gorge
ANTONYMS: summit, promontory, pinnacle

2. befall
(bi fôl′)

(*v.*) to happen, occur; to happen to

It is only natural to worry from time to time about the ills that may someday _____ us.

SYNONYM: come to pass

3. crucial
(krü′ shal)

(*adj.*) of supreme importance, decisive, critical

In many adventure films, the hero always arrives just at the _____ moment.

SYNONYM: pivotal
ANTONYMS: insignificant, inconsequential

4. dregs
(dregz)

(*n. pl.*) the last remaining part; the part of least worth

The _____ of bitterness are all that is left of our former friendship.

SYNONYMS: grounds, lees, residue, leftovers
ANTONYMS: elite, upper crust, cream of the crop

5. embody
(em bäd′ ē)

(*v.*) to give form to; to incorporate, include; to personify

The villain in a melodrama _____ cold-blooded ruthlessness.

SYNONYM: encompass

6. exasperate
(eg zas′ pə rāt)

(*v.*) to irritate, annoy, or anger

Small children sometimes _____ adults with endless questions.

SYNONYMS: vex, try one's patience
ANTONYMS: soothe, mollify, please, delight

7. fiasco
(fē as′ kō)

(*n.*) the complete collapse or failure of a project

With the bases loaded, our star pitcher gave up a home run, turning a close game into a _____.

SYNONYMS: disaster, flop, bomb
ANTONYMS: complete success, triumph, hit

8. garnish
(gär′ nish)

(*v.*) to adorn or decorate, especially food; (*n.*) an ornament or decoration, especially for food

The chef _____ our salad with colorful edible flowers.

When it comes to mystery novels, I prefer those that have a _____ of wit.

SYNONYMS: (*v.*) embellish, gussy up

9. heritage
(her′ ə tij)

(*n.*) an inheritance; a birthright

A rich _____ of human history and creativity is housed in the world's libraries and museums.

SYNONYMS: legacy, descent, pedigree

10. inert
(in ərt′)

(*adj.*) lifeless, unable to move or act; slow, inactive

In order to keep patients _____ during surgery, doctors use various general anesthetics.

SYNONYMS: motionless, sluggish, lethargic
ANTONYMS: vigorous, energetic, volatile, lively

11. mercenary
(mər′ sə ner ē)

(*adj.*) acting or working for self-gain only; (*n.*) a hired soldier, a soldier of fortune

A fortune hunter's motives are _____ rather than romantic.

A country that does not have a standing army may need to call upon _____ to fight in its wars.

SYNONYMS: (*adj.*) grasping, avaricious
ANTONYMS: (*adj.*) unselfish, disinterested, altruistic

12. negligent
(neg′ lə jənt)

(*adj.*) marked by carelessness or indifference; failing to do what should be done

A driver who is _____ about obeying traffic regulations may end up causing an accident.

SYNONYMS: careless, neglectful, remiss, derelict
ANTONYMS: careful, attentive, conscientious

13. oblivion
(ə bliv′ ē ən)

(*n.*) forgetfulness, disregard; a state of being forgotten; an amnesty, general pardon

Down through the ages, poets have described sleep as a kind of _____ that brings relief from woe.

SYNONYMS: obscurity, nothingness
ANTONYMS: fame, renown, celebrity

14. opus
(ō′ pəs)

(*n.*) an impressive piece of work, especially a musical composition or other work of art

Many scholars consider Michelangelo's Sistine Chapel paintings to be his greatest _____ .
SYNONYMS: work, composition, piece, oeuvre

15. pallid
(pal' id)

(*adj.*) pale, lacking color; weak and lifeless

A long illness may leave a person looking extremely frail and _____ .
SYNONYMS: colorless, bloodless, ashen, dull
ANTONYMS: ruddy, sanguine, racy, colorful

16. parable
(par' ə bəl)

(*n.*) a short narrative designed to teach a moral lesson

Sermons are often based on _____ from the New Testament.
SYNONYMS: moral tale, fable, allegory

17. rational
(rash' ə nəl)

(*adj.*) based on reasoning; able to make use of reason; sensible, reasonable

Calm and _____ analysis should lead you to a solution to most problems.
SYNONYM: logical
ANTONYMS: mad, insane, illogical, absurd

18. reciprocal
(ri sip' rə kəl)

(*adj.*) shared; involving give-and-take between two persons or things; working in both directions; (*n.*) (*math*) a number that, when multiplied by another number, gives 1

A _____ understanding of each other's likes and dislikes is important in a close friendship.

The fraction 4/3 is the _____ of the fraction 3/4.
SYNONYM: (*adj.*) mutual
ANTONYMS: (*adj.*) one-sided, unilateral

19. stricture
(strik' chər)

(*n.*) a limitation or restriction; a criticism; (*medicine*) a narrowing of a passage in the body

Most religions impose dietary _____ of some sort on their followers.
SYNONYM: restraint
ANTONYMS: compliment, praise, accolade, swelling

20. veneer
(və nēr')

(*n.*) a thin outer layer; a surface appearance or decoration; (*v.*) to cover with a thin layer

Some people may adopt a thin _____ of friendliness to hide their true feelings toward others.

Furniture makers often _____ sturdy but common wood with a finer, more costly variety.
SYNONYMS: (*n.*) facing, overlay, façade, pretense
ANTONYMS: (*n.*) nucleus, inner core

Completing the Sentence

From the words for this unit, choose the one that best completes each of the following sentences. Write the word in the space provided.

1. The administration intends to propose legislation to cut back on customs duties and relax other _____ on foreign trade.

2. In this, the third century of our nation's history, let us try to be worthy of our _____ of freedom!

3. In high school you will make many decisions _____ to your future, but determining what to wear to the prom isn't one of them.

4. To our dismay, the running back didn't get to his feet after being tackled on the play but lay _____ on the field.

5. A number of famous Roman emperors were clearly madmen for whose actions no _____ explanation can possibly be devised.

6. She was a famous novelist in her own day, but her work has now passed into _____.

7. Would you like your new desk finished with a walnut, maple, or mahogany _____?

8. Astrologers claim that they can discover what will _____ a person by studying the movements of various heavenly bodies.

9. My mother doesn't think that a plate of food is ready to serve unless she has _____ it with a sprig of parsley or a slice of tomato.

10. The old adage "I'll scratch your back if you'll scratch mine" aptly describes the kind of _____ arrangement he has in mind.

11. During her confinement in a Nazi concentration camp, she drained the cup of human suffering to the _____.

12. Since many composers don't publish their works in the order in which they were written, the number given to a particular _____ may not tell much about the date of its composition.

13. Of course she didn't look well after her stay in the hospital, but a few days at the beach took care of that _____ complexion.

14. In no time at all, poor management turned what should have been a surefire success into a costly _____.

15. Winston Churchill warned the English people that if they gave in to the Nazis, they would "sink into the _____ of a new Dark Age."

16. The ancient story of the Prodigal Son is a(n) _____ that helps us understand problems and situations of present-day life.

17. Nothing _____ me more than neighbors who play their television sets at high volume late at night.

18. The brief code of laws known as the Ten Commandments _____ basic moral values.

19. Without pretending that he cared about the public welfare, he told us frankly that his interest in the project was purely _____ .

20. The judge imposed a heavy fine on the _____ landlord who had failed to provide heat during the cold weather.

Synonyms

*Choose the word from this unit that is **the same** or **most nearly the same** in meaning as the **boldface** word or expression in the given phrase. Write the word on the line provided.*

1. a thoroughly selfish and **grasping** individual   _____

2. the artist's most popular **work**   _____

3. remained **motionless** for a long time   _____

4. a bad habit that really **irritates** me   _____

5. one who **personifies** courage and strength   _____

6. a **fable** with an important message   _____

7. known to have a very **logical** mind   _____

8. built a bridge over the **gorge**   _____

9. a state of **forgetfulness**   _____

10. stared at my **ashen** reflection   _____

11. **remiss** when it comes to returning phone calls   _____

12. an artistic success but a financial **disaster**   _____

13. claimed the property that was their **birthright**   _____

14. unprepared for what **occurred**   _____

15. **decorated** with red radish roses   _____

Antonyms

*Choose the word from this unit that is **most nearly opposite** in meaning to the **boldface** word or expression in the given phrase. Write the word on the line provided.*

16. a series of **insignificant** clues   _____

17. a **unilateral** agreement   _____

18. received **accolades** from the committee   _____

19. a place frequented by the **upper crust** of society   _____

20. an **inner core** of self-confidence   _____

Choosing the Right Word

*Circle the **boldface** word that more satisfactorily completes each of the following sentences.*

1. Any significant (**dregs, stricture**) of the passages leading to the heart will hinder the normal flow of blood to that organ and cause cardiac arrest.

2. If you are (**negligent, reciprocal**) about small sums of money, you may find that you will never have any large sums to worry about.

3. If our leadership is timid and (**mercenary, inert**), we will never be able to solve the great problems that face us.

4. Such familiar stories as "Little Red Riding Hood" are really (**parables, veneers**) that tell a child something about the conditions of human life.

5. Since he undertook that big job without any sound preparation, all of his ambitious plans ended in a resounding (**stricture, fiasco**).

6. What a relief to turn from those (**pallid, negligent**) little tales to the lively, vigorous, earthy stories of Mark Twain.

7. In this early novel by Dickens, we have an (**abyss, opus**) that gives us a wonderful picture of life in nineteenth-century England.

8. After his crushing defeat in the election, the candidate returned to his hometown and disappeared into (**heritage, oblivion**).

9. Experience teaches us that many of the things that seemed so (**crucial, inert**) when we were young are really of no ultimate importance.

10. Once the war had been won, the victors laid aside their high-minded ideals and became involved in a (**mercenary, pallid**) squabble over the spoils.

11. My uncle, who was a West Point graduate, (**garnished, embodied**) all the qualities suggested by the phrase "an officer and a gentleman."

12. A descendant of one of the Founding Fathers of this country, she strove all her life to live up to her distinguished (**opus, heritage**).

13. It's hard for people to admit that some of the misfortunes that (**exasperate, befall**) them are really their own fault.

14. Underneath the (**veneer, oblivion**) of her polished manners, we recognized the down-to-earth young woman we had known in earlier years.

15. Isn't it tragic that the religious groups fighting each other are separated by an (**parable, abyss**) of misunderstanding?

16. Since decent people would have nothing to do with him, he soon began to associate with the (**dregs, fiasco**) of humanity.

17. There are times when it is good to let your imagination run free, instead of trying to be strictly (**rational, crucial**).

18. "The heroism of these brave men and women speaks for itself," the senator remarked, "and needs no (**oblivion, garnishing**)."

19. Her constant chattering while I'm trying to do my vocabulary exercises (**exasperates, embodies**) me more than I can say.

20. The plan of the two schools to exchange members of their faculties proved to be of (**rational, reciprocal**) advantage.

*Read the following passage, in which some of the words you have studied in this unit appear in **boldface** type. Then complete each statement given below the passage by circling the letter of the item that is **the same** or **almost the same** in meaning as the highlighted word.*

Sunken Treasures

(Line)

There are shipwrecks resting in the depths of the oceans and other bodies of water all over the world. Historical records tell us what **befell** some of these ships. Some vessels went down in turbulent weather or because of navigational errors. Others became unseaworthy, perhaps because crew members were **negligent** in some way. Still others fell victim to attacks by enemies in wartime or by pirates. But (5) in some cases, we may never know the causes.

Treasure hunters dream of finding gold and jewels in the wrecks of pirate ships, but the real treasures are the ships themselves. For that reason, scientists and historians believe it is **crucial** to safeguard these underwater sites from those with purely **mercenary** interests.

Diver examining a shipwreck

A wreck believed to be the pirate (10) Blackbeard's warship, *Queen Anne's Revenge*, was located off the coast of North Carolina in 1996. Although underwater archaeologists did not find the pirate's loot, they did find priceless (15) artifacts, including cannons, anchors, and a brass bell dated 1709. At the bottom of Lake Champlain, marine explorers have discovered a Revolutionary War gunboat from the victorious fleet commanded by (20) Benedict Arnold in 1776.

The wrecks of ancient wooden ships are vulnerable to the damage caused by water and by wood borers, tiny sea creatures that feast on rotting timbers. Often little is (25) left of such ships except the remains of their cargoes. But in 2000, explorers made an amazing discovery: an elaborately carved wooden ship from the Roman era. It is believed to be about 1,500 years old, and its deck is intact. The ship lies at the bottom of a 650-foot **abyss** in the Black Sea. At that depth, the waters are almost still, and there is no oxygen. Without oxygen, wood borers perish, but that same lack of oxygen (30) has preserved the ship. Who knows what treasures this spectacular wreck will yield?

---

1. The meaning of **befell** (line 2) is
   a. sank
   b. launched
   c. happened to
   d. haunted

2. Negligent (line 4) most nearly means
   a. attentive
   b. careless
   c. skilled
   d. distracted

3. Crucial (line 9) is best defined as
   a. critical
   b. foolish
   c. trivial
   d. sensible

4. The meaning of **mercenary** (line 9) is
   a. suspicious
   b. avaricious
   c. unknown
   d. charitable

5. Abyss (line 29) most nearly means
   a. valley
   b. channel
   c. place
   d. chasm

Analogies

In each of the following, circle the item that best completes the comparison.

1. tedious is to **bore** as
a. gratifying is to vex
b. pithy is to falter
c. trying is to exasperate
d. wry is to yawn

2. veneer is to **thin** as
a. mountain is to flat
b. barn is to red
c. abyss is to deep
d. tide is to high

3. composer is to **opus** as
a. writer is to oeuvre
b. painter is to easel
c. actor is to stage
d. sculptor is to marble

4. vendor is to **sell** as
a. waif is to malinger
b. author is to ransack
c. mercenary is to loiter
d. pirate is to plunder

5. impediment is to **speech** as
a. infinity is to space
b. gridlock is to traffic
c. telephone is to communication
d. critic is to stricture

6. irascible is to **patience** as
a. arrogant is to pride
b. haughty is to greed
c. naive is to youth
d. inert is to energy

7. steadfast is to **falter** as
a. stubborn is to yield
b. silly is to simper
c. kindred is to agree
d. bland is to loiter

8. dovetail is to **together** as
a. attest is to apart
b. ransack is to together
c. estrange is to apart
d. disdain is to together

9. epoch is to **time** as
a. fiasco is to triumph
b. heritage is to occupation
c. oblivion is to number
d. niche is to place

10. dregs is to **bottom** as
a. veneer is to top
b. parable is to bottom
c. foreboding is to top
d. heritage is to bottom

11. amplifier is to **volume** as
a. clock is to time
b. generator is to temperature
c. thermostat is to quality
d. accelerator is to speed

12. foreboding is to **before** as
a. prelude is to after
b. epilogue is to before
c. hindsight is to after
d. finale is to before

13. pallid is to **complexion** as
a. forlorn is to size
b. pithy is to texture
c. reciprocal is to value
d. bland is to taste

14. waif is to **forlorn** as
a. greenhorn is to naive
b. stoic is to irascible
c. vendor is to solvent
d. mercenary is to monetary

15. arrogant is to **haughty** as
a. wry is to cynical
b. crucial is to decisive
c. steadfast is to treacherous
d. kindred is to dissimilar

16. solvent is to **bankrupt** as
a. humble is to haughty
b. imperative is to urgent
c. negligent is to frivolous
d. infinite is to timely

17. garnish is to **salad** as
a. jet plane is to transportation
b. epic poem is to limerick
c. hood ornament is to car
d. department store is to consumer

18. pallid is to **unfavorable** as
a. naive is to favorable
b. pithy is to favorable
c. ramshackle is to favorable
d. rote is to favorable

 **Word Associations**

In each of the following groups, circle the word that is best defined or suggested by the given phrase.

1. "Everything that could possibly go wrong has gone wrong!"
a. rote   b. epoch   c. fiasco   d. dregs

2. Pliocene, Miocene, or Oligocene
a. abyss   b. niche   c. kindred   d. epoch

3. the team's heralded invincibility
a. haughty   b. tedious   c. irascible   d. vaunted

4. a noted critic's reservations about the quality of a new Broadway play
a. impediments   b. parables   c. fiascos   d. strictures

5. to turn the house upside down searching for the key
a. estrange   b. ransack   c. exasperate   d. falter

6. the beautiful spirituals that have come down to us from earlier generations
a. heritage   b. armistice   c. garnish   d. kindred

7. a state of forgetfulness or obscurity
a. enormity   b. armistice   c. oblivion   d. foreboding

8. has a tendency to smirk
a. falter   b. loiter   c. simper   d. malinger

9. the cherries and lemon twists people use to gussy up the drinks they serve
a. opuses   b. veneers   c. garnishes   d. enormities

10. fitting together like the pieces of a jigsaw puzzle
a. loiter   b. dovetail   c. amplify   d. embody

11. a funny story with a touch of bitterness
a. wry   b. negligent   c. forlorn   d. bland

12. a job that's just right for you
a. plunder   b. niche   c. heritage   d. abyss

13. a simple story that has an important lesson for all of us
a. solvent   b. parable   c. niche   d. armistice

14. "Whatever happens, I'm ready for it."
a. befalls   b. vilifies   c. disclaims   d. attests

15. the great work that occupied the last two years of the composer's life
a. impediment   b. dregs   c. enormity   d. opus

16. "I had nothing to do with their plans to crash the party."
a. falter   b. loiter   c. disclaim   d. simper

17. "What's in it for me?"
a. mercenary   b. forlorn   c. rational   d. naive

18. declared a cease-fire
a. enormity   b. armistice   c. imperative   d. impediment

19. one who treats people in a high-handed and scornful way
a. reciprocal   b. mercenary   c. irascible   d. arrogant

20. what waves do to footprints in the sand
a. obliterate   b. loiter   c. embody   d. ransack

Vocabulary in Context

*Read the following passage, in which some of the words you have studied in Units 13–15 appear in **boldface** type. Then complete each statement given below the passage by circling the item that is **the same** or **almost the same** in meaning as the highlighted word.*

Secrets of the Mummies

(Line)

When most people think of mummies, they probably think of the kings of ancient Egypt, whose pyramid-shaped tombs are filled with
(5) fabulous riches. But the Egyptians were not the only people who mummified their dead. The Inca Empire of Peru, which flourished long before the Spanish arrived in the
(10) Americas, left behind thousands of mummies. Archaeologists have discovered huge underground burial chambers. The mummies within these tombs and the objects buried with
(15) them are proving to be a treasure trove of clues to how the Inca lived.

At its peak, the Inca Empire was the largest native state that has ever existed in the Western Hemisphere,
(20) with a population of more than 10 million. When an Inca ruler died, his body was mummified and placed within a royal tomb, along with food, drink, weapons, clothing, and
(25) mummified "helpers," including **steadfast** servants and animals. For a year after a ruler's death, his mummy was cared for as if it were still living. At the end of the year, the
(30) mummy was entombed in a great

burial hall with other royal mummies, each seated on a throne. The vast wealth amassed by the kings was placed in the burial hall with them.
(35) In Inca culture, mummies formed a link between the living and the dead. At festival times, **kindred** carried the mummies through the streets. This practice proved to people that the
(40) rulers had actually lived and that their descendants, who owned the mummies, were part of the royal line.

In the 1990s, burial chambers were discovered on a cliff high in a
(45) temperate rain forest in the Andes. Other mummies were found preserved in ice at the top of mountains regarded by the Inca as sacred places. Some of these burial sites are intact. Others
(50) have been **ransacked** by thieves seeking to **plunder** gold and precious artifacts buried with the mummies. Each new discovery is helping scientists to **amplify** their knowledge of
(55) these ancient people. The study of these **inert** remains is yielding details of Inca life before and after the arrival of Europeans in the Western Hemisphere. Slowly but surely, the secrets of the Inca
(60) mummies are being revealed.

---

1. The meaning of **steadfast** (line 26) is
a. polite
b. elderly
c. faithful
d. meek

2. Kindred (line 37) is best defined as
a. strangers
b. relatives
c. friends
d. workers

3. Ransacked (line 50) most nearly means
a. visited
b. burned
c. emptied
d. scoured

4. The meaning of **plunder** (line 51) is
a. loot
b. preserve
c. uncover
d. sell

5. Amplify (line 54) is best defined as
a. increase
b. publish
c. diminish
d. prove

6. Inert (line 56) most nearly means
a. ancient
b. priceless
c. fragile
d. lifeless

Choosing the Right Meaning

Read each sentence carefully. Then circle the item that best completes the statement below the sentence.

The enormity of the task of reconstructing Europe after World War II and the single-minded determination with which the United States went about the job still boggle the mind. (2)

1. In line 1 the word **enormity** most nearly means
a. heinousness   b. difficulty   c. immensity   d. atrocity

"While men believe in the infinite, some pools will be thought to be bottomless." (Thoreau, *Walden*) (2)

2. The best meaning for the phrase **the infinite** in line 1 is
a. an incalculable number   c. a supreme being
b. the idea of boundlessness   d. the limitless reaches of space

Long experience has taught me that a gentle bit of ribbing is a guaranteed solvent for jittery nerves or cold feet in the clutch. (2)

3. The phrase **solvent for** in line 2 is best defined as
a. cause of   b. explanation for   c. component of   d. solution to

"The taper feebly lights the dregs of night
As up the stairs the weary scholar climbs."
    (A. E. Glug, "The Art of Tilting at Windmills," 131–132) (2)

4. In line 1 the word **dregs** most nearly means
a. heavy burden   c. last hours
b. least valuable parts   d. pitchy blackness

Since I seem to be the last leaf on the grapevine, such waifs of gossip as come my way are few and far between, out-of-date, and thoroughly unreliable. (2)

5. The best definition for the word **waifs** in line 1 is
a. stray bits   b. street urchins   c. short statements   d. wild rumors

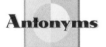

Antonyms

*In each of the following groups, circle the word or expression that is most nearly the **opposite** of the word in **boldface** type.*

1. negligent
a. careful
b. selfish
c. calm
d. thoughtless

2. reciprocal
a. one-sided
b. self-centered
c. thoroughgoing
d. halfhearted

3. ramshackle
a. quiet
b. faded
c. wise
d. sturdy

4. steadfast
a. kind
b. slow
c. wavering
d. pleased

5. irascible
a. fearful
b. good-natured
c. narrow
d. self-centered

6. estrange
a. joke
b. unite
c. arrange
d. threaten

7. gratify
a. satisfy
b. destroy
c. displease
d. overtake

8. crucial
a. mechanical
b. pivotal
c. flexible
d. minor

9. forlorn
a. homeless
b. blithe
c. wealthy
d. woebegone

11. attest
a. accept
b. reject
c. offer
d. disprove

13. vilify
a. denounce
b. praise
c. embarrass
d. overturn

15. kindred
a. smart
b. unrelated
c. disturbed
d. angry

10. loiter
a. cause
b. rush
c. annoy
d. promise

12. pallid
a. shared
b. fair
c. simple
d. ruddy

14. haughty
a. cruel
b. pretty
c. silly
d. humble

16. solvent
a. sturdy
b. untrue
c. boasted
d. bankrupt

Word Families

A. *On the line provided, write the word you have learned in Units 13–15 that is related to each of the following nouns.*
EXAMPLE: solvency—**solvent**

1. vilification, vilifier _____

2. blandness _____

3. malingerer, malingering _____

4. amplifier, amplification _____

5. exasperation, exasperating _____

6. adaptation, adapter, adaptability _____

7. naiveness, naïveté, naivety _____

8. infiniteness, infinitude, infinity _____

9. inertia, inertness _____

10. pithiness, pith _____

11. disclaimer _____

12. estrangement, estranger _____

13. loiterer, loitering _____

14. tediousness, tedium _____

15. embodiment, embodier _____

B. *On the line provided, write the word you have learned in Units 13–15 that is related to each of the following verbs.*
EXAMPLE: forebode—**foreboding**

16. rationalize _____

17. vend _____

18. impede _____

19. neglect _____

20. reciprocate _____

Two-Word Completions *Circle the pair of words that best complete the meaning of each of the following passages.*

1. "Though I am certainly _____ that most critics gave my new play rave reviews," the author remarked, "I can't help feeling a little hurt by the _____ of those who panned it."
   a. vaunted . . . parables
   b. exasperated . . . disclaimers
   c. estranged . . . enormities
   d. gratified . . . strictures

2. Acquiring a foreign language can be a particularly _____ chore because it involves so much memorization. If a person didn't have to learn everything by _____, the task would be a good deal less time-consuming.
   a. foreboding . . . epoch
   b. exasperating . . . niche
   c. tedious . . . rote
   d. irascible . . . heritage

3. "You don't need to address issues that will clearly have no effect on the outcome of this election," the campaign manager told the candidate. "But it is _____ for you to take a firm stand on those that may prove _____."
   a. tedious . . . bland
   b. naive . . . reciprocal
   c. gratifying . . . pallid
   d. imperative . . . crucial

4. "All my critics claim that my support for human rights has never been anything but halfhearted," the senator remarked. "However, the record clearly shows that I have been _____ in my commitment to this great cause. Indeed, I take great pride in the fact that I have never _____ or wavered in my allegiance to it."
   a. bland . . . malingered
   b. steadfast . . . faltered
   c. inert . . . adapted
   d. negligent . . . loitered

5. Most immigrants in this country have found it necessary to modify or _____ the traditions they brought with them in order to meet the needs of life in a new environment, but few have totally abandoned the rich _____ of their ancestors.
   a. adapt . . . heritage
   b. vilify . . . impediment
   c. plunder . . . veneer
   d. amplify . . . kindred

6. Though police officers in my neighborhood are sometimes accused of _____ or otherwise lying down on the job, let me point out that the diligence and efficiency with which they solve most cases clearly _____ their overall devotion to duty.
   a. malingering . . . attests to
   b. inertia . . . obliterates
   c. negligence . . . disclaims
   d. steadfastness . . . dovetails with

Building with Classical Roots

fect, fic, fy—to make

This root appears in **amplify** (page 157), "to make bigger, increase." Some other words based on the same root are listed below.

beneficial	clarify	deify	exemplify
certify	defective	edify	personify

From the list of words above, choose the one that corresponds to each of the brief definitions below. Write the word in the blank space in the illustrative sentence below the definition.

1. favorable, helpful, producing good ("*making good*")

The _____ influence of teachers has helped many young people to realize their full potential.

2. to instruct so as to encourage intellectual, moral, or spiritual improvement

A sermon should _____ those who hear it.

3. faulty, not perfect, not complete

Manufacturers will often replace _____ products free of charge.

4. to make clear or easier to understand

A flowchart can be used to _____ the steps in a computer operation.

5. to make a god of; to worship as a god

The ancient Romans _____ Julius Caesar and Augustus posthumously.

6. to guarantee; to declare true or correct ("*make certain*")

A notary public _____ that documents such as deeds and contracts are authentic.

7. to be an example of; to show by example

Awards were presented to students whose conduct _____ the principles of good citizenship and service to the community.

8. to be the embodiment of; to represent the qualities of

In an old-fashioned melodrama, the hero _____ courage and virtue.

From the list of words above, choose the one that best completes each of the following sentences. Write the word in the blank space provided.

1. Instead of repeating your confusing remark over and over again, why don't you try to _____ it for us?

2. There is strong scientific evidence that regular aerobic exercise is _____ both to the heart and to overall health.

3. Tomorrow, I plan to return to the manufacturer the microwave oven that proved to be

_____.

4. The statue of Venus de Milo _____ my idea of feminine beauty.

5. Stained-glass windows were originally intended to _____ illiterate worshipers with pictorial depictions of Bible stories and parables.

6. The officials of the bank will have to _____ this check before we can accept it.

7. Since 1947, the Japanese have regarded their emperor as a mere mortal rather than as a(n) _____ person.

8. This disorganized mess _____ what can happen when we rush into a project without having a definite plan worked out and agreed on in advance.

---

*Circle the **boldface** word that more satisfactorily completes each of the following sentences.*

1. Adoring fans may sometimes forget that their superstar idols are human beings and (**edify, deify**) them instead.

2. The characters in the medieval play *Everyman* (**personify, clarify**) abstract ideas such as Fellowship and Good Deeds.

3. A moderate amount of rainfall is (**beneficial, defective**) to crops, but prolonged heavy rain can do a great deal of damage.

4. One purpose of a judge's charge to a jury is to (**clarify, exemplify**) the law as it applies to the particular case that is being tried.

5. At registration time, a school will ask parents to (**personify, certify**) that their children have received all the required inoculations.

6. Doctors can use glasses, contact lenses, or surgery to correct (**defective, beneficial**) eyesight.

7. Many painters and writers of the Victorian era were moralists who sought to (**edify, clarify**) and uplift the public through their work.

8. Unscrupulous robber barons such as Jay Gould (**certified, exemplified**) the spirit of unrestrained capitalism in nineteenth-century America.

Read the following sentences, paying special attention to the words and phrases underlined. From the words in the box below, find better choices for these underlined words and phrases. Then use these choices to rewrite the sentences.

WORD BANK				
abyss	befall	falter	infinite	ransack
adapt	crucial	gratify	kindred	stricture
amplify	disclaim	heritage	negligent	tedious
attest	epoch	impediment	oblivion	veneer

An Amazing Sap

1. During the <u>distinct period of time</u> of European exploration of the Americas, Old World adventurers first came into contact with an amazing sap produced by a jungle tree. This sap, which the Quechua Indians called *caoutchouc*, was rubber.

_____

_____

2. Native Americans had been familiar with rubber for thousands of years. They perfected the <u>long and boring and repetitious</u> method of collecting the sap and then heating and mixing it to reduce its odor and stickiness.

_____

_____

3. The native peoples found an almost <u>endless and exceedingly great</u> number of uses for the versatile sap.

_____

_____

4. For example, they applied a <u>thin outer layer or covering</u> of the cured sap to clothing and shoes to make those garments waterproof.

_____

_____

5. When the explorers returned to Europe, they could <u>affirm to be true or genuine</u> to the remarkable properties of *caoutchouc*, but rubber remained a mere curiosity.

_____

_____

6. In 1839, Charles Goodyear, an American inventor, found a way to cure the rubber sap. Rubber was thus rescued from <u>a state of being forgotten</u>.

_____

_____

7. Technological innovation has made rubber a valuable substance that can be <u>adjusted or changed to suit conditions</u> for a variety of applications.

_____

_____

Analogies *In each of the following, circle the item that best completes the comparison.*

1. bland is to **caustic** as
a. gaunt is to emaciated
b. curt is to pithy
c. haggard is to ungainly
d. pallid is to ruddy

2. elite is to **dregs** as
a. niche is to antics
b. bonanza is to windfall
c. fiasco is to plaudits
d. promontory is to abyss

3. barter is to **trader** as
a. sell is to vendor
b. rehabilitate is to waif
c. endow is to recipient
d. cite is to author

4. venerate is to **vilify** as
a. dovetail is to converge
b. magnify is to minimize
c. obliterate is to preclude
d. attribute is to attest

5. unflagging is to **waver** as
a. steadfast is to falter
b. enterprising is to vie
c. fervent is to wallow
d. overbearing is to loiter

6. crucial is to **pivotal** as
a. churlish is to personable
b. predominant is to subordinate
c. haughty is to willful
d. dire is to calamitous

7. parable is to **moral** as
a. sentence is to question mark
b. adage is to happy ending
c. joke is to punch line
d. stricture is to logical flaw

8. irascible is to **vex** as
a. jaunty is to anguish
b. impartial is to prejudice
c. impatient is to exasperate
d. disgruntled is to appease

9. foreboding is to **premonition** as
a. acme is to pinnacle
b. citadel is to dungeon
c. vigil is to night
d. residue is to ingredient

10. grapple is to **implement** as
a. tether is to machine
b. epitaph is to tombstone
c. bludgeon is to weapon
d. bolster is to utensil

 **Choosing the Right Meaning** *Read each sentence carefully. Then circle the item that best completes the statement below the sentence.*

"I know that the opinions I hold are not popular," she replied, "but they are the result of much thought, and nothing will induce me to abdicate them." (2)

1. The word **abdicate** in line 2 is best defined as
a. discard   b. disown   c. display   d. disinherit

Though gold and copper are highly tractable materials, iron is not because it requires extremely high temperatures to melt. (2)

2. The word **tractable** in line 1 most nearly means
a. malleable   b. docile   c. precious   d. amenable

The Nuremberg trials set a precedent that makes it extremely unlikely that any government would in future consent to an act of oblivion for war criminals. 2)

3. The word **oblivion** in line 2 most nearly means
a. recrimination   b. amnesty   c. forgetfulness   d. obscurity

After a little over a decade of nonstop growth, the economy suddenly began to
falter and sink into depression. (2)

4. The best meaning for the word **falter** in line 2 is

a. hesitate   b. stammer   c. weaken   d. fluctuate

I realized that my suggestion was not destined to fly when my boss made a wry
face at the mere mention of it. (2)

5. The word **wry** in line 1 most nearly means

a. droll   b. peculiar   c. angry   d. twisted

Two-Word Completions

Circle the pair of words that best complete the meaning of each of the following sentences.

1. The civil rights movement made significant advances when the Supreme Court threw
out the "separate but equal" _____ in effect for years and
_____ all sorts of unfair laws and practices based on it.

a. accord . . . asserted
b. decree . . . perused
c. stance . . . bolstered
d. doctrine . . . invalidated

2. At no time in our history have Americans been so divided as during the
_____ of the Civil War, when a great many families had
_____ on both sides and "brother fought brother."

a. epoch . . . kindred
b. intrigue . . . mercenaries
c. sequel . . . cronies
d. enormity . . . jurisdiction

3. Sharks have been aptly described as "insatiable feeding machines" because their
_____ appetites never seem to be _____.

a. staid . . . appeased
b. ample . . . regaled
c. indiscriminate . . . stinted
d. voracious . . . gratified

4. Delightful though they truly are, her personal _____ and
eccentricities are so pronounced that no _____ of manners and
polish can ever hope to mask them.

a. tenets . . . milieu
b. defects . . . crusade
c. quirks . . . veneer
d. enmities . . . residue

5. In Arthurian legend and romance, Sir Galahad is an idealized figure who
_____ purity, nobility, and all the other _____
associated with a virtuous knight, whereas Sir Lancelot is much more human and
consequently falls short of the mark.

a. embodies . . . attributes
b. proclaims . . . fallacies
c. entails . . . epitaphs
d. negates . . . repercussions

Enriching Your Vocabulary

Read the passage below. Then complete the exercise at the bottom of the page.

On the Money

Money in one form or another is as old as human history. Ancient people did not use paper money and coins to acquire goods or accumulate wealth. Instead, they relied on *barter* (Unit 10), an exchange of goods and services. For example, a farmer

Quarters commemorating the admission of the individual states to the Union

might give an animal to another farmer in exchange for a quantity of grain. Eventually, items such as beads, seashells, stone disks, and even cattle were adopted as standardized means of exchange. Various metals, especially gold and silver, have been used as money for at least 4000 years, and standardized coins have been used for nearly 3000 years. By the seventeenth century, paper notes were also common.

For centuries, nations have used coins and paper notes to honor famous people and commemorate important events. The faces of Roman emperors appeared on coins, just as portraits of American presidents appear on our coins and bills.

The gold one-dollar coin introduced in 2000 features a portrait of Sacagawea, the Shoshone guide who accompanied Lewis and Clark on their historic expedition. In 1976, the U.S. Mint issued a special quarter to mark the nation's bicentennial; and in 1999, it began issuing quarters honoring each of the fifty states.

In Column A below are 10 more money words. With or without a dictionary, match each word with its meaning in Column B.

Column A

_____ **1.** currency
_____ **2.** revenue
_____ **3.** fiscal
_____ **4.** expenditure
_____ **5.** divest
_____ **6.** asset
_____ **7.** liability
_____ **8.** dividend
_____ **9.** depression
_____ **10.** capital

Column B

a. something one owns
b. financial
c. a form of money
d. the wealth of a business
e. to rid oneself of an investment
f. something one owes
g. income
h. expense
i. money earned on an investment
j. a period of general decline in business activity and employment

Selecting Word Meanings

*In each of the following groups, circle the word or expression that is **most nearly the same** in meaning as the word in **boldface** type in the given phrase.*

1. a **forlorn** expression on my face
   a. happy   b. woebegone   c. puzzled   d. surly

2. **kindred** languages
   a. foreign   b. modern   c. ancient   d. related

3. the **citadels** of power
   a. drawbacks   b. trappings   c. strongholds   d. uses

4. **basked** in the limelight
   a. reveled   b. hid   c. flourished   d. faded

5. a **legendary** character
   a. foreign   b. mythical   c. fascinating   d. historical

6. **menial** jobs
   a. well-paid   b. interesting   c. low-level   d. professional

7. tried to **convey** my ideas
   a. disclaim   b. amplify   c. express   d. defend

8. tries to appear **blasé**
   a. calm   b. interested   c. knowledgeable   d. bored

9. a **calamitous** fire
   a. sudden   b. minor   c. devastating   d. brief

10. an **imperative** duty
    a. essential   b. expensive   c. terrifying   d. burdensome

11. **devised** a method
    a. discarded   b. invented   c. borrowed   d. explained

12. **divergent** points of view
    a. similar   b. interesting   c. conventional   d. differing

13. **cowered** in their cages
    a. growled   b. slept   c. cringed   d. roared

14. plans that go **awry**
    a. amiss   b. slowly   c. forward   d. smoothly

15. a **cryptic** reply
    a. sensible   b. pleasing   c. hostile   d. puzzling

16. a **curt** note
    a. childish   b. humorous   c. brusque   d. courteous

17. **indiscriminate** slaughter
    a. unreported   b. unplanned   c. unselective   d. unusual

18. flaunt their wealth
   a. conceal   b. show off   c. enjoy   d. use

19. came upon a **bonanza**
   a. monster   b. problem   c. disaster   d. windfall

20. audacious plans
   a. careless   b. successful   c. bold   d. unflagging

21. traveled **incognito**
   a. disguised   b. alone   c. luxuriously   d. safely

22. whatever may **befall** us
   a. please   b. amuse   c. help   d. happen to

23. wallow in the mud
   a. roll   b. grow   c. play   d. work

24. full of **quirks**
   a. failures   b. peculiarities   c. ideas   d. mistakes

25. to **oust** the intruders
   a. fight   b. greet   c. expel   d. discover

Synonyms

*In each of the following groups, circle the **two** words or expressions that are **most nearly the same** in meaning.*

26. a. steadfast   b. oblique   c. pithy   d. resolute

27. a. obsess   b. invalidate   c. assert   d. annul

28. a. inaudible   b. crucial   c. pivotal   d. vaunted

29. a. habituate   b. maim   c. incapacitate   d. loiter

30. a. sustain   b. belittle   c. minimize   d. venerate

31. a. pertinent   b. rational   c. relevant   d. abashed

32. a. hover   b. articulate   c. muster   d. amass

33. a. foreboding   b. stricture   c. premonition   d. unison

34. a. vex   b. ostracize   c. exasperate   d. rehabilitate

35. a. aloof   b. prone   c. apt   d. predatory

36. a. nullify   b. proclaim   c. tether   d. negate

37. a. aghast   b. wanton   c. willful   d. exotic

38. a. waver   b. wallow   c. convey   d. falter

39. a. bolster   b. plunder   c. grope   d. ravage

40. a. facetious   b. overbearing   c. personable   d. arrogant

Supplying Words in Context

In each of the following sentences, write in the blank space the most appropriate word chosen from the given list.

Group A

ensue	pallid	shiftless	proximity
evolve	purge	malinger	elite
ransack	embody	avail	vie
peruse	fend	estrange	ethical
endow	disdain	retentive	ornate

41. Before you fill out the job application, you should _____ the instructions carefully.

42. How can the employers expect any one applicant for the job to _____ *all* the qualities they are seeking?

43. Unless he improves his _____ ways, he will not be successful at that job.

44. A riot may _____ if the crowd is not properly controlled.

45. We had to _____ every room in the house in order to find the missing book.

Group B

dexterous	finesse	solicitous	devoid
opus	levity	fallacy	scavenger
decoy	myriad	stoical	parry
disgruntled	waif	vilify	impending
glut	preclude	renown	vigil

46. The fans were _____ because they were convinced that their team had lost as the result of bad officiating.

47. Jane Addams won great _____ for her noble work to help people living in the slums.

48. Of all the _____ woes of humankind, is there anything worse than a toothache?

49. The defense attorney remarked with satisfaction that the lack of solid evidence against her client would _____ his conviction.

50. With my friend serving as a(n) _____ to attract their attention, we managed to get away without their seeing us.

Word Pairs

In the space provided before each of the following word pairs, write:

S—if the words are synonyms or near-synonyms.
O—if the words are antonyms or near-antonyms.
N—if the words are unrelated in meaning.

51. _____ pert—jaunty

52. _____ haggard—gaunt

53. _____ captivate—estrange

54. _____ deplore—rue

55. _____ prodigal—frugal

56. _____ genial—churlish

57. _____ capacious—rote

58. _____ haughty—unassuming

59. _____ heritage—veneer

60. _____ regale—attest

Words Connected with History

Some words that are used in connection with historical events are listed below. Write the appropriate word on the line next to each of the following descriptions.

transition	decree	mercenary	embargo
abdicate	crusade	doctrine	reciprocal
armistice	epoch	turncoat	tenet
plebeian	scapegoat	repercussion	mediate

61. A great undertaking, such as the effort by Europeans to conquer the Holy Land in the eleventh and twelfth centuries _____

62. A temporary halt in a war, such as the one that ended World War I in 1918 _____

63. A word applied to a trade agreement between the United States and Canada, in which each nation gives something that the other wants _____

64. A soldier hired to fight for money—for example, a Hessian who served in the British army in the American Revolution _____

65. Any event or period of time that marks a major development in history _____

66. A statement of ideas or policies, such as the one President Monroe issued in 1823, when he warned European governments to stay out of the New World _____

67. A policy of cutting off trade with other nations, as the United States did with France and England before the War of 1812 _____

68. To attempt to settle a dispute between two other parties, as the United States did in the Russo–Japanese War (1904–1905) _____

69. The change that occurs when one president gives up power and the next president takes over

_____

70. A term applied to Benedict Arnold because he sold out to the British during the American Revolution

_____

Word Associations

In each of the following, circle the word or expression that best completes the meaning of the sentence or answers the question, with particular reference to the meaning of the word in **boldface** type.

71. Two ways in which you can **bludgeon** someone are with
a. sweet talk and promises
b. a club and arguments
c. courtesy and fair dealing
d. financial help and good advice

72. **Apparitions** would be likely to play an important part in
a. your history book
b. ghost stories
c. a TV news program
d. a math examination

73. Which of the following would be likely to be **ungainly**?
a. an Olympic gymnast
b. an overweight ballet dancer
c. a bankrupt merchant
d. an eagle on the wing

74. The word **teeming** would not be applied to
a. the streets of a busy city
b. a heavy rainfall
c. a jungle
d. an empty room

75. Which of the following might aptly be classified as **wry**?
a. a loaf of bread
b. a sense of humor
c. twinge of conscience
d. a mole

76. A **recluse** usually prefers to be
a. out-of-doors
b. in good company
c. in a position of power
d. alone

77. Which of the following would be most likely to **simper**?
a. your dentist
b. a foolish, self-conscious person
c. a judge sentencing a prisoner
d. a student taking a tough exam

78. People who have reached an **accord**
a. play musical instruments
b. are at the last stop of a bus line
c. are in agreement
d. work at similar jobs

79. When you say that an argument is **porous**, you mean that it
a. is very strong
b. will hold up in a court of law
c. is well stated
d. is full of logical holes

80. A **tractable** person is one who
a. can operate a tractor
b. owns a large tract of land
c. is easily influenced by others
d. is unbearably stubborn

81. Which of the following is outstanding for **longevity**?
a. a famous movie star
b. a 99-year-old person
c. an all-American halfback
d. a popular teacher

82. To be successful, a **mendicant** must master the art of
    a. lying
    a. stealing
    c. begging
    d. fencing

83. If you are at the end of your **tether**, you are
    a. in good physical shape
    b. ready to graduate
    c. sitting down
    d. in a desperate situation

84. Which of the following animals spends a great deal of time **delving** in the earth?
    a. a porcupine
    b. a beaver
    c. an otter
    d. a mole

85. From a friend with a **volatile** personality, you would expect
    a. high moral standards
    b. great stubbornness
    c. an interest in politics
    d. sudden changes in mood

86. A speaker who is **tedious** is one who probably
    a. has prepared the talk carefully
    b. uses simple, direct language
    c. deals with an important topic
    d. speaks too long

87. The **residue** of a chemical experiment refers to
    a. the equipment in the lab
    b. what is left over after the experiment
    c. the purpose of the experiment
    d. the chemicals used

88. To be successful, a **vendor** should be good at
    a. accounting
    b. selling
    c. carpentry
    d. diagramming sentences

89. If you have **qualms** about something you have done,
    a. you are proud of yourself
    b. your conscience is bothering you
    c. you expect a reward
    d. you want to do the same thing again

90. The **jurisdiction** of a court refers to
    a. the kinds of cases it can decide
    b. where the court is located
    c. the qualifications of the judges
    d. the money needed to run the court

91. A **pseudonym** is most likely to be used by
    a. someone traveling incognito
    b. a waif
    c. a police officer
    d. a leading citizen of your community

92. To do something without **stinting** is to be
    a. careful
    b. stingy
    c. generous
    d. in bad taste

93. Which of the following might be called **tawdry**?
    a. a well-managed farm
    b. a center for cancer research
    c. a one-room schoolhouse
    d. cheap, loud decorations

94. A **promontory** would be a good place to
    a. play volleyball
    b. let children play unattended
    c. raise potatoes
    d. look out to sea

95. Someone who constantly **scoffs** might well be called a(n)
    a. Doubting Thomas
    b. Artful Dodger
    c. Dapper Dan
    d. Nervous Nelly

96. Which of the following would probably be **upbraided**?
   a. a worn-out coat
   b. an unruly student
   c. a newborn baby
   d. a heroic firefighter

97. A **parable** uses a story to
   a. trap a liar
   b. make arithmetical computations
   c. describe an event
   d. clarify a moral idea

98. A person who serves as your **proxy** is
   a. a servant
   b. a medical specialist
   c. one who acts in your place
   d. a close friend

99. An **avowed** pickpocket is one who
   a. admits to his or her crimes
   b. has never been caught
   c. is helping the police
   d. is exceptionally skillful

100. If your knowledge of words is **prodigious**, you will probably
   a. misuse many words
   b. have a small but useful vocabulary
   c. become an English teacher
   d. score close to 100% on this final test

INDEX

The following tabulation lists all the basic words taught in the various units of this book, as well as those introduced in the *Vocabulary of Vocabulary, Working with Analogies, Building with Classical Roots,* and *Enriching Your Vocabulary* sections. Words taught in the units are printed in **boldface** type. The number following each entry indicates the page on which the word is first introduced. Exercise and review materials in which the word also appears are not cited.